12/63

EAST AND WEST

BY C. NORTHCOTE PARKINSON

PARKINSON'S LAW

THE EVOLUTION OF POLITICAL THOUGHT

THE LAW AND THE PROFITS

IN-LAWS AND OUTLAWS

EAST AND WEST

EAST AND WEST

C. NORTHCOTE PARKINSON

HOUGHTON MIFFLIN COMPANY BOSTON

THE RIVERSIDE PRESS CAMBRIDGE

1963

FOR ANN

Grateful acknowledgment is made to the following authors and publishers for permission to quote from the works cited:

Harvard University Press: Geoorge Sarton, *History of Science*.

Holt, Rinehart and Winston, Inc.: *The Vision of Asia* by L. Cranmer-Byng. Copyright 1933, copyright renewed © 1961 by L. Cranmer-Byng. Excerpts reprinted by permission of Holt, Rinehart and Winston, Inc.

John Murray, Ltd.: L. Cranmer-Byng, *The Vision of Asia*; Freya Stark, *Alexander's Path*.

Penguin Books, Ltd.: Herodotus, *The Histories*, translated by Aubrey de Selincourt.

John Baker: Lancelot Lawton, *Empires of the Far East*, published by Grant Richards.

Routledge & Kegan Paul, Ltd.: Jules Toutain, *The Economic Life of the Ancient World*.

Dr. Ralph Turner, *The Great Cultural Traditions*.

PREFACE

EAST AND WEST are terms in constant use, pregnant with meaning but hard to define. We speak of individuals or groups as "Oriental" or "Western" in character. We hear of an Asian viewpoint, unacceptable to the West, of a Western colonialism causing resentment in the East. East is East, we remember reading, and never the twain shall meet. "But they must meet!" say the idealists, and so the debate goes on. But what exactly is being discussed? What is the East and where does it begin? Where is the West and at what point does it end? Our ideas are more vehement than precise. We know how we feel, but we have no idea what we mean. Having located this area of confusion and obscurity, I have tried to dispel the mists and reveal what lies beyond our vague generalities. This book is the result.

I write as an historian, not as a satirist, and my approach has been chronological. I have tried to go back to the earliest period at which the terms "East" and "West" had any but a geographical meaning. I have tried to show how the conflict and contrast have developed through the centuries. I have tried to indicate some of the differences which persist. The story I have to tell is comprised in the twenty chapters which follow. On the events as thus outlined I have based a theory of history which is contained in the Introduction. Whoever grasps the theory can apply it to the narrative. Whoever reads the narrative can decide for himself how far the theory is supported by the facts. But the reader who may be inclined to accept the argument should realize that a theory of history is merely a point of view. While

possibly valid in itself and useful even to the statesman, it does
not exclude other points of view. The same tree will be differently described or drawn by observers whose viewpoint is different. The several descriptions may all be accurate even though
no two of them will tally. It is only the amateur historian who
seizes upon one viewpoint, one specified angle, height, and distance, arguing that all other descriptions are illegal, immoral,
and wrong. Karl Marx was one such amateur, who wrote that,
"The history of all known society, past and present, has been the
history of class struggles." This statement is not wholly untrue.
Marx could, it is true, know relatively little about history and
relatively less about economic history, which had been little
studied at the time at which he wrote, but he had perceived an
aspect of the truth. To somebody whose chief interest is class
struggles, all history must center upon them. Nor need his narrative be false. To put it, however, in its proper perspective, we
must remember that other narratives, from other points of view,
are equally valid. To somebody whose chief interest is medicine,
the history of all known society has been the history of disease.
To someone whose chief interest is roads and bridges, the history
of all human society has been the history of communications.
In this way the histories of commerce, dentistry, sanitation,
music, drama, navigation, and art all have their own validity.
Only the student self-centered to the point of lunacy will claim
— as Marx did — that his viewpoint must supersede all others.
Of that error I am guiltless. My view of history is one of many
and no more accurate than any other. All that I can claim for
my interpretation is that it may be thought specially relevant to
the age in which we live.

On the assumption that the reader is so far in agreement, I
have a further warning to utter. Because I observe a certain pattern in events I do not mean to suggest that their sequence is
inevitable. I do not see mankind as tied to the wheel of fate. It
was Karl Marx again who predicted the unavoidable conse-

quences of the trend he had observed. His predictions were
falsified partly, at least, because he had failed to foresee the
effect of his own preaching. His antagonists took heed of the
books which his followers often excusably found unreadable.
They steered wide of the rocks to which he had drawn their
attention, proving once more that the fatalist is wrong. In my
own view, for what it is worth, the endless repetition of the same
pattern of events is probably avoidable. The sharp conflicts of
contrasting civilizations might well be averted. As against that,
the obliteration of human differences would lead to a cultural
stagnation — a greater evil, perhaps, than any which is likely to
result from conflict. But if conflict is to continue, we might do
well to cushion the future impact of the one civilization upon
the other, lessening the antagonisms and replacing emotions,
where possible, with knowledge.

Toward modifying the destructive force of future collisions,
this book may be some slight contribution in itself. For an
awareness of the movements which sway mankind cannot but
lessen resentments and save regret. I remember once swimming
from a sunlit beach in Trinidad, where blue-green breakers
foamed, seething, toward a shell-white sand. The surf riders and
swimmers included people of differing speech and color — Europeans and Indians, Negroes and Chinese. Only the South Africans stood aghast on the shore. In such tumbled waters it was
natural that folk should sometimes collide, as indeed they did.
Surfacing after some such mishap, the good swimmer would
merely laugh. Where people collide ashore, by contrast, it is
usually the fault of one or the other, thus proving the cause of
at least temporary antagonisms. As each can go where he will,
the responsibility lies between them for any predicament in
which they should land. In the surf, by contrast, all are swayed
by the same elemental forces, their own efforts counting for
little until the wave is spent. No one blames another for what
none can help. Where a child might cry or a fool might rage,

the swimmer does not even expect an apology. And this good-natured atmosphere is the result, basically, of knowledge. Each bather knows the force of the waves, and it is this knowledge that turns resentment into mirth.

In some such fashion I am trying here to explain what tides there are in the affairs of men. A knowledge of these impersonal forces and their useful purpose may do something to mitigate our antagonisms. It can do nothing, admittedly, to reduce the shock of impact. On this subject, however, I shall have something to say, more especially on the relationship between diet and energy. How we react to our environment may depend, more than we realize, upon what we eat.

Given a more suitable diet, as recommended by the food reformers (plain food, uncooked and Spartan), I might perhaps have had the energy to ransack libraries. I might myself have typed the manuscript of the present work. Instead, I have relied upon the results of a desultory reading and have called upon others repeatedly for aid. Conscious of my own limitations as an orientalist, I have quoted at length from the works of known authorities. Where my own opinion weighs least I have appealed to the learning of those whose word the reader must respect.

I must thank Mrs. Valentine and Miss Vidamour for typing my manuscript, and Miss Nancy Robin for excluding unwanted though well loved intruders from the room in which I work. To Ann my thanks are more difficult to express, for without her encouragement the book would never have begun or finished; nor, without her, would the effort have been worthwhile. To Ann, for that reason, this book is dedicated.

C. Northcote Parkinson

Guernsey,
January 12th, 1963

CONTENTS

MAPS

INTRODUCTION

THIS BOOK deals with civilizations, not with the world as a whole. It does not touch upon areas in Africa which have never produced a civilization, nor upon such countries as Australia which are capable, mainly, of future development. The ancient civilizations of South America are equally ignored, as lacking a continuity with the present day. The story here told will center upon the Eurasian continent, with North Africa as geographically annexed, and modern America — North and South — as its historical extension. The civilizations with which we are concerned originate in roughly the same area, but have diverged sufficiently to give us our concepts of East and West, based broadly upon Asia and Europe.

The first and obvious fact to emphasize is that Europe and Asia are merely the opposite sides of the one continent. They are traditionally divided by the Ural Mountains, Ural River, Caspian Sea, Caucasus, Black Sea, and Dardanelles. Asia Minor has been the disputed area, but the frontier has been otherwise fairly stable; not as a political concept, but at least as a cultural fact. East and west of that great divide the land masses are not altogether dissimilar, with plains in the north, a mountain barrier forming their boundary on the south, and a number of peninsulas, like Italy and Malaya, jutting further south again. But the basic similarity goes little further than that, giving place to some significant contrasts. In the first place, Asia is far larger, with four times the area and double the population. In the second place, while most of Europe is north of 40 latitude, most of the Asian centers of population lie to the south of it. In the third place, the European land areas are broken up by water — the Black Sea, Mediterranean, and Baltic — while the habitable parts of Asia are more effectively divided from each other by mountain and desert.

These three basic differences — and there are others — have had their permanent results. Between East and West there has been a traditional relationship of the many to the few, lessened no doubt since the development of America, but well represented by the difference in scale of the political unit. The historical importance assigned in the West to Greece, Portugal, or Sweden would be paralleled in the East by the grandeur of India or China — countries not strictly comparable in scale. As regards climate, moreover, the warmer and colder lands do not exact the same response. On this subject Lord Curzon observed that:

> . . . Greater heat has produced less capacity of resistance; and just as in India all the masculine races have their habitat above the 24th degree of latitude, so in the Far East is there the greatest contrast between the peoples of China, Korea and Japan, lying north of that parallel, and those of Burma, Siam, Malaysia and Annam, which lie below it . . .*

Too much can be made of this, but life clearly demands less of mankind in lands where food is easily procurable and where cold is unknown.

Last of all, the landlocked waters of Europe have made for an ease of communication which Asia affords only to a lesser extent. This was a major factor in European oceanic expansion. Apart from that, however, it gave Europe a cultural solidarity which Asia has never had in the same degree. While European political units have been relatively small, they have existed for

* Rt. Hon. G. N. Curzon, *Problems of the Far East* (London, 1898), 7.

much of their history within the framework of the one civilization to which they all belong. The same can hardly be said of India, China, or Persia, where admittedly larger kingdoms have been coextensive with the civilizations from which their cultures derived. In a comparison between East and West, we have to deal on the one hand with three related but distinct civilizations; on the other with a single civilization recognizably the same from the Urals to the Atlantic; and from there, indeed, to the Pacific coast of America.

So distinct are the Asian civilizations that some orientalists would deny the validity of any theory which treated them as one. What is there in common, they would ask, between a Korean, an Arab, and a Parsee? Nothing, they would answer, and there is a sense in which they would be right. There is another sense, however, in which they might be wrong. For the three could resemble each other in having a wristwatch, a smattering of English, a contempt for the Negro, and a reluctance to be seen doing manual work. They could also resemble each other in their attitudes to the West. For if geographical factors form the background to men's thinking, it is history that fills the foreground. And while the Oriental civilizations are distinct from each other, many of the Orientals themselves have some history in common. Such unity as exists between the countries of Asia, like the far greater unity which links the countries of the West, is based upon such feelings of hostility as they may happen to share.

Almost throughout recorded history there have been conflict and rivalry between East and West. That rivalry, the theme of this book, has not attracted the attention of many historians. They have been too specialized to see far beyond their own civilizations and periods. The relationships, therefore, of East and West have formed a somewhat neglected field of scholarship, a subject too vast for analysis, too vast even to have attracted attention. But current and probable events must force us to study what we have hitherto chosen to ignore. To understand the East-West conflict is vitally important. More than that, it is becoming daily more urgent. We must substitute knowledge for emotion, and it is in the light of this knowledge that our decisions should be made.

In studying the history of relationships between East and West, between the opposite sides of the Eurasian continent, we come to realize that there have been alternating phases of Oriental and Western ascendancy. Periods of high civilization are found to have lasted from one to two thousand years (more or less), and scholars can break these periods down into phases of origin, growth, achievement, and decay. And whatever their life span, whatever the height or splendor of their flowering, all civilizations known to us have ended in decadence. Why? The answer to that question would be a book in itself. Are the causes biological? Is there a decline in virility, a numerical inequality of the sexes with the male fatally predominant? Is there a disgenic sequel to prolonged periods of war? What actually goes wrong and why? We have learned to associate decay with overtaxation, but is that a symptom or a result? Overtaxation is again the cause of a growing burden of useless — and worse than useless — bureaucracy; but has that also a biological aspect? We recognize that decay, at a given period, may be more advanced in one country than another, but what is the yardstick by which we are to measure the difference?

Amid a number of uncertainties, the one evident fact is that national decadence is at least accompanied by the individual's loss of energy. And energy derives presumably from diet. Research might show that people depend for energy on the nature of their soil, what Shakespeare calls "the mettle of their pastures." We might at least suspect that the more complex civilization removes people from their best supplies of food, leaving them to depend upon the imported, the preserved, and the stale. We might guess that dental troubles could reflect the state of malnutrition and that these might in turn affect digestion. History tells us repeatedly of settled and prosperous populations being conquered by nomadic herdsmen who live, presumably, nearer to nature and further from soil erosion. From facts such as these we might conclude that energy may dwindle with each generation further removed from the countryside. This was commonly believed by thinkers of the past, who attributed all sterling qualities to the open-air life. As keen an observer as Ibn Khaldûn thus attributes human energy to the avoidance of a rich diet. "The Spaniards," he cites as an example, people "whose country produces no butter and who live mainly on millet and in whom we can observe a sharpness of mind and a readiness for learning and a bodily grace which are unique." We may well believe that the Conquistadors must have had something which their descendants have often seemed to lack. Was it something which is gone forever, or was it an energy which we could seek to replace?

Whatever our answer to that question or however complete is our ignorance on the subject, we are left with the fact of decadence. The energy dies away, the arts become sterile, policy becomes timid, and the outposts are abandoned. And it is this decay which creates the vacuum into which another and more virile civilization is drawn. As between East and West, it is clear that their periods of high civilization have never been simultaneous. Instead, there have been alternate periods of ascendancy, the decadence of one coinciding with the highest achievements of the other. These alternate phases of expansion assume a military form, and we are at first inclined to see these vast movements of mankind as the overspilling of energy, the exuberance of an achievement which can no longer be kept within its original frontier. Such overspillings do undoubtedly occur; but further study may incline us to think that the vacuum is the more powerful force. For the trade routes which link the two civilizations are the pipeline along which the invasion is drawn. And failure to maintain the pipeline at one end draws the experts in from the other. One of the strongest motives for human interference is the spectacle of a fumbling ineptitude. "Oh, for heaven's sake," we burst out, "I'll do it for you!" The roof destroyed in a typhoon is not so much pushed over as sucked off, rather, by the vacuum formed in the building's lee. So the offensive begins and will continue until its force is spent.

The nature of the offensive is easy to misunderstand. It is natural, in the first place, to study the military movement as an isolated event rather than the dramatic assertion of a superiority already established, and one extending in fact to other fields. The suction created by a progressive decay draws in a flow of ideas, fashions, inventions, and words. It attracts missionaries, travelers, merchants, and teachers, with agents both commercial and secret, trade missions, cultural delegations, military advisers, and high-powered diplomatists. The actual invasion comes later, as a rule, being followed up by tax collectors, administrators, surveyors, and philologists, architects, engineers, art critics, and crooks. Where the peaceful pressure is sufficiently unopposed, no actual invasion may be needed. More than that, the pressure may continue even after an invasion has failed. The offensive is only perhaps incidentally of a military kind, the campaigns being more dramatic but not necessarily more important than the influences otherwise brought to bear. This is a fact of which we too readily lose sight. It is as easy again to attribute military conquest to a technical superiority in weapons; such a superiority as we should expect to find linked with a generally rising level of accomplishment. There is sometimes a basis for this conclusion, but the facts as often refuse to fit the theory. Technical superiority is as often the result as the cause of achievement. The voyages of Columbus had the effect of encouraging progress in nautical astronomy; they were not made possible by the progress that had already been made. The German conquest of France in 1940 was not primarily the work of parachutists and mechanized columns. The invaders consisted largely of infantry units with horsedrawn transport, sucked into France by the French collapse — very much as the British and American armies were later drawn into Italy without set purpose, merely because of the Italian disintegration. The technical improvements tend to come *after* the first victories have been won. As for the Japanese, who conquered Southeast Asia by the most humdrum methods, their technical progress never took place at all. Campaigns often give dramatic emphasis to a defeat which took place before the war had even begun. And the defeatism of the one side may be more important than the confidence acquired by the other.

If the nature of the first offensive, as between East and West, needs some explanation, its sequel requires none. For every such movement must sooner or later create a resistance. The mere ascendancy of the one civilization, quite apart from any racial discrimination or economic oppression, must eventually create an atmosphere of resentment. Nor is the hostility directed against tyrannical rulers as such. Hatred springs rather from being treated, however kindly, as inferiors. It first comes to the boiling point, moreover, among people who have admitted their inferiority and who hate themselves for it. In a country where there has been no conquest or oppression, but only a willing acceptance of things alien, the revulsion may be more explosive than among the so-called victims of imperial rule. But whatever the story has been, there will be an eventual movement of rebellion. By understudying their masters, the underlings will have lessened the technological gap between them. By rejecting some part of the imperial culture, they will have found a basis for moral resistance. By reviving the memories of their own earlier achievements or conquests (real or imagined), they will have laid claim to an equality of rank. So begins the revolt against what is nowadays called "colonialism"; the ascendancy of one people over another.

Among those brought up in the traditions of the American or Russian revolutions there is a belief in the morality of revolt as contrasted with the wickedness of imperialism. We have to realize, however, that no such contrast has ever existed. If imperialism leads to eventual revolt, the revolt leads as inevitably to a new imperialism. Successful rebels who cry "One man is as good as another" go on instantly to add "And better!" — thereby announcing their own ascendancy over some other group. English rebels against Spain were quick to enforce their own rule over Ireland. American rebels against England would stand no nonsense from Mexico. The Javanese had scarcely gained their independence from the Netherlands before they began to oppress Sumatra and look for conquests to the eastward. How could it be otherwise? The forces of resistance — whether emotional, psychological, military, or economic — are left unopposed as a result of their own success. They instinctively seek new opponents as justification for their own being. Younger sons on the make do not so readily sheathe their swords for lack of argument — as Henry V's successors discovered for themselves. They find another argument, and so it has always been. Ascendancy creates resistance, and resistance turns into a new ascendancy.

Once set in motion, this gigantic and clumsy engine, this alternating ascendancy of East and West, must seemingly pound on. In its decay each civilization creates a cultural vacuum into which the forces of the rival — and rising — civilization must tend to flow. By the time this transfusion has created a resistance, and so brought about a recovery, the source of new vigor has itself decayed, creating a new vacuum in another place. So the piston moves back to its previous position, not without friction, sparks, and noise. This is a rough description of what might be thought a crude and inefficient piece of indifferent plumbing. To the idealist, who may agree to the accuracy of this description, the engine may appear not merely crude but highly dangerous. Should it gain speed and momentum, this piston action could destroy us all. With grounds for apprehension based upon the current applications of science, the idealist would seem justified in demanding that the engine be stopped, leaving the human race to live in peace. He might see hope in the possibility of assimilation. He might plead, as others have urged before, that all societies should merge and mingle and that the contrasting civilizations should end as one.

This concept of assimilation, whether practicable or not, attracts many people whose opinions must command respect. It is an ideal, nevertheless, with which the present author must profoundly disagree. For most human progress, in the past, has been the result of that friction which the peace-loving idealist would seek to abolish. The brightest sparks of invention have resulted from the impact of civilizations and the clash of contrasting ideas. Where such friction has been long avoided, mental stagnation has been the result, such a stagnation as must always characterize a society which exists in isolation. Given the most primitive way of life, a stable society might be thought attractive. Given a high level of civilization, it is not even possible, for the absence of growth is itself the first sign of decay. And what fails to develop must fail to survive.

Granted then that the conflict must continue and that it serves an essential purpose, it might still be considered desirable to lessen somewhat the shocks of future impact. Could the area of conflict be restricted in any way? Could it be confined, in any degree, to the fields of intellect and culture? Something of the sort may well be possible. We could cushion the shocks by ensuring that their nature becomes widely known. We could check the momentum of the process by slowing down and modifying the progress of decay. But this depends again upon our having learned to recognize decay when we see it. Once we have admitted to ourselves that civilizations are liable to decay and that our own is no exception, we can begin to ask the right questions. How are we to judge whether or not a society, our own or another, is decadent? Few people realize that historical research may be quite as important as research in organic chemistry. This is nevertheless the fact, and a program to analyze the decay of civilizations would yield results at least as valuable as might be expected from an attempt to measure the life of electronic components. That many historians waste their time on trivialities may be true, but so do many scientists. And the fact remains that progress in historical knowledge has been at least as significant as progress in any other field of research. Nor is the opportunity past for making discoveries which would be exciting in themselves and relevant to the twentieth century.

In studying the chapters which follow, the reader will do well to remember the central theme. But in comparing the East and West he must try to avoid the opposite mistakes. Intolerant and narrow-minded people stress the differences to the point of concluding that Orientals or Westerners, as the case may be, are scarcely human, being no more than "chinks" or "foreign devils." Philanthropists ignore the differences to the point of saying "We are all human beings — people are everywhere the same." Neither theory is particularly helpful, and the upholders of these contrary opinions, both mistaken, make, in effect, the same mistake — that of applying a preconceived idea to a subject of which one knows practically nothing. The differences exist and serve a purpose. They need to be measured, analyzed, and compared. To exaggerate them is manifestly wrong, but to ignore them is obviously worse.

In attempting to understand the dynamics of the East-West relationship, a possibly useful analogy can be found in the smaller, national society in which most of us live. For that, too, is a machine, achieving a similar purpose, but drawing its power from another source. Here the energy is of the sort developed by a waterfall: its potential being related to the weight of the water and the difference in level, its immediate force being related to the number and size of the channels through which the water is allowed to fall. By this analogy, the high and barren slopes represent the levels of society which are exposed to hardship, poverty, and want. The ravines which lead down to the sheltered and fertile plains are the avenues open to individual or family ambition. The water is the population, or that part of it which seeks a better environment. In descending, it drives the dynamos of intellect before gaining the level at which it is destined to collect. The potential energy of a society is thus the difference in status between its most and its least privileged. The useful application of the force available must depend on the number and nature of the channels open to ambition. Where there is none, the society is static until the dam breaks in violent revolution. Where there are too few, the dam takes longer to collapse but will break in the end. Where the channels have been nicely adjusted, the maximum power is generated from a system which will remain relatively stable. But where the streams are too many and scattered, with all careers open to everyone, the water dribbles uselessly over the hillside, bypassing the turbines, and the society ceases to be dynamic. Most power is generated in the most steeply graded societies, where the greatest effort brings the greatest reward in terms of status. No power can be generated in a society where all begin, and remain, on the same level.

Here then is a picture of the dynamic as compared with the static society. Force is generated from movement. The same is true of East and West. On a far vaster scale the movements generated by decay and expansion have been made to drive the machinery of progress. But here too there is presumably an optimum volume and speed. Too little movement would produce a stagnation of thought. Too violent a movement could destroy one of the two cylinders on which the machine's efficiency must depend. And a still greater violence could destroy the whole plant. There are grounds, therefore, for concluding that the dynamics of the East-West relationship are worthy of study throughout the world. In a single volume planned on a modest scale, it would be impossible to bring such a study to its end. It is enough perhaps to claim, at this stage, that the work has at least begun.

1

THE ANCIENT EAST

ALL HISTORIES used to begin with the opening lines of *The Iliad*:

> Sing the wrath, O Goddess, the baleful wrath of Achilles son of Peleus, that laid on the Achaeans ten thousand sorrows, and sent away goodly souls of heroes to Hades, and themselves it gave to dogs and all the birds; and the counsel of Zeus was fulfilled, from the day when first Atreides, king of men, and the divine Achilles quarrelled and stood apart. Who among the gods set them twain to fight?

Here is a good beginning to one of the greatest stories, and what is the story about? It concerns the quarrel between Agamemnon and Achilles, begins with the intervention of Apollo, and ends with the funeral of Hector. Homer thus typifies many later authors to whom the rivalries on one side have seemed more interesting than the conflict as a whole. But *The Iliad*, dealing with peoples already civilized, points the way back to an earlier period. We are bound to ask at the outset where civilization really began. And while there may be disagreement about the rival claims of Mesopotamia and Egypt, it is generally agreed that civilization has its origin in one or the other. With some hesitation scholars have fixed on 2169 B.C. as the date on which Babylon's first dynasty was founded. And whereas the Egyptian Old Kingdom may date from 3000 B.C., there were older civilizations in Sumer and Akkad from which both Egypt and Babylon

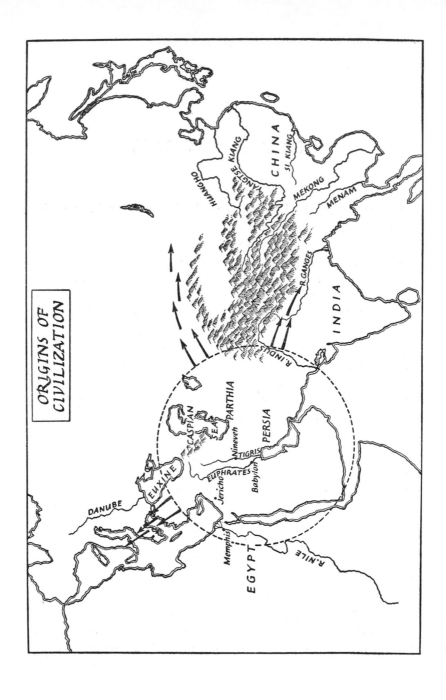

ORIGINS OF CIVILIZATION

CHINA

HUANG-HO
YANGTSE KIANG
SI KIANG
MEKONG
MENAM

R. GANGES
R. INDUS

INDIA

PARTHIA
CASPIAN SEA
Nineveh
PERSIA
TIGRIS
EUPHRATES
Babylon
Jericho

EUXINE
DANUBE

Memphis
EGYPT
R. NILE

derived. If world civilization has any one cradle, it would seem to have been somewhere between Babylon and Memphis. So far as is known, the civilizations of India and China were of rather later date, whether derivative or not. There were cities in the Indus Valley from about 3000 B.C. (Harappa and Mohenjo-Daro), and the first recorded dynasty in China (the Shang, c. 1450 B.C.) ruled over peoples long since civilized. On all evidence so far available, it is clear that civilization began in the Middle East, and appeared soon afterwards in India and China.

But what do we mean by civilization? We mean, literally, the art of living in cities. But this follows, historically, the rise of agriculture as opposed to the earlier and pastoral type of economy. Without the plow, without the basis of settled cultivation, no city — and therefore no civilization — is even possible. Whether the cultivation of barley began in Egypt or Mesopotamia, Syria or Moab, we know that it transformed the life of its discoverers. Villages, essential to agriculture, became towns and towns became cities. With agriculture came the worship of the gods, without which the crops would not ripen, and, from that, divine kingship under which whole river valleys could be unified. Under these ancient monarchies some great progress was made in irrigation, architecture, and metalwork. The Sumerians evolved a form of writing, and also an arithmetic based on the number sixty. To this we can trace the 360 degrees of the circle, as also the sixty minutes in the hour. They may have discovered the wheel and the chariot, for they used both at an early period. The Egyptians had produced a fairly accurate calendar by 3500 B.C., with 365 days in the year. They had the seagoing sailing ship by 2500 B.C., and the shadow clock by 1500. In the building of the pyramids, they displayed a respectable knowledge of mathematics and engineering. All this achievement long antedated anything in Europe that could be called civilization. The pioneers of progress were all more or less Oriental, and they all based their civilization on their central institution of monarchy. Religion, security, order, and justice all depended upon a more or less deified king.

The rise of Babylon may be said to have begun with the conquest of Ur by the Amorites in about 2200 B.C. Under the Babylonian kings, of which line Hammurabi was the sixth and greatest, Babylon became famous for its laws, its architecture, its wealth, its metallurgy and textiles. The use of iron originated apparently with the Hittites of Asia Minor, who may have obtained the ore from Armenia. It was also from the Hittites that the people of Babylon learned how to train horses and make chariots. Among the most remarkable of the Hittite documents so far discovered is a treatise on horsemanship dating from about 1360 B.C. The author of this work, which also shows some Indian influence, describes a training period of six months. Beginning with the selection of the faster horses, he deals with their feeding and watering, their training at the walk, amble, and gallop, and every other detail of a daily routine. Horses may have been brought to Babylon by the Kassites themselves, from Mitanni. Scarcely known in the time of Hammurabi, they became more numerous after 1750 B.C. and were even exported to Egypt. They were so valuable, even then, as to form an acceptable gift from one king to another. They were used only to draw chariots, whether for purposes of ceremony or war. From Babylon, the uses of iron and of the horse-drawn chariot spread to adjacent lands, to Egypt and the Aegean. The purposes for which the chariot was used are sufficiently described in *The Iliad*, and were evidently much the same in Egypt, India, Tibet, China, and Europe.

It was when Babylon and Egypt remained the twin centers of civilization, with the former stagnant and declining under its Kassite rulers, the latter, under Rameses III, that Troy fell to the Greeks. This seems to have been in about 1250 B.C. — modern archaeologists having come to the conclusion that Herodotus was right, as indeed he often was. Being written in 850 B.C., or

thereabouts, *The Iliad* and *The Odyssey* represent an oral tradition rather than a contemporary narrative. But they vividly
describe a Greek invasion of Asia Minor and one which undoubtedly took place. Led by Agamemnon and Menelaus of
Sparta, the Achaeans were campaigning near the entrance to the
Hellespont. And the fall of Troy heralded a regular conquest of
the whole coastline from Phocaea to Miletus. The Ionic cities
of Asiatic Greece had all, apparently, existed before the Ionian
invasion, the previous inhabitants being expelled or absorbed.
They would seem to have fallen to the Greeks at some period
before 776 B.C. Inland of these coastal settlements was the Lydian monarchy of Sardes, formidable from 700 B.C. on, and representing perhaps an earlier movement from the west. All the
peoples west of the river Halys seem to have had a certain kinship; beyond that river were peoples of more typically Asian
origin and Semitic character. This movement of tribes from
Europe extended to the Black Sea, its furthest reach being represented by the legend of the *Argo*. All these territories west of
the Halys came to be absorbed finally in the kingdom of Lydia,
ruled by King Croesus.

In the movement between East and West the Achaean invasion of Asia Minor represented an early phase. Was it, in fact,
the first? Or were the Achaeans reacting to an earlier invasion,
the movement which had first brought the arts of civilization
into the Aegean? While that would seem probable, the actual
story is hard to reconstruct. Of this, however, we can be certain:
that the pendulum had begun to swing, the East-West engine
had been set in motion, by 1250 B.C. It was from the beginning
a complex process, involving a struggle for supremacy in either
camp. Asia Minor was the principal theater of conflict and was
so to remain for centuries. It is there, to this day, that the East-
West contrast is most clearly visible in its architectural form.
There is here a Greek column and there a Turkish battlement, a
church here and a mosque there, the superimposed relics of
Persia and Macedonia, Rome and Islam. The invasion of Asia

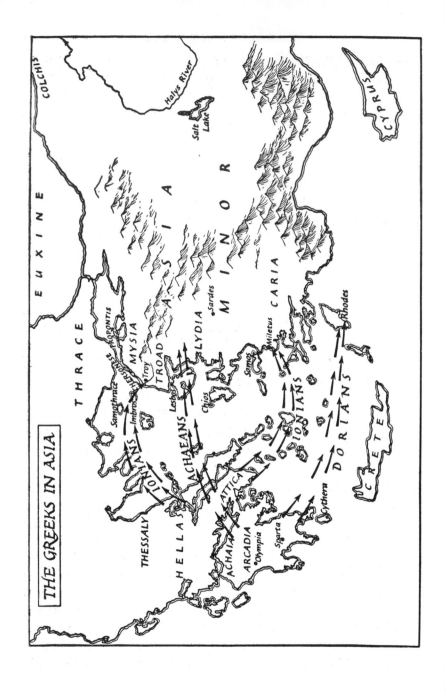

THE GREEKS IN ASIA

COLCHIS

CYPRUS

Halys River

Salt Lake

EUXINE

ASIA MINOR

THRACE

CHERSONESE
Samothrace
Imbros
Propontis
MYSIA
Troy
TROAD
Lesbos
Chios
Samos
Miletus
Sardes
LYDIA
CARIA
Rhodes

THESSALY

IONIANS

HELLAS

ACHAEANS

ATTICA

IONIANS

DORIANS

CRETE

ACHAIA
ARCADIA
Olympia
Sparta
Scythera

had lost its momentum by the time of Croesus, whose legend and whose monetary innovations may well represent the character of an Affluent Society, a civilization that has found in comfort a substitute for adventure. Opposite Lydia the energies of Asia were collecting. And the first question, as always, was one of leadership. Of the various racial groups, which was to give direction? Which would spearhead the Asian reaction to the European assault? There was a period of rivalry, a trial of strength, and then the Medes and Persians stood forth as the leading people of the East. After the story, therefore, of Agamemnon and Achilles, we pass to the story of Cyrus and Darius. It remains to describe how their leadership was established and to what great movement, from East to West, it was the necessary prelude.

The Bronze Age had come to an end by about 1200 B.C., and with it the old empire of Babylon. Indo-European invaders had subdued Babylon in 1600, making it the center of the Hittite Empire. Although armed with iron, the Hittites failed against Egypt, and were themselves conquered by the Assyrians and their war chariots. They established a new capital at Nineveh, and conquered Egypt in 668–625. Nineveh fell to a new group of people, the Chaldeans, in 612, and this led to the revival of Babylon. Finally, the Chaldeans were subjugated by the Medes and Persians under Cyrus the Great in 550–530 B.C. Cyrus was a Persian whose leadership had been accepted by the Medes in 549, and who, by his own account, took Babylon "without a battle." This was the occasion, in 539, described by the prophet Daniel, when Belshazzar, King of Babylon, had given a banquet for a thousand of his lords, wives, and concubines. Then came the mysterious writing on the wall, as interpreted by Daniel: MENE — God hath numbered thy kingdom, and finished it; TEKEL — Thou art weighed in the balance, and art found wanting; PERES — Thy kingdom is divided, and given to the Medes and Persians . . . In that night was Belshazzar, the king of the Chaldeans, slain. And Darius the Median took the kingdom, being about three score and two years old. It was Cyrus, in fact, who conquered Babylon so smoothly, and the fall of Belshazzar would seem to have been the result of a palace intrigue and one in which Daniel was presumably involved. But Cyrus actually treated the dethroned king with consideration, and went into mourning when (in 538) his prisoner died. Having already conquered Lydia, capturing Sardes from King Croesus and occupying the whole of Asia Minor, Cyrus now tried to secure his eastern frontier against the nomads of Central Asia. Being killed in battle, he was succeeded by his son Cambyses in 530. An expedition against Egypt had been planned by Cyrus, and now went forward under Cambyses's leadership. The Egyptians were defeated, Memphis fell, and Cambyses became the new pharaoh. He died soon afterwards, and was succeeded, after a period of civil war, by Darius, son of Hystaspes, the satrap of Parthia. It was under Darius that the Persians established an empire destined to last for two centuries, an empire which might easily have absorbed the whole known world. In the story of the relationship between East and West, the Persians play a decisive role. Of the four great Oriental civilizations — Mesopotamia, Egypt, India, and China — the Persians managed to absorb three into one political organization. The mere size of their achievement is difficult to grasp, and yet, without a knowledge of Persia, the rest of the story becomes incomprehensible.

Although Darius was the great king in Persian history, Cyrus had prepared the way for him. And what Cyrus had done was to gain possession of Asia Minor, conquering both Lydia and the Ionian cities of the coast. The invasion from the West, of which there is some early hint in the story of Jason's voyage from Thessaly to Colchis, had reached its furthest extent, perhaps, in 700 B.C. But it had provoked a movement from the opposite direction, one which began at some period after the eastward movement had lost its impetus. By the time of Cyrus, the tide

had gone in the other direction. Cyrus was no ruthless conqueror and, as Ghirshman says: "Few kings have left behind so
noble a reputation," * but he had perceived the advantages which
his kingdom could derive from the trade between East and
West. It was Darius who now pursued this policy to its logical
conclusion. It was he who gathered together and summarized
the entire achievement of the ancient East. It was he who
brought nearly the whole of the civilized world under a single
centralized government. In the history of the world, Darius
played, as we shall see, a most important part.

* R. Ghirshman, *Iran*, trans. by the author (London: Pelican, 1961), p. 133.

2

DARIUS THE KING

Saith Darius the King: By the favour of Ahuramazda these are
the countries which I seized outside of Persia; I ruled over them;
they bore tribute to me; what was said to them by me, that they
did; my law — that held them firm; Media, Elam, Parthia, Asia,
Bactria, Sogdiona, Chorasmia, Drangiana, Arnchosia, Sattagydia,
Gandara, Sind, Amyrgian Scythians, Scythians with pointed caps,
Babylonia, Assyria, Arnbiz, Egypt, Armenia, Cappadocia, Sardis,
Ionia, Scythians who are across the sea, Skudia, petasos wearing
Ionians, Libyans, Ethiopians, men of Maka, Carians.

Saith Darius the King: Much which was ill-done, that I made
good. Provinces were in commotion; one man was smiting the
other. The following I brought about by the favour of Ahura-
mazda, that the one does not smite the other at all, each one is
in his place. My law — of that they feel fear, so that the stronger
does not smite nor destroy the weak.*

This inscription, which still remains on a tablet found at
Susa, describes accurately the extent of the Persian Empire.
Darius did, in fact, rule from Thrace to the Indus, from the
Caucasus to the Indian Ocean. It took him some years to establish his rule, which was difficult besides to sustain, but the facts
remain generally true: his law it was that kept them, more or
less, in their place. Most of the empire was his by right of conquest, but it was ruled with a benevolence of which Cyrus had
set the example. No attempt was made to turn unity into uniformity. Each territory kept its own language and religion, and
the man who was king at Susa was known as pharaoh in Egypt.

* Ghirshman, *op. cit.*, p. 153.

Under Cyrus (559–530 B.C.), the most generous of rulers, this policy of decentralization had gone too far, compelling his successors to begin the conquest all over again. Learning from this, Darius (522–486 B.C.) set up a far stronger organization. He divided the empire into twenty provinces, each under a governor, or satrap, chosen from among the Persian nobility. Each satrap had with him a military commander, a chief secretary, and a principal tax collector, all responsible directly to the king. To make assurance doubly sure, there were also traveling inspectors who could arrive, unexpected, and ask to see the accounts. From the considerable revenue that was collected, Darius could maintain his court and administration, his royal bodyguard — the Ten Thousand Immortals — his building projects, and his provincial garrisons. His rule would seem to have been very effective indeed.

What was novel about the Persian Empire was its lack of geographical cohesion. The cultures from which the Persians derived their civilization had each arisen on a single river system: the Nile, the Euphrates, the Tigris, and the Indus. Parallel and connected civilizations had developed on the banks of the Huangho, the Yangtze, the Menam, and the Mekong. The elaboration of the culture had been closely connected with the length of the river.*

> The rivers that were carrying to the sea not only water but men, goods, ideas, had to be pretty large to provide a sufficient concentration and competition in the lower reaches. Any culture, even the least developed, is so complex that it cannot be created by small groups, but only by relatively large ones — thousands or millions of men. To appreciate the immensity of the tasks that had to be accomplished, one need think of only one element, language, the perfection of which implied a multitudinous, anonymous, unconscious fermentation of unimaginable intricacy.†

* The Nile is 3473 miles long, the Yangtze 3200, the Indus 1800.
† George Sarton, *History of Science* (Oxford, 1953), p. 19.

In areas less civilized, the main river was often not long
enough. What Darius attempted was to combine in one empire
the river valleys of the Tigris, Euphrates, Nile, and Indus, with
possible extension to the Ganges, the Danube, and Dnieper.
His first need was for a system of communication between one
river and another. This could take one of two forms, the construction of roads or the building of ships. In practice, there
would need to be both, with fast horses on the one, and ample
tonnage on the other. But the road which is intended basically
for official purposes — for the messenger with letters of recall,
for the reinforcements sent to the frontier — comes to be used
by the merchant as well. It cannot be otherwise, for it is to
the merchant that the troops will send their booty and from
whom they will purchase their supplies. The harbor intended
for warships will soon, in practice, shelter the merchantman as
well. Again, it cannot be otherwise, for it is to the merchant that
the admiral will turn for his timber and cordage. There was
trade before the time of Darius, but under his rule, and unified
by his law, appeared the first great trade route of the world.
Herodotus calls it the Ancient Royal Road. He tells us, moreover, that it went from Susa across the Euphrates, to the Cilician
Gates, and so across Asia Minor to Sardes and Ephesus. There
was an alternative northern route, on the other side of Tay
Chela (the great salt lake), which went south of the Black Sea
and across the basin of the Halys River, and so to the Bosphorus and to Smyrna. In the opposite direction was the road
to Ecbatana, Herat, and India, with an extension from Herat
to Bactria, Yarkand, and China.

At intervals all along the road are recognised stations, with
excellent inns, and the road itself is safe to travel by, as it never
leaves inhabited country. In Lydia and Phrygia, over a distance
of 94½ parasangs — about 330 miles — there are 20 stations. On
the far side of Phrygia one comes to the river Halys; there are

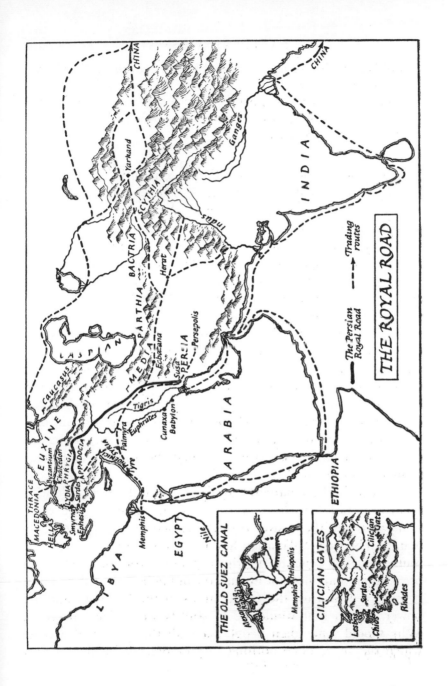

THE ROYAL ROAD

—— The Persian Royal Road
- - - → Trading routes

THE OLD SUEZ CANAL

CILICIAN GATES

gates here, which have to be passed before one crosses the river.
The post is strongly guarded. Once over the river, and into Cappadocia, a distance of 104 parasangs with 28 stations, brings one
to the Cilician border, where the road passes through two sets of
gates, both guarded . . .

Herodotus goes on to describe the three months' journey from
the coast to the Palace of Memnon, counting 111 stations or
posthouses between Sardes and Susa, and describing the ferries
and gates. What took the merchants ninety days was covered
by the royal envoys in a week, using relays of horses. Nor was
the road a mere track. It was so well leveled and paved that some
parts of it still exist. It represented an elaborate and costly piece
of organization, surveyed and mapped, planned and constructed,
policed and staffed, maintained and guarded. Nor did Darius
neglect to provide the alternative routes by sea, canal, and river,
with quaysides and organized ports. More than that, he completed the ship canal between the Nile and the Red Sea, a work
begun by the Egyptian pharaoh Necos, and left unfinished after
the expenditure of 120,000 lives. "The greater part of Asia was
discovered by Darius," says Herodotus, going on to explain how
the coast was explored from the Indus back to Egypt. "After the
voyage was completed, Darius subdued the Indians and made
regular use of the southern ocean."

But why did he *subdue* the Indians? Could he not trade with
them peacefully? In the story of imperial expansion, this question recurs and the answer is often framed in terms of megalo-
mania. The true explanation lies in the very nature of the trade
route. Having gone to all the expense involved, whether in
breakwaters and pilots, or in culverts and police, the ruler cannot
be expected to leave the far terminus in the hands of another
power. To do that would be to stultify the whole operation.
Why should some alien people have all the benefit of a trade
which they have done nothing to promote? Why should they

be allowed to levy a toll without rendering any service? And, apart from that, will merchants ever use a route on which no safety can be guaranteed beyond a certain point? Even purely technical considerations would point to the same conclusion. For, without a dependable source of supplies at the far end, the return journey or voyage may well prove impossible. And what about warehouses? Ideally, the goods which the ship or caravan is to bring back should be collected in advance under cover and under the eye of a watchman. A resident agent should have done the buying at leisure and should be free to sell at leisure after the carrier has gone. There should be credit facilities and under-writers, implying a known system of commercial law. All this implies a measure of political control. Having subdued the Indians, Darius could make regular use of a trade route which was effectively his. And, having subdued the Ionian cities, he could feel as secure in the opposite direction. As the Persian saying went, "Darius was a tradesman."

With the trade route in full operation, Darius could draw on the technical knowledge of his own empire. Himself "an Achaemenian, a Persian, son of a Persian, an Aryan, having Aryan lineage," * he could draw in the first place on the traditions of his own racial group. His tombstone, as Strabo records, reads as follows: "I was a friend to my friends; as horseman and bowman I proved myself superior to all others; as a hunter I prevailed; I could do everything." † This was all profoundly true; so much so that the various points deserve separate emphasis. He was a friend, first of all, to his friends. He stood by his fellow nobles and officers, looked after his troops, and protected his allies. Nor did he place himself on so high a pedestal as to make friendship impossible. He was no earthly god or robed image, but an active soldier claiming the obedience of those below him in rank. And his claim to authority rested, first and

* Ghirshman, op. cit., p. 153.
† Ibid., p. 152.

foremost, on his soldierly reputation. As horseman and bowman he had proved himself the best. How? By rising to the
command of the Ten Thousand Immortals, the household
troops, the post he had held before he obtained the throne. As
for horsemanship, it was to that that he owed his throne. Among
the seven conspirators who had ended the previous regime, the
choice of king was to fall on whichever one's horse was the first
to neigh after sunrise on the following morning. With the help
of his groom, Darius ensured his own success, and afterwards
built a commemorative monument on which the horse was portrayed and the groom named. Pegasus apart, this is one of the
most famous horses in history, and the incident is the more significant in that the horse was not yoked but ridden. The competition was one among horsemen, not among the drivers of
chariots. By the time of Darius, in fact, the Persian gentleman
was never seen on foot.

Horsemanship was a part of the King's Persian inheritance,
but the cavalry tradition owed something to the other parts of
the empire. Horses had first been trained in the steppe country
east of the Caspian Sea. They were used at first in chariots, as
described in *The Iliad*, appearing first in about 2000 B.C. "No
cavalry was used until Sennacherib put mounted archers into the
Assyrian forces in 800 B.C., and the horse's head was held by a
man on foot." * Having learned their cavalry tradition from
the Assyrians, the Persians put a high value on horses, and
especially upon the white horses they used to sacrifice at the
tomb of Cyrus. But the Lydians were also horsemen and far
more skilled than the Greeks. This fact is brought out by Herodotus in the story of King Croesus and his plan for building
ships — a plan he abandoned on being told that his subjects
would be at as great a disadvantage at sea as their Greek opponents would be on horseback. These references to riding do not
prove that the chariot was obsolete. On the contrary, Darius

* Astley J. H. Goodwin, *Communication Has Been Established* (London, 1937),
p. 48.

is represented in his famous cylinder seal as shooting a lion from his chariot, and with evident success. What they do prove is that horses had been bred of a size that could be ridden. And this was an important factor in the Persian campaign, as it was also in the system of communications by which the empire was held together.

Other techniques came from other sources. Weights and measures and business practices were derived from ancient Babylon. The idea of law came from the ancient code of Hammurabi. The language of common use, Aramaic, came from the region of Damascus. The art of stonecutting came from Ionia via Sardes, the art of brickmaking from Babylon, the art of bas-relief from the Assyrians. From the Hittites came the arts of coining money and using iron. From Lydia came the bimetallic currency, the invention of Croesus, itself a powerful factor in the development of commerce. From ancient Mesopotamia was derived the practice of banking, with deposits, loans, and rates of interest. From Egypt came the art of writing on papyrus, and also a number of astronomical discoveries and the use of the shadow clock. From the Phoenicians came the alphabet. And the trade which brought the Persians into contact with the Indians had its indirect extension to the Ganges Valley and indeed to China. As for the claim made by Darius — "I could do everything" — it was roughly true. Nor would anyone be able to do much more for many centuries to come. For the technology of the Greeks and Romans was not superior to that of Persia, as modern historians of technology have pointed out. "The curve of technological expertness tends to dip rather than to rise with the advent of the classical cultures." * The Persians had inherited almost every technical skill which was to be available before the beginnings of modern history. With very few exceptions, these techniques were derived from the East.

Having control of the world's main trade route, Darius wished

* C. Singer, E. J. Holmyard, and A. R. Hall, A History of Technology (Oxford, 1954–58), II, 753.

— and logically — to extend his control in either direction. In India his operations may have extended to the Peshawar district, and his troops certainly reached the Indus. In the west he first turned his attention to Scythia — to what we should now describe as southern Russia. This would seem to have been the first move in a campaign against the Greeks, and as such it was a partial success. It left him in possession of Thrace and Macedonia, with a useful bridgehead from which to stage a further advance. Against the Scythians proper he had little success because he failed to overtake them or bring them to battle. They would neither fight nor surrender, having limitless space in which to withdraw and no cities which they felt bound to defend. Darius had the sort of frustration later felt by Napoleon and Hitler. This campaign gave his Greek opponents a perfect opportunity to attack the Hellespont, cut his line of communication, and prevent his return to Persia. But the Greeks lacked the necessary cohesion. Some of the Ionians were actively assisting Darius, while the Athenian democrats, led by Hippias, were in favor of appeasement. Nothing was done until after Darius had extricated himself. It was then, and not until then, that the Ionian cities saw their opportunity. This was the moment they chose for their revolt against Persia. They were actively assisted by Greeks from across the sea, but to little purpose. The rebellion was crushed and the cities of the "Ionian League" were successively captured. Byzantium and Chalcedon were destroyed, and the population of Miletus was removed to Persia. Chios and Lesbos fell and preparation followed for an attack on Greece itself. In the Greeks, Darius had sensed an alien opposition to his plans. Nor was he the first Persian king to look upon them with distaste. Said Cyrus once, according to Herodotus, "I never yet feared the kind of men who have a place set apart in the middle of the city in which they get together, and tell one another lies under oath." His attitude was reasonable, but we need to ask, at this point, what kind of men they really were.

3

T.HE TALE OF TROY

Think of a time when the wheeling constellations did not yet exist; when one would have looked in vain for the sacred Danaan race, finding only the Apidanian Arcadians, who are said to have lived before the moon itself was there, feeding on acorns in the hills. These were the days before the noble scions of Deucalion ruled the Pelasgian land, when Egypt, mother of an earlier race, was known as the corn-rich country of the Dawn . . .*

So wrote Apollonius of Rhodes, setting his modern readers no easy task. It is only by a great effort that we can think of the exact period to which he refers. We feel more confident of the chronology in Hesiod or Homer; and it is from Homer, indeed, that our earliest classical history is derived. In *The Iliad,* he describes part of a campaign fought in Asia Minor, an early phase of that movement which was to establish the Greeks on that coast. Their opponents, the Trojans, are believed to have been a Phrygian tribe, culturally different from the Hellenes but racially much the same. If there was a difference between the two armies, however, there were at least comparable differences among the allies themselves on the invading side. "Think of a time," says Apollonius, when "the sacred Danaan race" did not exist. Was the Homeric period such a time? Had the Achaeans much sense of affinity among themselves?

The Achaeans, as they are known, were, it seems, the builders of the cities of Tiryns, Mycenae and Orchonenos, and the heirs

* Apollonius of Rhodes, *The Voyage of the* Argo, trans. by E. V. Rieu (London: Penguin, 1959), p. 154.

of the Minoan sea empire which . . . they overthrew about
1400 B.C. In the Mycenaean Age (1400–1200 B.C.) they dominated the coasts along the Aegaean Sea, warring with one another, and fighting all comers. Chief among these opponents
was Troy, which occupied the ancient site that dominated the
Hellespont. The Trojans were a branch of the Phrygian people
who penetrated Asia Minor when the Hittite powers began to
weaken; apparently, they occupied the site near the entrance of
the Hellespont about 1500 B.C. . . . Shortly after 1200 B.C. the
Achaeans under the leadership of Mycaenae, which suffered from
Trojan competition in the pottery trade, united to attack this
stronghold. Whether they triumphed by trickery, as narrated by
Homer, or carried the city by storm is unknown; at any rate, they
captured it, reduced the walls and burned its citadel. The date
now usually assigned for the Trojan War is 1194–1184 B.C.*

To descend from the deathless story of Helen's abduction to
the more sordid level of competition in the pottery trade is
almost too abrupt; a fall from cloud-capped Ilium to Stoke-on-
Trent. And it is arguable, surely, that there was more to it than
that. For *The Iliad* scarcely includes any mention of the Hellenes as such, nor are their opponents described as "foreigners."
Chryse, it is true, begins his appeal "My lords, and you Achaean
men-at-arms," but there is much talk thereafter of the Argives,
the Locrians, the Myrmidons, and Dolopes. The Trojan allies
were of still more differing origin, according to Homer, had no
language in common, and "used many different cries and
calls." † The Greeks were so many tribal groups assembled from
the scattered islands and mountain valleys of their homeland.
How far they were united, it is difficult to say. But the basic
geographical fact governing their lives was the lack of any one
river system on which their culture might be based. The civili-

* Ralph Turner, *The Great Cultural Traditions* (New York, 1941), I, 235.
† Homer, *The Iliad*, trans. by E. V. Rieu (London: Penguin, 1950), p. 88.

zations of the ancient East had each grown up along a single
river. The Persian empire linked by road and sea the different
civilizations which it had with difficulty absorbed. The Hellenes
had no river of any length, and no large agricultural plain from
which a city of any size could draw its food. Their unity, such
as it was, depended upon the sea, and their cities, as they arose,
depended increasingly on their trade with other lands. Having
no foodstuffs or raw materials to export, they relied from the
start on industry and trade. Essential to them was their trade
with the Hellespont and Euxine, their main source of corn and
dried fish. Even to maintain this vital trade, they needed timber
for shipbuilding, which came to them from the Euxine, and iron
for their weapons, which came from the same direction and originally from Asia Minor. For profit, as opposed to subsistence,
they looked to a further traffic in luxury goods — a traffic, in
fact, with the East. So the great trade route which Darius looked
upon as essentially his, was regarded by the Greeks as essentially
theirs, at any rate at its western end. If the Persians relied upon
the East–West trade for their imperial unity, the Greeks relied
upon it for their mere existence. Their instinct was to secure
control of the ports through which the trade must pass, beginning naturally, with those of the Hellespont and Bosphorus. It
is no coincidence that nine cities were built in succession on
the same Trojan site. Control of the straits had been in dispute
from early times. What movement there had been in either direction during centuries of prehistory, it may never be possible
to say, but the city sacked by Agamemnon, son of Atreus and
King of Mycenae, was not the first but the seventh. The
Achaeans fairly swept over the coasts of Asia Minor — as we
have seen (p. 5) — and their descendants were there when
Darius came to deal with them. His was a belated counterattack,
response to an invasion which took place centuries before, and
which may, itself, have been the sequel to some previous movement in the other direction. By the time of Darius (522–486

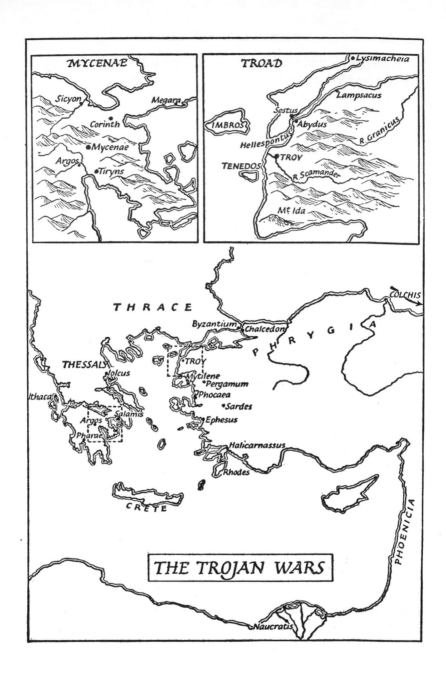

MYCENAE

Sicyon

Megara

Corinth

• Mycenae

Argos

• Tiryns

TROAD

• Lysimacheia

Lampsacus

Sestus

IMBROS

Abydus

Hellespontus

R. Granicus

• TROY

TENEDOS

R. Scamander

Mt Ida

THRACE

COLCHIS

Byzantium

Chalcedon

P H R Y G I A

THESSALY

• TROY

Iolcus

Mytilene

• Pergamum

Ithaca

• Phocaea

• Sardes

Argos

Salamis

• Ephesus

Pharae

Halicarnassus

Rhodes

CRETE

PHOENICIA

THE TROJAN WARS

• Naucratis

B.C.), the pendulum had been set in motion. The Hellenes were alien intruders on territory which was rightfully his, and our first task is to discover in what sense they were alien.

Returning again to *The Iliad*, we find there one or two indications of a contrast between the Achaeans and their Trojan opponents — a first hint or two of Greek peculiarities. They were, to begin with, more interested in ships than in horses. Homer refers constantly to "the horse-taming Trojans" as contrasted with "the bronze-clad Achaeans." That is not to say that the Achaeans were uninterested in their horses and chariots, for this would be untrue. But some were less interested than others, and all would have been ready to admit that the better horses were in the Trojan camp. It was perhaps because they were big men and bronze-clad that the Achaeans did not ride, their small dun-colored horses being scarcely up to their weight. Significant in this context is the incident of Dolon, Odysseus, and Diomedes.* The Trojans sent Dolon to reconnoitre the Achaean camp. He was promptly captured and interrogated by Odysseus. After giving full information about the Trojan order of battle, Dolon reveals that the newly arrived Thracian king, Rhesus, is encamped at the very end of the line, his white horses being the biggest and finest ever seen. The result is the raid by Odysseus and Diomedes, from which these heroes returned *on horseback*, leaving fourteen men dead beside the Thracian campfire. Nestor hails Odysseus as "flower of Achaean *chivalry*," and adds, "I have never seen or imagined horses like these." It was with this pair that Diomedes won the chariot race at the funeral games held in memory of Patroclus, and they came, significantly, from Thrace.

For horse breeding, the Achaeans were badly placed. They had small pastures, scanty forage, and a terrain mostly unsuitable for cavalry. They may have become obsessed at times with their opponents' superiority in this respect. Such an obsession

* *The Iliad*, Book X, p. 190.

might underlie the story of the Wooden Horse. Was such an effigy likely to be of particular interest to the horse-loving Trojans? And was this an interest which the Persians felt for later horses, both living and carved in bas-relief? Darius thought of himself, first and foremost as "horseman and bowman." Persian boys of noble birth were brought up to ride, use the bow and speak the truth.* The Achaean method of upbringing had no such emphasis. They did not ride and, while they used the bow, their heroes did not fight with it. Archers they had, but they were, as Oman points out "light troops without horse, lance, shield, or defensive armour . . . mere furtive hoverers on the edge of battle," † and while Odysseus certainly shot down the suitors for Penelope, he had caught them, remember, without shield or armor. As for truth, the Persians had some grounds for thinking the Hellenes their inferiors in veracity. For Herodotus remarks (and *he* should have known), "The Greeks in general have a weakness for inventing stories with no basis of fact." ‡ They can thus be said to have lacked the qualities which the Persians had been taught to value. As against that, the Greeks of the Homeric period had, by Homer's account, some characteristics which other peoples lacked. On three of these it will be proper now to comment. They had a special interest in athletics. They had the beginnings of a sense of humor. They placed a great value on seamanship.

Take first their interest in athletics. When reading *The Iliad*, one has no great sense of contrast between the opposing armies. They would seem to have been much the same sort of people, as indeed they probably were. What sharp difference there is would seem to be revealed in their funeral customs.

---

* Herodotus, *The Histories*, trans. by Aubrey de Selincourt (London: Penguin, 1954), p. 68.
† Sir Charles Oman, *The Art of War in the Middle Ages* (London, 1924), I, 25.
‡ Herodotus, *op. cit.*, p. 120.

When Hector dies, his body is burned on a funeral pyre, the bones are buried under a mound of earth, and the mourners attend a banquet. *The Iliad* ends, indeed, with these words: "Such were the funeral rites of Hector, tamer of horses." But the funeral of Patroclus centers upon an athletic meeting. It begins with a chariot race, replete with accusations of jostling and crowding, accompanied by eager betting, and leading to a dispute as to who gets the second prize. Then there is a boxing match, won by a knockout to the jaw. An all-in wrestling contest ends in a draw, but Odysseus wins the race on foot. There follows then a fencing match, putting the weight, and archery. The last event, javelin throwing, is canceled for lack of time, and the soldiers disperse to supper. Each of these funerals, remember, took place under a truce made with the enemy. The Trojans could have held games, had this been their custom; the Achaeans had all they needed for a banquet, had that been a necessary part of the rites. But they had different ideas as to what should be done, and the Hellenic idea is one of special interest.

Some people may question whether the sports meeting took place as described. Homer, they might object, is believed to have written at some period before 700 B.C. — say 450 years after the fall of Troy. Could he have learned the true facts from oral tradition? Some of the facts he certainly did learn, but much of his description might be thought more applicable to his own time than to the period of Agamemnon and Aeneas. Granted that this may be the fact, he still describes a well-established athletic tradition. The first Olympic games are supposed to have been held in 776 B.C., but they can have been no novelty even then. As for Homer's description, it has everything. Nestor gives Antilochus some hints on gamesmanship. Achilles, who distributes the prizes, makes it clear that he would himself have won the main event, had he been competing. There is a consolation prize for a gallant loser. Nestor has to explain that, when younger, he was in a class by himself and won pretty well every event — except, of course, when the two Moliones cut in unfairly during the chariot race. The heavyweight boxer predicts his own victory. The crowd applauds the discus thrower, and all present are lost in admiration for the champion archer. A prize goes (without competition) to the president of the association, who gives it in turn to the man who announced the competitors and results. In its essentials, the whole meeting could have happened yesterday — save only that the occasion was a funeral.

Here then, at a very early period of their history, the Hellenes showed themselves peculiarly athletic. Had they invented the competitions in which they engaged? It seems that they did not. Athletics can be traced to Egypt and to the period following the Battle of Megiddo in 1468 B.C. Thutmose III was a keen archer and Amenhotep apparently keener still. "He could not be overtaken in running races. He was strong of arm, never tiring when pulling the oar." * But the Egyptian taste for athletics seems to have depended upon the Pharaoh's whim. It disappeared under monarchs whose physical prowess was less obvious. Among the Greeks, the love of games would seem to have been at once exceptional and consistent.

In sharp contrast we have the attitude of the Chinese, summarized by Confucius in the words "Gentlemen never compete." Actually, the Chinese did have competitions in archery, but these tended to become competitions in politeness. The Greeks were at once more athletic and more intent on winning, and certain consequences of this peculiarity need emphasis. To begin with, their leaders had to compete. The athletes at the funeral of Patroclus included Menelaus, King of Sparta, Odysseus, King of Ithaca, Aias, King of Salamis, and Diomedes, King of Argos. As for Agamemnon, King of Mycenae and overlord (in some rather vague sense) of all Achaea, he would have won the javelin-throwing competition had not the event been

* John A. Wilson, *The Burden of Egypt* (Chicago, 1951), pp. 195–98.

scratched; or so Achilles assured him. While it is true that these "kings" were the rulers of rather small territories and the leaders of relatively small contingents, they were the only royalty the Achaeans had. Agamemnon has some shadowy precedence over the rest — enough to gain him a prize, ex-officio — but the others can be rude to him on occasion, and Achilles flatly disobeys his orders, calling him drunkard, coward, and bully. From the whole story of *The Iliad*, it is apparent that these kings are — or are believed to be — the best soldiers and athletes in the army. Their authority is not that of the divinely appointed and untouchable despot, enthroned, remote, and mysterious. Agamemnon cannot even direct the battle without having Achilles call him a mere staff officer. These chieftains have to prove themselves, and show their superior prowess. And while Nestor, King of Pylos, derives a little authority from his experience and age, it is clearly less than the others derive from their current reputations. Those with the highest status are in the prime of life. As the old Egyptian priest said to Solon: "Ye ever remain children, in Greece there is no old man." * While this may not have been entirely true, we might fairly conclude that age in Greece was accorded little respect as such. The highest admiration was reserved rather for the athletic, the good-looking, and the brave.

A further point to note in connection with the Hellenic taste for sport is that the competitors were almost or completely naked. There was little mystery left to the Achaean chieftain when the games were over. No robe of office made him seem more than he was. He could scarcely be shown to have won, when he had actually lost. He could not pretend a strength or youth or virility that he did not possess. What he amounted to, all could see for themselves. Godlike he might claim to be, but not merely by descent. For the Achaean gods were very human indeed, and commonly stripped for action. Those who

* S. Davis, *Race Relations in Ancient Egypt* (London, 1951), p. 23.

could claim kinship with them had to show their divine qualities in battle, in sport, and in the nude. Realistic or idealized representation of the human body was to be a chief characteristic of Greek art. This was highly distinctive, contrasting sharply with, say, Chinese art, in which the nude is practically unknown. In this practice of public nudity the Greeks had a basis for some ideas of equality. For, while the common soldier's lesser value was made pretty obvious, his leader's superiority was in human terms. The democratic politician, fairly represented by Thersites, is promptly smacked down by Odysseus. "We cannot all be kings here," he points out to the infantrymen, "and mob rule is a bad thing." But Homer gives no great weight to that hero's higher status. He is essentially a bigger and stronger man, experienced, cunning, handsome, and quick. His leadership derives from qualities he is known to possess, and which others might presumably imitate. As for divine descent, these Achaean chiefs are virile men with an eye for the prettiest girls. As generations pass, their godlike ancestry will become the fairly common attribute of a widening circle of descendants. Their children, like their gods, could be very like themselves.

The Homeric characters, whether human gods or godlike men, have also the beginnings of a sense of humor. It may not amount to much, but it must not pass unnoticed. One's first impression might be wrong in this respect. The occasions for laughter seem few. The gods roar with laughter to see Hephaestus bustling up and down the hall, though we are not told exactly why. There is a general laugh when Thersites is beaten by Odysseus. Hector and his wife, Andromache, have to laugh when their little boy is frightened of his father's helmet and plume. Odysseus returns laughing from his raid on the Trojan lines.* There is nothing in all this to suggest that Homer himself had much sense of humor, and his characters, after ten years of war, might be excused, perhaps, for their failure to see the funny side of it. As against

* Homer, op. cit., pp. 39, 47, 129, 196.

this, the scenes which take place between the immortals themselves, with no humans present, have an atmosphere which is
not entirely serious. While not exactly farcical, they are far
removed from the solemnities of the Old Testament. And
Homer presumably intends a joke when he makes Athene join
Diomedes in his chariot, and adds that "the beech-wood axle
groaned aloud at the weight it had to carry." * There is not much
sign, in Homer's work, of laughter softening the asperities current among men, but there is humor enough to make the gods
seem less frightening. At least, by comparison with some other
peoples, the Hellenes would not pass for particularly religious
men.

It would be natural to ask, at this point, why the Greeks were
to differ in this respect from other people. The nature of their
landscape may have had much to do with it. A background of
mountain, hillside, headlands, and isles offers an interest which
is concentrated, in flat country, on the sky. There is then a
contrast between the mental habits associated with woods and
wildflowers and those associated with the brooding immensities.
The point is not that the Greeks turned against their gods,
preferring others, but that they gradually found them more amusing than real. This was the more possible for them in that their
own numbers were small. They were seldom so numerous as to
become victims of any mass hysteria. The army before Troy
was small enough to collect round a single speaker — the more
easily, no doubt, after sickness had reduced its initial strength.
Relatively few in numbers, and without any wish to become
more numerous, the Greeks always remained individual. They
were never as so many grains of sand measured in the light of
eternity. It was their sense of individuality that underlay their
sense of humor. Theirs was a world in which men could resemble gods, and gods still more could resemble men.

Another factor in Greek humor was their use of wine. Hel-

* *Ibid.*, p. 114.

lenic territory grew wine and olives, and in some places little else. Wine was always to play an important part in their way of life, their own being a rather inferior stuff by current standards — Samos perhaps excepted — but constantly mentioned in all their literature. Whether wine can assist the processes of thought may be a matter for dispute, but it certainly helps to create that convivial atmosphere in which things at first thought tragic are seen to be merely funny. Some of the simpler jokes of mankind center upon infirmities, of which intoxication is one. So the effect of the wine is to help the imbiber to see the humorous side of things, the effect of further potations being to make him a source of amusement to others. In some other countries, the jokes have mostly been on a low social level — stories about beggars and fishermen and woodcutters — the rulers and nobles, being so closely connected with the gods, are too dignified to afford any subject for mirth. One effect of wine drinking is to allow the same man to be awe-inspiring at one time and extremely relaxed at another. Jokes which pull the highest things down to human level are more characteristic, perhaps, of wine-drinking peoples than of people reared on milk and water. Ganymede, who became cupbearer to Zeus, had no sinecure, and the other gods who laughed at Hephaestus were already less than sober. When a quarrel develops between Zeus and Hera, the tactful Hephaestus quickly stands the goddess a drink — the text making it clear, incidentally, that the decanter already went clockwise. From the beginning, wine and laughter have gone together.

A last characteristic of the Achaeans, as portrayed in *The Iliad* and *The Odyssey*, was their emphasis on seamanship. The ancient civilizations of Mesopotamia, Egypt, India, and China had been based on river systems. Boats had played an important part, therefore, in their systems of communication. From river estuaries their interest had gradually extended to the sea, to their own coasts, and to the more easily accessible islands. They came to have their ships and seamen, their seaports and customs revenues. But the sea was marginal to their way of life. Sailors and fishermen were useful men, but low in the social scale. For the king to have *seen* the sea might be thought exceptional. For a seaman to become king was hardly a possibility that anyone need consider. But the Greek kings were all seamen before they were anything else. Among their earliest legends was the tale of the *Argo*, the ship commanded by Jason, son of the King of Iolcus in Thessaly. His companions included Admetus, King of Pherae, Periclymenus, the eldest son of King Neleus, Orpheus from Thrace, and great Hercules himself. Whatever substance there might be in this tale of a voyage to Colchis, no Greek hearer thought it strange to have so much royalty aboard. As for *The Iliad*, it tells the story of a combined operation. And *The Odyssey* is no more than the tale of how Odysseus sailed back home to Ithaca.

It is the seascape of the Aegean which provides a further key to the Greek character. Within the confines of a rowing vessel, no one man could have been much of a mystery to the rest. His abilities as a seaman were almost instantly assessed. His prestige must have depended, essentially, on what he could do and not upon what he purported to be. The ship's master, like the leader of a nomadic tribe in the desert, had to be the best man there. But the respect he managed to exact from his shipmates was not due from him to anyone else. He was beyond the effective control of any overlord or priest. He was not easily made subject to law or tax. Like the nomad on the desert fringe, he had behind him an immensity into which he could vanish; what Homer calls "the friendly sea." It gave him a spirit of independence, which was modified in practice by his desire for gain. While he was not easy to overawe, he was often to be bought, and the independence of his spirit applied not only to superiors but to equals. To persuade the Greeks to act together — as they did for the first time against Troy — was a task for legendary heroes, and scarcely feasible for the merely mortal. Imaginative and untruthful, freedom-loving but unreliable, quarrelsome and adventurous, spellbound by beauty, and susceptible to bribes, the Greeks already had a character of their own.

Given their known characteristics, the Greeks could never have civilized themselves. Instead, they took their civilization from the ancient East, from Babylon, and still more from Egypt via Crete. That they should have looked to Egypt in the first place was inevitable, for, of the ancient river cultures, that was the only one which opened on the Mediterranean. Nor had the Greeks themselves any illusions on the subject. They tended, indeed, to overstate their indebtedness to Egypt, so as to minimize their debt to Persia. From Egypt mostly had come their knowledge of architecture, sculpture, and medicine. In point of fact, however, they had also drawn upon Babylon and Assyria for their culture, business practice, and language, with Lydia as their point of contact. Much of their religion had come from the Phrygians, and their alphabet, like their knowledge of trade, came from the Phoenicians in about the tenth century B.C. During the great period of Greek expansion (11th–7th centuries B.C.), the Ionian migrants had colonized part of Asia Minor, while other emigrants had gone to Italy and Sicily. But their contact was maintained with Egypt, or at least revived during the second half of the seventh century. Amasis, King of Egypt, was the man who brought this about, having actually married a woman from Cyrene. How far he was under Greek influence might be inferred from his known achievements, interests, and habits. As Herodotus said of him:

> He used to organise his working day on a regular principle; from dawn till the time when the markets fill up at mid-morning he gave all his attention to such business as was brought to him, after which he spent the rest of the day in frivolous amusement, drinking and joking with friends . . . [When his advisers re-

monstrated with him] . . . Amasis replied . . . 'a bow always
kept strung would break, and so be useless when it was needed.
It is the same with a man; anyone who was always serious, and
never allowed himself a fair share of relaxation and amusement,
would suddenly go off his head, or get a stroke . . .' *

This profound truth Amasis might have learned from his
Greek friends. He certainly saw enough of them. With his
approval, they founded Naucratis, the Greek city in the Nile
Delta (615–610 B.C.). Amasis also had a bodyguard of Ionian
and Carian mercenaries — the Carians being the people from
whom the Greeks had learned how to put crests on their helmets,
as well as handles and painted devices on their shields. All the
Greek contacts with Egypt ended when that land was conquered by Cambyses in 525 B.C., becoming a Persian province.
From that time, the Greeks stood very much alone.

* Herodotus, op. cit., p. 172.

4

THE PHOENICIANS

HAD THE GREEKS been the only seafaring people of the Mediterranean, there would have been something of a deadlock between Persian and Greek aspirations. Darius wanted to extend his trade route westward, the Greeks wanted to extend theirs to the head of the Euxine and as much further as they could go. And, although the Persian monarchy was immensely powerful, the Greeks were far from easy to coerce. Fortunately, from the Persian point of view, there was a rival people to whom Darius could turn. In the Phoenicians he had seafaring allies, the more useful in that their original seaports were within his own empire. And before the Greek movement of expansion, the Phoenicians had been monopolists. As Toutain points out:

> Formerly the Phoenicians had been, for the Greeks themselves and for the other peoples of the Mediterranean, the sole providers of the industrial products which could not be made in the family. It was they who had brought the many creations of the arts and industries of the East to the beaches of the Aegaean and Ionian Seas. When they had been driven from those seas and markets by the Greeks, the Hellenic industries found outlets and customers there . . . trade needing to be fed by industry and industry owing its prosperity to trade.*

The Phoenician cities lay along the Levant coast, the most important being Aradus, Byblos, Sidon, and Tyre. Behind them

* Jules Toutain, *The Economic Life of the Ancient World,* trans. by M. R. Dobie (London, 1930), p. 24.

lay the forests of Lebanon, their source of shipbuilding timber. Their narrow strip of territory produced little else, but formed a corridor connecting Mesopotamia and Egypt. They lived in a restless borderland, fruitful mainly in dispute and ideas, and derived their culture more from Babylon than from Egypt. They soon extended their activities to Cyprus and Crete, and so across the Mediterranean. A Semitic people akin to the Jews, they were most closely allied to them from about 970–940 B.C., when Hiram of Tyre provided Solomon with materials for the temple at Jerusalem. It was mostly after that period that the Phoenicians expanded their trading activities westward. By the eighth century, they held the center of the Mediterranean, with settlements established at Carthage (814 B.C.), Utica, Motyca, and Malta, and more distant trading stations in Sardinia and as far westward as Cadiz. In the other direction, their ships went down the Red Sea to Mesopotamia and India, and the caravans which crossed the desert seem to have been part of the same organization. For some five hundred years, their commercial ascendancy was assured, and the more so in that the Greeks were relatively quiescent. From about 1400 to say 1100 B.C., the Mycenaeans had been pushing into Asia Minor, but their effort had died away. From about 1100, it was the Phoenicians who were the more active, pushing their settlements westward to Lebda, Susa, Utica, and (in 814 B.C.) to Carthage. The Greeks also spread westward to Italy and Sicily and (in 600 B.C.) to Massalia in the south of France. Their only important colony on the African coast was Cyrene, and there was some sort of agreement, in about 500 B.C., by which the Greeks ceded the rest of the African shore to their rivals. Beyond the central narrows of the Mediterranean, beyond Malta and Motyca, the Phoenicians' influence predominated. There was thus no question of Greek rivalry in Spain, nor apparently in Minorca, and none but the Phoenicians had passed the Pillars of Hercules. After the fall of Tyre, in 574 B.C., the leadership of the Phoenicians passed to Carthage. Tyre and

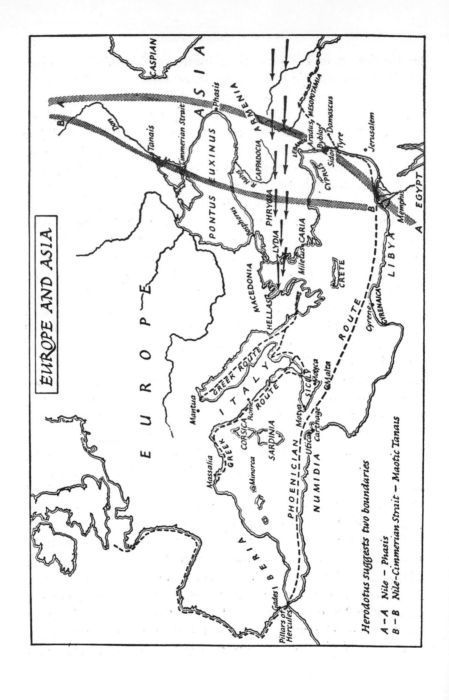

EUROPE AND ASIA

CASPIAN

ASIA

Phasis

Don

ARMENIA

Tanais

Cimmerian Strait

MESOPOTAMIA

Aradus

Damascus

Byblos

Sidon

Tyre

Jerusalem

PONTUS EUXINUS

CAPPADOCIA

Halys

Bosphorus

CYPRUS

Memphis

PHRYGIA

LYDIA

CARIA

Miletus

MACEDONIA

HELLAS

CRETE

EGYPT

LIBYA

ROUTE

Cyrene

CYRENAICA

Mantua

ITALY

GREEK ROUTE

SICILY

Motya

Malta

Rome

CORSICA

Utica

Massalia

GREEK

SARDINIA

Carthage

Minorca

PHOENICIAN

NUMIDIA

IBERIA

Pillars of
Hercules

Gades

Herodotus suggests two boundaries

A – A   *Nile – Phasis*

B – B   *Nile–Cimmerian Strait – Maeotic Tanais*

Sidon came to be a part of the Persian empire in 539, forming with Syria and Cyprus a single province in that vast organization.

If there was a marked difference between the Greeks and Persians, there was a still greater difference, and a natural hostility, between the Greeks and Phoenicians; as also incidentally, between the Greeks and Jews. There was, of course, a rivalry in trade, but there was more to their difference than that. As Sarton points out, their hostility went deep.

> About the twelfth century, when the Cretans lost the strength to rule the sea, Phoenician sailors were ready to succeed them and they did . . . They soon became the masters of Mediterranean trade, with no rivals except the Greeks . . . Almost everywhere they were competing with Greeks, and their rivalry was not only commercial but naval. The Greeks hated them and accused them of greed and unfairness; these accusations and the hatred prompting them were probably reciprocated. The rivalry between Greeks and Phoenicians . . . remained under one form or another one of the main themes of ancient history . . .*

Almost the first Greek references to the Phoenicians are to be found in Books XIV and XV of *The Odyssey*. When Odysseus, disguised, tells his imaginary life history to the swineherd, Eumaeus, he describes his visit to Egypt:

> I passed seven years in the country, and made a fortune out of the Egyptians who were liberal with me one and all. But in the course of the eighth I fell in with a rascally Phoenician, a thieving knave who had already done a deal of mischief in the world. I was prevailed on by this specious rogue to join him in a voyage to Phoenicia, where he had a house and estate; and there I stayed with him for a whole twelve-month. But when the days and months had mounted up, and a second year began its round of season, he put me on board a ship bound for Libya,

* George Sarton, *op. cit.*, p. 107 *et seq.*

on the pretext of wanting my help with the cargo he was carrying, but really that he might sell me for a handsome sum when
he got there . . .*

The swineherd turns out to be himself the son of the King
of Syrie, kidnapped from home with the connivance of his
Phoenician nurse, and eventually sold as a slave to Laertes.

> One day the island was visited by a party of those notorious
> Phoenician sailors, greedy rogues, with a whole cargo of gewgaws
> in their black ship. Now there happened to be a woman of
> their race in my father's house, a fine, strapping creature and
> clever too with her hands. But the double dealing Phoenicians
> soon turned her head. One of them began it by making love
> to her when she was washing clothes, and seducing her by the
> ship's hull, and there's nothing like love to lead a woman astray
> be she never so honest . . .†

The repetition of the words used — with no other Phoenicians
described more favorably — gives a clear picture of the folk from
Tyre and Sidon as seen by their Greek competitors. They were
greedy, thieving, and double-dealing. Above all, they were treach-
erous — each anecdote being an instance of betrayal under the
cover of a pretended friendship. Had the great library at Carthage
survived we should have Phoenician literature to study; epics,
perhaps, in which the Greeks always appear as talkative, unreliable, and piratical liars. These would at least serve to remind us
that dishonesty on the one side is no proof that those on the
other side are upright. Granted, however, that the Phoenicians
had virtues and the Greeks had faults which Homer failed to
emphasize, it is interesting, nevertheless, to realize that these are
not passages of indiscriminate abuse. Homer does not accuse the

* Homer, *The Odyssey*, trans. by E. V. Rieu (London: Penguin, 1950), pp.
222–23.
† *Ibid.*, p. 241.

Phoenicians of idleness, cowardice, dirtiness, or even cruelty. He accuses them mainly of treachery, and there is good reason to conclude that he was right.

In the history of the Phoenicians, scholars tend to ignore Phoenicia itself after the Persian conquest of 539. From that period on, Carthage, a colony settled from Tyre, assumed the leadership of this race. The efforts of the Carthaginians were directed toward Sicily, Sardinia, and Corsica, and these formed the overture to later conflicts with Rome. But the merchants of Phoenicia, absorbed into the Persian Empire, were none the less prosperous for their loss of autonomy. They enjoyed Persian protection, and a considerable share of the trade. There was a Persian royal palace in Sidon, but Tyre was still a city of importance. It was from Phoenicia that Darius was to draw his fleet and recruit his seamen. Nor can there be any doubt that their ships were among the best obtainable. As for the seamen, they had no reluctance about destroying their chief rivals in trade. From their point of view, it was a trade war between Phoenician and Greek, with the Persians called in as allies of the former. Many of the Greeks must have seen the conflict in the same light. In the growth of their national feeling, the difference they recognized between themselves and the Persians was perhaps initially less than their sense of contrast with the men of Tyre and Sidon. Whatever differences there were came to be emphasized as the war went on. They came to regard their opponents as increasingly alien. But while this is true of many Greeks, others were affected differently by the Phoenician example, and also by the attitude of many Greeks resident in Asia Minor. They were far from united against Persia. Some of them saw Darius as a friend.

To understand this divergence of view, we must return again to the trade route. By the time of Darius, trade from the East reached the Mediterranean at various points, including Miletus in the north and Sidon in the south. The northern route was extended along a line of Greek colonies which ended at Massalia now Marseilles. The southern route was extended along a line of Phoenician colonies which ended at Gades now Cadiz. Each group would have preferred a monopoly, and each was prepared to defend the share it had. But the Greeks could seek no commercial advantage from a conflict with Persia. Economically, they might gain more from being a part of the Persian Empire, obtaining special privileges — perhaps even at the expense of the Phoenicians. Any Greek merchant would wish to remain on good terms with Darius, even if it meant, possibly, some loss of autonomy. And in the past, remember, the Greek cities in Asia Minor had been allowed a great measure of freedom. The Persian rule had been benevolent. Nor had the Greeks been without influence at Susa. Their trade had gained from Persian protection and patronage, their craftsmen had worked at Persepolis. The sensible thing to do was to make the best terms possible, and yield a token submission to the Persian monarchy. For Darius was the ruler, after all, of the civilized world, having no rivals, only subjects.

Many Greeks thus argued for accepting Persian rule. But others argued for resistance to the death. Why? And why did resistance become the accepted policy? The first historian to attempt any answer to these questions was Herodotus, whose aim, he said, was to do two things:

> to preserve the memory of the past by putting on record the astonishing achievements both of his own and of the Asiatic peoples; secondly, and more particularly, to show how the two races came into conflict.
>
> Persian historians put the responsibility for the quarrel on the Phoenicians . . .*

What had they done? They kidnapped Io, daughter of Inachus, King of Argos. Later, some Greeks, or possibly Cretans,

---

* Herodotus, *op. cit.*, p. 11.

abducted Europa, the king's daughter, from Tyre. Followed the voyage of the *Argo* and the abduction of Medea from Colchis. Forty or fifty years afterwards, Paris, son of King Priam, carried off Helen, the wife of King Menelaus of Sparta.

> Thus far there had been nothing worse than woman-stealing on both sides; but for what happened next the Greeks, they say, were seriously to blame; for it was the Greeks who were, in a military sense, the aggressors. Abducting young women, in their opinion, is not indeed a lawful act; but it is stupid after the event to make a fuss about it. The only sensible thing is to take no notice, for it is obvious that no young woman allows herself to be abducted if she does not wish to be. The Asiatics, according to the Persians, took the seizure of the women lightly enough, but not so the Greeks; the Greeks, merely on account of a girl from Sparta, raised a big army, invaded Asia and destroyed the empire of Priam. From that root sprang their belief in the perpetual enmity of the Grecian world towards them — Asia with its various foreign-speaking peoples belonging to the Persians, Europe and the Greek states being, in their opinion, quite separate and distinct from them.*

The generally accepted view is that Herodotus lived from about 484 to 425 B.C., writing his *Histories* in later life. If we suppose them to have been written between 440, say, and his death, he is describing events fairly near to him in time. So that he can be assumed to represent his generation in making a sharp distinction between European and Asian; as indeed in recognizing a geographical boundary between Europe and Asia. The talk of the day was of a feud going back for centuries, such a feud as may or may not have existed. But the conflict was certainly obvious when Herodotus wrote, and he was perhaps the first man to describe it. More than that, he described the European reaction to Asian pressure. He was aware of the piston movement as between East and West and lived at a time when

* *Ibid.*, p. 14.

the East was unquestionably in the ascendant. Asia was a different world and one against which the Greek states had to defend themselves and so defend Europe. But what, to him, did the word "Europe" signify? On this subject he was fortunately explicit:

> . . . all Asia, with the exception of the easterly part has been proved to be surrounded by sea, and so to have a general geographical resemblance to Libya.
>   With Europe, however, the case is different for no one has ever determined whether there is sea either to the east or to the north of it, all we know is that in length it is equal to Asia and Libya combined. Another thing that puzzles me is why these distinct names should have been given to what is really a single land-mass — and women's names at that; and why, too, the Nile and the Phasis — or according to some, the Maeotic Tanais and the Cimmerian Strait — should have been fixed upon for the boundaries. Nor have I been able to learn who it was that first marked the boundaries, or where they got the names from . . .*

Herodotus uses the word "Libya" for Africa, states that Asia is called after the wife of Prometheus, and Europe after Europa, the king's daughter abducted from Tyre. Between Asia and Europe his boundary line is the Nile and the Rion at the eastern end of the Euxine — bringing the whole of Asia Minor into Europe. According to others, as he admits, the boundary is marked by the Don and the Bosphorus. There was room here for disagreement, but that was not what the conflict was about. For the effect of a Persian victory, had it taken place, would have been to absorb Europe into Asia. Nor would this have been geographically absurd. It was strange, rather, as Herodotus remarks, to apply different names to the opposite ends of the same continent. This was now being done, and it marks the hardening of a cultural frontier.

* *Ibid.*, p. 256.

But if the frontier was there, we must beware of giving it a greater significance than it merits. For, as Sarton points out, the situation was confused.

The importance of that conflict between Asia and Europe can hardly be exaggerated; it is one of the greatest conflicts in the history of the whole world and one of the most pregnant; the final victory of the Greeks determined the future . . . to call it a conflict between Asia and Europe, however, or between East and West, however true on the surface, is misleading. Many of the Greeks had lived for generations in Asia or Egypt, and on the other hand the Phoenicians, the naval allies of Persia, were scattered all over the Mediterranean, and could threaten the Greeks from the West. Neither was it a conflict between the Aryans and the Semites, for the Persians were as Aryan as the most Aryan Greeks . . .*

All this is perfectly true. But while the conflict was not exactly one of Asia against Europe, it did serve to decide whether there was to be a Europe at all. With the details of the struggle we are not concerned, except in so far as they illustrate the difference between the antagonists. Suffice to say that Darius launched his first attack soon after establishing his invasion base at Miletus. An army under Mardonius was ferried across the Hellespont and marched overland with Athens as one of its objectives. Macedonia was conquered, but the accompanying fleet was wrecked on the promontory of Mount Athos. Mardonius withdrew, therefore, to Asia Minor and was superseded by new generals, Datis and Artaphernes. These collected another and larger fleet in 490 B.C., embarked an army, and sailed straight for the Aegean. After sacking Eritrea, the Persians headed for Attica, and made their landing at Marathon, not far from Athens. They landed only a part of their army, which was defeated by the Athenians with heavy loss. Darius instantly

* George Sarton, *op. cit.*, p. 222.

began his preparations for a new campaign, but the news of Marathon produced a revolt in Egypt, which was still in process when Darius died. His son and successor, Xerxes, dealt first with the Egyptians, and then resumed the campaign against Greece. Said Xerxes (if we are to believe Herodotus), "I will bridge the Hellespont and march an army through Europe into Greece," and he went on to explain his further objectives in these words:

> . . . we shall so extend the empire of Persia that its boundaries will be God's own sky. With your help I shall pass through Europe from end to end and make it one country, so that the sun will not look down upon any land beyond the boundaries of what is ours. For if what I am told is true, there is not a city or nation in the world which will be able to withstand us, once Athens and Sparta are out of the way.*

From wanting to round off their commercial system, the Persian rulers had gone further in their plans. Unavoidably, the conquest of Greece had become a matter of prestige. How could the rest of the empire be held together if it became known that Xerxes had accepted defeat? "We Persians have a way of living," said the King, and appeasement was no part of it. In 480 B.C., he raised a vast army and led it in person across the Hellespont, passing the strait by a bridge of boats — at the second attempt — and once more taking the land route via Thrace and Macedonia. With great difficulty, Xerxes forced the pass of Thermopylae, and occupied the deserted city of Athens. His fleet, however, was defeated at Salamis, and the Persian king returned to Asia. The next year (479 B.C.), the Persians were decisively defeated at Plataea. They did not venture into the Aegean again until 467 B.C., when their navy was defeated again. Thenceforward the Persian threat was greatly diminished. The initiative now lay with the Greeks.

From the point of view of the relationships between Asia and

* Herodotus, *op. cit.*, pp. 416–17.

Europe, the most significant fact about this conflict was the com-
position of the Persian army. It comprised, besides Persians,
Medes, and their immediate allies, contingents from Syria, Bactria, India, Parthia, Arabia, Ethiopia, Libya, Phrygia, Lydia, and
Thrace. It was an army fully representative of Asia as a whole,
with other groups drawn from the territories through which
Xerxes marched. Its strength lay in its cavalry, which had no
chance to operate in suitable country. Its weakness lay in the
fact that the infantry, apart from the Persian, Median, and
Lydian divisions, had no helmets. For engaging the Greek infantry, masses of lightly-armed bowmen and spearmen were sin-
gularly ill-equipped. "The Indians were dressed in cotton; they
carried cane bows and cane arrows tipped with iron." Of the
well-armed, a proportion were of doubtful loyalty. Themistocles
attributed the Persian defeat to the gods, "who were jealous that
one man in his godless pride should be King of Asia and of
Europe too." More prosaically, Herodotus says of the Persians
at Plataea: "The chief cause of their discomfiture was their
inadequate equipment; not properly armed themselves, they were
matched against heavily armed infantry." As for the fighting at
sea, Herodotus remarks very justly that "the Persians were, indeed, bound to get the worst of it, because they were ignorant of
naval tactics and fought at random without any proper disposi-
tion of their force." As for the Phoenicians, their morale may
have suffered from the Persians' attitude toward them. They
were good seamen and genuinely hostile toward the Greeks.
"Amongst those who sailed . . ." writes Herodotus, "it was the
Phoenicians whose heart was most in the business." * But if the
Greeks thought little of them, there is some indication that the
Persians thought less.

The story is told that Xerxes' tent fell into Greek hands after
the battle of Plataea. Pausanias told the captured servants to
prepare the sort of meal a Persian commander-in-chief would

* Herodotus, *op. cit.*, p. 365.

expect. They laid gold and silver tables with a magnificent display. For a joke, Pausanias then told his own servants to prepare an ordinary Spartan dinner.

> The difference between the two meals was indeed remarkable, and, when both were ready, Pausanias laughed and sent for the Greek commanding officers. When they arrived, he invited them to take a look at the two tables, saying, "Gentlemen, I asked you here in order to show you the folly of the Persians, who, living in this style, came to Greece to rob us of our poverty." *

* *Ibid.*, p. 584.

5

THE HELLENES

In the war between the Persians and Greeks, the turning point was not Salamis, clearly, but Thermopylae. It was there that Leonidas attempted to hold the pass against the entire Persian army. His thousand Spartans and Thespians were killed, almost to a man, leaving an immortal legend and a badly shaken enemy.

> Go tell the Spartans, you who read,
> We took their orders, and are dead.

So heavy had been their casualties that the Asian troops' morale declined sharply and never recovered. Persian soldiers saw no prospect of success against better armed troops who were ready (it seemed) to fight to the death. But the significant contrast was not in fighting qualities, but in mere numbers. According to Herodotus, the Asian forces numbered 2,641,610 soldiers and sailors, with as many camp followers again, making 5,283,320 in all. Whatever may be thought of these figures, Xerxes clearly had very large forces indeed. Even dividing the historian's estimate by ten, we still have 500,000 men arrayed against the Greek detachments, no one of which amounted to more than a handful. It is in these relatively small numbers that we can perceive the basis of the Greek character. They were few enough to be individuals. They had also every reason to emphasize the divergence between themselves and their opponents. They were deliberately different from the Phoenicians and Persians, from the peoples of the mainland, from Asians generally, from *Orientals*.

In what, however, did their difference consist? Three basic characteristics are observable, all rooted in their geographical surroundings: they were relatively few, and averse to multiplying; they were relatively poor, and regarded ostentatious wealth with disapproval; they were relatively uninterested in a future life and far more concerned with the world they knew. Take the question of numbers first. As dwellers on islands and in mountain valleys, they wanted no more than a certain population in a given area. They restricted their numbers, therefore, by birth control, "exposing" unwanted babies, particularly females and those thought to be unhealthy or deformed. They also resorted to emigration when the population passed the optimum number. In his description of the ideal city, Plato fixes the number of citizens at 5040, no more and no less. He and other Greek thinkers reject both the solitude of the desert and the teeming millions of the plain. They prefer a settled community of a socially desirable size, and one in which the individual (as apart from the family or clan) can have his place. Isaiah, the Jew, reduces the individual to nothing in the sight of God. Gautama wants to merge the individual with God. Confucius thinks of the individual as part of the family. The Greeks made *individual* perfection their aim, their gods being little more than human beings made perfect. With their attitude toward numbers, they saw no merit in large families, no crime in being childless, no great eccentricity in being unmarried. Having only the one wife (and she sometimes neglected), they seemed to think more of beauty than of sex. Being few, they could experiment with forms of government in which a high level of physique, intelligence, and education could be assumed. In education they could give the individual that attention which becomes impossible when the family is large.

Relatively few, they were also relatively poor. Slaves were a form of wealth, and one which gave them leisure, but they otherwise scratched rather a scanty living from a rather poor soil. It is a human tendency to boast of adverse circumstances which we cannot improve, so the Greeks, like the Scots, made a virtue of living frugally. They made a cult of simplicity, just as a man who cannot afford wine will make a boast of abstinence. Wealth was neither very common among them nor very much admired. Hellas was thus able to provide examples of men who kept to a simple diet and simple dwelling and simple clothes, not from poverty but from choice. But their simplicity was not asceticism. We hear little of any Greek doing as the Indian Brahman may do — discarding his possessions to become a beggar. We hear little of fasting or contemplation, and as little again of illness due to excess. The Greeks of the classic period have given us, instead, a different word: Spartan. That term signifies a plain and scanty diet, a hard bed, a tough physical condition, a stoical endurance of fatigue, discomfort, or pain; and all this not from necessity, not from religious devotion, but merely from self-respect.

What, finally, of the Greek attitude to religion? That they were religious up to a point is clear, their temples being the structures to which they devoted the greatest care. They took less trouble over graves, tombstones, and burial customs, producing no equivalent to the monumental masonry of Egypt. Small states produce no remote and deified rulers and hence as a rule no undue obsession with a state-supported cult. The priesthood in Hellas seems to have had only a limited influence, perhaps through having no monopoly of learning, poetry, music, or art. It was the Greek half-heartedness about religion which weakened, without quite abolishing, the institution of kingship as it had existed among them. They tended to deprive their kings of any but minor religious duties. They had thus no monarch of the deified sort, to be approached on hands and knees; and their nobles, while admittedly descended from gods and heroes, had only a vague prestige. The result was that they had no elaborate ceremonial or etiquette, but addressed each other plainly and directly. The Athenians were informal in manner, and the Spartans, saying as little as possible, left us the word "laconic" to describe the sort of conversation they approved. And, as the story about Pausanias may suggest (p. 45) they had every motive to accentuate their peculiarities and underline their "European" or "Hellenic" qualities. When Herodotus says of the Egyptians, "They are religious to excess, beyond any other nation in the world," * or of the Babylonians, "They grow their hair long, wear turbans, and perfume themselves all over," † he is pointing a contrast between the Hellenes and the rest. While the Greeks might differ from each other, they differed still more from everyone else.

If the Greeks were moderate in numbers, moderate in wealth, and moderate in religion, we can fairly say that moderation was the basis of their characters. The better word, however, is "proportion." Rejecting extremes, as of asceticism or luxury, they chose the middle way. Proportion is the relationship between the parts and the whole. It was the Greeks who discovered that an unequal division of something in length should produce a certain ratio between the parts: namely, the golden mean or $\sqrt{5} - 1 : 2$. Proportion was, for them, the secret of beauty, of conduct, and of learning. They found beauty, as no other people have done, in the proportions of the human body: neither too tall (as in a giant), nor too short (as in a dwarf); neither too fat (as in the common representation of Buddha), nor too thin (as in the emaciated figure of the Hindu ascetic); neither too muscular (as are the biceps of the modern "strong man"), nor too feeble (like the constricted feet once admired in Chinese women). They reserved their admiration for the proportionate figure associated with youth, health, and fitness. They inevitably developed homosexual tendencies, other peoples copying them, apparently, in pederasty. They bestowed high honors on their

* Herodotus, *op. cit.*, p. 115.
† *Ibid.*, p. 93.

nude athletes — with women not excluded — and commemo-
rated all that they most admired in their sculpture. Representation of the unclothed human figure remained for them the highest form of art.

The same sense of proportion was applied to architecture.
Building their temples in stone or marble (of which they had
plenty), they adhered to a simple plan, rejected elaboration,
relied for effect upon a strict proportion between the parts. They
wanted no excessive height, as in the Empire State Building.
They wanted no vast extent, as in the Pentagon. They sought
only proportion and achieved it by the most precisely calculated
means. Nor was the same sort of proportion absent from their
manners. Polite they must have been, for politeness is a Greek
word, but they did not abase themselves. By Asian standards,
their mode of address was brusque, brief, and rude. They were
civil, to use the Roman word, but not ceremonious. They differed again from others in their attitude toward learning. What
knowledge they had was not enshrined in any ancient language,
nor was it the monopoly of any specially learned class. It was
not, as in China, particularly difficult to acquire. Learning,
whether poetry, drama, or music, was accessible to all, and the
learned man was seldom just that and nothing more. There was
no reason why the same man should not be a tradesman, soldier,
scholar, athlete, and poet. And here again, the sense of proportion intervened, for the Greeks were opposed, in general, to the
mysterious. The Greek philosopher or mathematician was usually prepared to reveal his art to anyone who would listen. There
were no hushed whispers, no vows of secrecy. Respect for learning was real, but not so obsessed as to make any great mystery
of it.

With the Greek sense of proportion went the Greek sense of
humor. We have already glimpsed its rudimentary origins in
The Iliad, but it was well developed by the time of Pericles.
With Aristophanes (b. circa 448, d. after 388 B.C.), it reached its

peak of achievement with a blend of political, social, and literary satire. Where it differed from the humor of the Orient was in its close relationship to contemporary institutions, persons, and events. The jokes of the world are basically few, and can be classified as follows: the joke about mishap resulting from physical or moral defect — blindness, intoxication, or cowardice; the joke concerning the contrast between what is expected and what exists; the joke about sex; and the joke which is purely verbal. In a yet deeper sense, however, the four basic jokes are one. They are all variations on the one theme, the contrast between what ought to be and what is. And that is why the Greeks, with their tremendous sense of proportion, had a leadership in humor. More than that, it affected, on occasion, their actual conduct of affairs. When Pausanias captured Xerxes' tent, furniture, and retinue, he could have reacted in several ways. He could have killed the servants. He could have made an inventory of the loot. He could have made a speech against the evils of luxury. He could have quoted Cyrus who said, "Soft countries breed soft men." He could have uttered any number of platitudes. Instead, however, he saw the joke, and invited his officers to share in it. "Here are these chaps laden with wealth, overfed to the point of bursting, and they have to invade Hellas — for what? To scrounge *our* rations!" Pausanias may not have seen the joke on every occasion — we know in fact that he did not. He did not even prove a particularly loyal Greek. But, without being Greek, we may doubt whether he would have seen the joke at all.

To summarize the contrasts we have found, we might conclude that a Greek of the time of Pericles would regard a Phoenician, Indian, or Persian as alien in a special way — resembling each other in several respects, but differing from him. As regards outward appearance, he might think the Asian too elaborately robed and adorned. The Asian's city he would think too crowded for comfort, with the individuals too lost in the mass. While the wealthy Asian might be too fat, his poor neighbor would be too thin. Asian women, he would find little in evidence, their figures well concealed but probably unathletic. He would find the Asian resolute in refusing to eat with a Greek for fear of defilement. Were he a scholar, the Asian would prove at once ceremonious in speech and evasive about his special knowledge. As for the Asian temples, they might be large and impressive but were mostly, for his taste, ill-proportioned and over-ornate. And what would the Asian think of the Greek? He might think him ill-fed and meanly dressed, so presumably poor, irreligious and irreverent, and so essentially ignorant. Greek manners he would think appalling. After all, a greatly inferior Persian would prostrate himself before a man of higher rank. These Greeks merely say "Hello, Euthyphro!" or "Hello, Glaucon!" with no respect shown to anyone. To make matters worse, the Greek must always ask questions about things which are none of his business, displaying his own paltry knowledge and throwing doubt on accepted custom and belief. The Asian might conclude, finally, that the Greek was a superficial and talkative person and totally lacking in respect for the decencies and mysteries of life.

In pointing the contrast between Persian and Greek, Herodotus says of the former: "Themselves they consider in every way superior to everyone else in the world, and allow other nations a share of good qualities decreasing according to distance, the furthest off being in their view the worst." * He adds, however, that "No race is so ready to adopt foreign ways as the Persian." In the aftermath of Plataea, their sense of superiority began to weaken and their taste for foreign ways was accentuated. Xerxes was assassinated in 465 B.C. and his son Artaxerxes I lost control of the Greek cities of Ionia. These fell again to Darius II, who made good use of the rivalry between Athens and Sparta. After the accession, however, of Artaxerxes II, there was a revolt, headed by his brother Cyrus who called in an army of ten thousand Greek mercenaries. Cyrus was killed at the Battle of

* Herodotus, *op. cit.*, p. 69.

Cunaxa (401 B.C.) in Babylonia, leaving the Greeks stranded in
a very alien land. They fought their way out under Xenophon's
leadership. What is significant about the story is, first of all, the
known Greek superiority as infantry. Cyrus called them in and
relied upon them as the best troops available. After his death,
the Greeks were pursued by the Persian general, Tissaphernes,
but nothing he could do made much impression on them. They
executed a creditable withdrawal, their main difficulty arising
from a lack of cavalry. In attempting to raise the Greek morale,
Xenophon reminded the troops of how the Persians had been
defeated on previous occasions:

> Now . . . when you know from experience that even if they are
> many times your number, they are not anxious to face you, what
> reason have you to be afraid of them any longer? Do not imag-
> ine that we are any the worse off because the native troops who
> were previously in our ranks have now left us. They are even
> greater cowards than the natives whom we have beaten, and they
> made this clear by deserting us and fleeing to the other side. It
> is far better to see people who want to be the first to run away
> standing in ones enemy's army than in ones own ranks.
>
> If any of you feel disheartened because of the fact that we
> have no cavalry, while the enemy have great numbers of them,
> you must remember that ten thousand cavalry only amount to
> ten thousand men. No one has ever died in battle through being
> bitten or kicked by a horse; it is men who do whatever gets done
> in battle. And then we are on a much more solid foundation
> than cavalrymen, who are up in the air on horseback, and afraid
> not only of us but of falling off their horses; we, on the other
> hand, with our feet planted on the earth, can give much harder
> blows to those who attack us and are much more likely to hit
> what we aim at. There is only one way in which cavalry have
> an advantage over us, and that is that it is safer for them to run
> away than it is for us.*

* Xenophon, *The Persian Expedition*, trans. by Rex Warner (London: Penguin, 1961), p. 108.

This is a typically Greek appeal to common sense. Faced with the same situation, the Jews reacted differently. "When thou goest out to battle against thine enemies, and seest horses and chariots and a people more than thou, be not afraid of them." So begins the Jewish Field Service Regulations (Deuteronomy XX) in which the next duty falls to the priest. It is for him to assure the troops that "the Lord your God is he that goeth with you, to fight for you against your enemies, to save you." A similar role was allotted to the Brahman in India. But the Ten Thousand were told, instead, that their opponents were inferior troops. This was not entirely true, and Xenophon ended by improvising a troop of cavalry, which did good service. What is true is that the Persians had no answer to the Greek phalanx, and that their cavalry, mere mounted archers, could only harass the enemy. What is more, the Persians always camped at least six miles from the Greek army, fearing a night attack, during which their cavalry would be useless. The whole story of the *Anabasis* illustrated the moral superiority of the Greeks. It was they who were operating in Persian territory. It was they who dominated each scene of action. And it was they who finally withdrew in good order, their formations intact to the end. The Persian empire was, in fact, declining, and with it the whole power of the Orient.

It was during this period, from 400 B.C. onwards, that Greek and European expansion began. Illustrating a recurrent theme in human history, the Greeks went over from the defense to the attack. For a period their energies had been concentrated on the defense of their country. In so far as they had achieved any unity, it was based upon a common hatred of Persia, and a common hostility toward the Oriental. As Hogarth points out:

> . . . in her retreat before that nation, she, Persia, drew her pursuer into a world which, had she herself never advanced into Europe, would probably not have seen him for centuries to come.

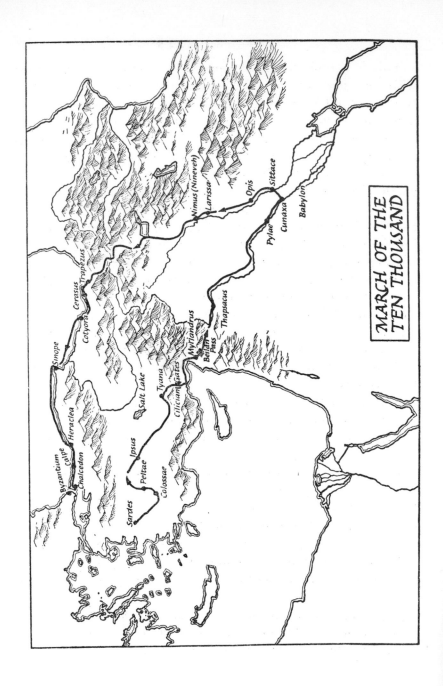

MARCH OF THE
TEN THOUSAND

Moreover, by a subsequent change of attitude toward her victorious foe — though that change was not wholly to her discredit — Persia bred in the Greeks a still better conceit of themselves and a better understanding of her weakness. The Persians with the intelligence and versatility for which their race has always been remarkable, passed very rapidly from overweening contempt to excessive admiration of the Greeks. They set to work almost at once to attract Hellenic statesmen and men of science to their own society, and to make use of Hellenic soldiers and sailors. We soon find western satraps cultivating cordial relations with the Ionian cities, hospitably entertaining Greeks of distinction and conciliating Greek political and religious prepossessions. They must have attained considerable success, while thus unwittingly preparing disaster . . . such an attitude towards Greeks was suicidal. It exalted the spirit of Europe while it depraved the courage and sapped the self-reliance of Asia.*

All this is true enough but it would be wrong to blame individuals for a mistake in policy. The whole movement of western expansion was bigger than that. The Persian retreat, taking the pressure off the Greeks, released their energies and ambitions. Simultaneously, it created the power vacuum into which the Greeks were drawn. And the European assault on Asia, sequel to the Asian attack on Europe, was not merely a military offense. It had, it is true, a military side. Trying to recover Egypt with Greek mercenaries in 380 B.C., Artaxerxes found more Greek mercenaries on the other side. Agesilaus of Sparta invaded Asia Minor in 397 and 394, proving that a march on Susa was a possibility to consider. The Greeks, in fact, were penetrating Asia, either by invitation or by face of arms. But their ideas outran their swords, traveling both faster and further. In Phoenicia, for example, Greek art made its impact in the 5th and 4th centuries and led to the extinction of the native style. Similar influences were felt in Persia itself, where sculpture showed Greek influ-

* D. G. Hogarth, *The Ancient East* (London 1914), p. 183.

ence. As Euripides wrote, "Asia serves as the slave of Europe."
To translate this growing ascendancy into terms of actual conquest, two things were needed: the replacement of democracy
and the improvement of the horse. No decisive result could be
achieved without leadership or without cavalry. The task was to
unite the Greek phalanx with the Persian cavalry, producing a
balanced force of all arms. Only in Macedonia could this be
done. Marginally Greek in culture, with pasture for horses and
plains in which to maneuver, ruled at one time as a Persian
province and thereafter as a kingdom, Macedonia assumed the
leadership of Europe.

While there may be historical doubts about the machinery of
East-West relationships before this period, the rise of Macedonia
marks the beginning of a movement about which our information is reasonably complete. From this period on, our picture of
the great engine of progress, the alternating ascendancy of East
and West, the piston driven by decay and expansion, is more
clear and precise. And this new phase of western expansion
under Macedonian leadership illustrates perfectly the theme of
this book. The Persian pressure upon Hellas followed an earlier
phase of Greek expansion and was caused by the Greek loss of
momentum and subsequent decay. At once reacting to the Persian threat and absorbing something of Persian tradition, the
Hellenes began to emphasize all that was distinctive about their
own way of life. They accorded a special veneration to the works
of Homer. Why? Because Homer sang of the last period of
European ascendancy over Asia, the period when Troy fell to
the Achaeans, when the East–West trade route was largely
under Greek control. Greeks of the Hellenistic period turned to
Homer just as later Europeans would turn to the story of Rome.
But a mere revolt against the Asian way of life would have
failed had its leaders not absorbed, without emphasizing, some
elements of Persian tradition. More than that, some Greek ideas
had to go. First of these was democracy. The Athenians had

developed their democratic institutions during a period of decline. These had served to rally the Greeks against Persia in the cause of freedom. For that strictly defensive purpose the Athenian political theories had (more or less) sufficed. For the period of European ascendancy that was to follow, democracy obviously had to go. Greeks who elected their officers could fight their way out of a declining Persian Empire. They would have to be reorganized on very different lines before they could fight their way in again. To the Persian technique of horsemanship they would have to add the Persian tradition of monarchy.

The Macedonians did more, however, than merely add up all that was effective in the Greek and Persian traditions. They added a new factor, the real cavalryman as contrasted with the mounted archer.

> . . . In the times anterior to Philip II (B.C. 359–336) the military force of Macedonia seems to have consisted, like that of Thessaly, in a well-armed and well-mounted cavalry, formed from the substantial proprietors of the country, and in vast numbers of targeteers. But until Philip formed his famous Phalanx after the model of the Theban system, established by Epaminondas, the Macedonian infantry was little more than a rabble of shepherds and cultivators. Philip did not merely discipline this raw material into the best infantry that the world had yet seen, armed with the sarissa, a pike 21 feet in length, but he paid equal attention to his cavalry, and it was to this army that he owed largely his superiority over the autonomous States of Greece and the Illyrians and Thracians. When Philip came to the throne, he bestowed great care upon all that appertained to horses and horse-racing. He sent both chariots and ridden horses to compete at Olympia.*

The stages of development are fairly clear. The dun and white horses of Asia and Europe, derived from the tarpan, were too

* William Ridgeway, *The Origin and Influence of the Thoroughbred Horse* (Cambridge, 1905), p. 302.

small to be ridden. They were used to draw the chariot as described in the literature of the ancient world. The far superior and much faster horses of North Africa, bay horses from Libya, often with white stockings or star, came to be ridden but only by small men, lightly armed. It was gradually discovered that a cross between the dun and the bay would produce, sometimes, a horse of strength and speed, able to carry a man in armor. The ridden horse event was introduced into the Olympic games in 648 B.C. Soon afterwards, in 632 B.C., was founded the Greek African colony of Cyrene destined to be the Greek source of Libyan horses. Only in Thrace, however, and Macedonia, were the pastures suitable for real horse breeding. There — and of course, in Persia — the true cavalry charger was bred. There are hints of the future in the *Anabasis*, for we read of Xenophon himself being mounted, more especially in the March to Kurdistan (Book III).

> Xenophon rode along the ranks on horseback, urging them on . . .
> Soteridas, a man from Sicyon, said: "We are not on a level, Xenophon. You are riding on horseback, while I am wearing myself out with a shield to carry."
> When Xenophon heard this, he jumped down from his horse, pushed Soteridas out of the ranks, took his shield away from him and went forward on foot as fast as he could, carrying the shield. He happened to be wearing a cavalry breastplate as well, so that it was heavy going for him . . . The other soldiers, however, struck Soteridas and threw stones at him and cursed him until they forced him to take back his shield and continue marching.*

This was not an incident that could have happened on the Persian side. But the Persians were already wearing armor on horseback, even if their weapon was still the bow. No one, said Xenophon, was ever killed in battle by a horse. The time was coming when this would no longer be true.

* Xenophon, *Anabasis*, p. 124.

6

TALK OF ALEXANDER

THERE IS a sense in which Alexander of Macedonia remains still unequaled among the rulers of the world. His was a greatness which we can scarcely measure. He was, as Auden might have said, a man "in the shadow of whose gigantic achievement we pitch our miserable tent." He came of a remarkable family, being the son of Philip and Olympias, nephew of the redoubtable Polyclea and brother of Cynane, "famous for her military knowledge" and an actual commander in the field. Not exactly a Greek — and yet sufficiently so to have competed in the Olympic games — he had been a pupil of Aristotle for three years. As S. C. Easton observes:

> Alexander's regard for reason and balance, his belief in the control of the body by the mind, his disinterested love of knowledge, and his spirit of inquiry could have been instilled into him by his tutor.*

So it could have been; and Alexander may well have absorbed much of what Aristotle had to teach. Of practical affairs, however, the younger man knew a great deal more; and in sheer imagination he was trammeled a great deal less. It was this combination of exceptional ability with outstanding vision that made Alexander the genius he was.

This is no place for his biography nor for an analysis of his military achievements. Mounted on his famous charger, Bucephalus, riding at the head of his Companions (a Royal Squadron of Heavy Cavalry), commanding some 3000 horsemen and

* Stewart C. Easton, *The Heritage of the Past* (New York, 1955), p. 272.

18,000 infantry, he swept through Asia Minor and Phoenicia, beginning with the capture of Miletus and Sardes, and ending this first phase with the capture of Tyre. From that moment the Persians had no Mediterranean base from which their ships could threaten Alexander's future lines of communication between Macedonia and Asia. Phase Two, the following year, involved the occupation of Egypt, where he was received as a liberator, his march taking him to Siwa and Memphis. He then founded the new city of Alexandria, planned and destined to take the place of Tyre. It was during this phase that he secured remounts from Libya itself — three hundred horses from Cyrene alone. Darius, who had been routed the year before at Granicus and Issus, now assembled another vast army for the defense of Persia. Alexander invaded the heart of the empire (331 B.C.) and defeated Darius for the third and last time near Nineveh, going on from there to occupy Babylon, Susa, and Persepolis. With surprising speed, the whole empire had collapsed. Darius having been killed by his own officers, Alexander assumed the title of "Great King" and hastened to establish his rule over the remaining provinces.

This last phase involved the invasion of India. From Persepolis, he marched north to Ecbatana and then followed the trade route into Bactria, founding new cities as he went (one named after his horse), and so down the Indus to Patala. On the way, he fought and won the Battle of the Hydaspes (327 B.C.) which established his authority over the Punjab. A return march through the deserts of Baluchistan — shorter in distance but far more difficult — brought his army back to Susa. He went soon afterwards to Babylon, where he died of swamp fever at the age of thirty-three (323 B.C.). His astonishing career was over.

What had Alexander achieved? He had established "Hellenistic" culture over the whole of what had been the Persian empire. The word "Hellenistic," as distinct from Hellenic, is used to describe this later cultural phase during which development had

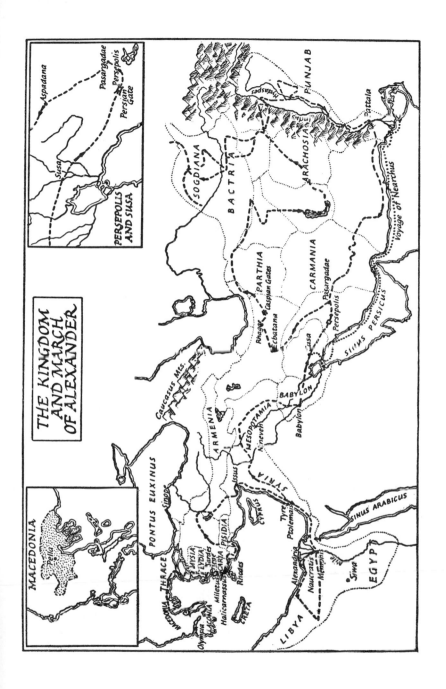

THE KINGDOM AND MARCH OF ALEXANDER

PERSEPOLIS AND SUSA

MACEDONIA

given way to dissemination. Macedonian culture might be compared with American, the extension of a civilization which had originated elsewhere. Put in other terms, the Greeks ceased to be discoverers when they became teachers. The cultural heritage of the Hellenistic world was, in fact, impressive, but the height of artistic expression already lay in the past. The immediate task was to share this heritage with the world; and the world of Asia stood ready to receive it. As we have seen, Greek ideas had traveled along the trade route before Alexander's march had begun. As Freya Stark points out, the tribes which Alexander overcame in Asia Minor were half Hellenized already. It was this discovery that proved to him what more was possible. To quote Freya Stark again, "no empire before or since has been so persuasive, nor has any conversion except a religious one been so complete and widespread as was his hellenizing of the Asiatic world." *
Scholars have argued as to how deep, or how superficial, this conversion was. That is not, however, to our present purpose. So far as this book is concerned, the question is, rather, what exactly did Alexander take with him? For this is the very heart of the matter. It is easy to say "the spirit of Hellas," but the statement is vague and probably not even true.

In so far as the Hellenistic idea can be put into a word, the term Humanism would have to be used. For it was the Greeks who discovered *man*.

In Ralph Turner's words:

> In art the dominant form was the human figure. In religion the primary concern was the human soul. In philosophy the great instrument was the human reason. In scientific speculation man was for the first time distinguished as a part of nature.†

They idealized the natural and proportionate, rejecting the

* Freya Stark, *Alexander's Path* (London, 1958), p. 113.
† Turner, *op. cit.*, p. 597.

grotesque and preferring the human scale. This is how their outlook was defined by an earlier scholar, D. G. Hogarth:

Hellenism meant, besides a politico-social creed, also a certain attitude of mind. The characteristic feature of this attitude was what has been called Humanism, this word being used in a special sense to signify intellectual interest confined to human affairs, but free within the range of these. All Greeks were not, of course, equally humanistic in this sense . . . But when Alexander carried Hellenism to Asia it was still broadly true that the mass of civilised Hellenes regarded anything that could not be apprehended by the intellect through the senses as not only outside their range of interest but non-existent. Further while nothing was held so sacred that it might not be probed or discussed with the full vigour of an inquirer's intelligence, no consideration except the logic of apprehended facts should determine his conclusion. An argument was to be followed wherever it might lead, and its consequences must be faced in full without withdrawal behind any non-intellectual screen. Perfect freedom of thought and perfect freedom of discussion over the whole range of human affairs; perfect freedom of consequent action, so the community remained uninjured — this was the typical Hellene's ideal.*

It was the ideal for which Socrates had died and which Plato had made current. But it rested upon the isolation of the individual, as detached from the family and tribe. No such argument is possible except among individuals, and individuality is lessened in communities which have grown beyond a certain size. Granted, however, that Humanism was the Hellenistic creed, its actual expression was, and naturally, in very concrete terms. What Alexander brought to Asia was the Greek city, complete with marketplace, acropolis, council house, gymnasium, stadium, and theater. In what sense, it might be asked at the outset, was the city an innovation? The ancient East had its

* Hogarth, op. cit., p. 231.

cities already, the cities indeed from which Greek civilizations
had derived: Memphis, Heliopolis, Babylon, Nineveh, and Susa.
These had been the cradles of a technological accomplishment
which the Greeks had not surpassed. They had been the seats
of government for kings, viceroys, and satraps: solidly fortified,
economically prosperous, and architecturally magnificent. What
they had lacked was a life of their own, as distinct from the government to which they belonged. The point of the Greek city
of the Hellenistic period was that the original constitution —
that of an independent state — had been preserved within the
framework of a larger political organization. It was still governed
in much the same way, even when its rulers had become merely
the members of a city council. It had the vitality of Birmingham
or San Francisco, as contrasted with the more artificial propri-
eties of Canberra, Ottawa, or Washington, D.C. It existed in
its own right whether the king were there or not.

This life of the Hellenistic cities, planted in Asia as exemplify-
ing the European way of life, centered upon the institutions
named. Take first the marketplace or "agora," as contrasted with
the Asian "bazaar." The Greek cities of Asia were planned from
the outset on a chessboard pattern first introduced, apparently,
at Miletus — a city completely destroyed by the Persians and
replanned, as well as rebuilt, after the Persian defeat in 479 B.C.
Hippodamus, the Milesian architect, went on to plan the Piraeus
at Athens, a similar pattern being followed at Rhodes, Halicarnassus, Priene, and elsewhere. Such town planning was not unknown in China, where Nanking, for example, has a grid plan
on a north–south axis and where other cities reveal an error of
11° or 13° reflecting the declination of the T'hang period. But
Hellenistic cities revealed a special civic character. They had
thus a definite market area; not an alley jammed with stalls, but
a center for the city's social, economic, and political life. It was
the place, as Cyrus had said (see page 18), where the Greeks
came together and told one another lies under oath. A daily

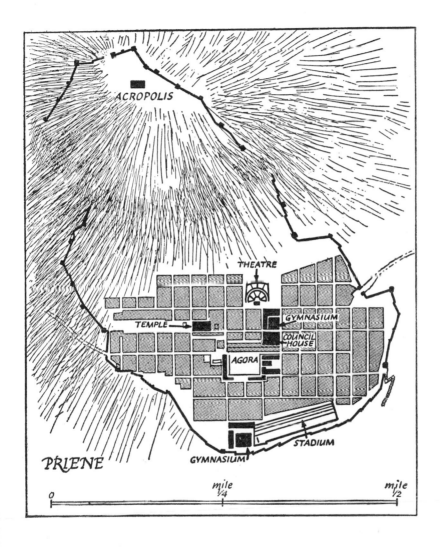

ACROPOLIS

THEATRE

TEMPLE

GYMNASIUM

COUNCIL HOUSE

AGORA

STADIUM

GYMNASIUM

PRIENE

mile 1/4

mile 1/2

0

appearance there must have been — for all practical purposes
compulsory — for in no other way would one hear the news —
often of vital importance. Some Greeks deprecated the idleness,
vulgarity, and gossip of the marketplace, and urged the provision
of a separate space for more serious affairs. This was sometimes
done, the "stoa," an arched arcade, being set aside for political
and legal purposes. But whether among the market stalls or set
apart, there was always a place of meeting, opportunity for the
orator, and the center where the news was passed round and
public opinion was formed. Among the Greeks, public opinion
mattered.

While the "agora" had been the basis of Greek democracy,
this no longer existed in Alexander's day. But while it had
proved impracticable at the national level, it remained an aspect
of local government. The Greek city could not rule an extensive
territory, but it could at least rule itself. It possessed, therefore,
a central focus, a dominating feature which the citizens could
regard with pride, and the stranger, it was hoped, with awe. This
was the acropolis, a group of temples placed, if possible, on a
salient feature of the site. In later days, when religion played
only a small part in their lives, the acropolis was sometimes
omitted, but the temples remained as a monument to the Greek
sense of proportion, order, and beauty. They never lavished
quite the same care on anything else. But the temples retained
a very human proportion and pulled their deities down to a very
human scale. The statues might be more than life-size but they
were seldom colossal, and they represented men and women who
were divine only in their calm aspect and shapely physique.
Having performed the proper ritual and shown the gods all the
respect they wanted (or all, anyway, the gods were going to get),
the city fathers could adjourn for serious discussion to the council house — a tiered semi-circular chamber designed especially
for debate.

If democracy was not essential to the Greek way of life — and it never had been — debate certainly was. We find the Greeks debating at the siege of Troy, and again in the *Anabasis*. Whatever their real form of government, they always had time to argue. The origin of this lay partly in their tradition of approximate equality. They might vary in reputation and status, but not to the point of prostration on the one hand, or esoteric superiority on the other, and the basis for the superiorities they recognized — whether in athletics, debate, beauty, or war — had at least to be apparent. So eloquence was among the gifts they valued. It took the place, to some extent, of authorship, for although they were literate — thanks to the Phoenician alphabet — the poetry and philosophy of their classic period was still largely oral. Theirs was the spoken word, which could scarcely have been possible among people who had no public places in which oratory could be practiced. Xenophon makes Socrates suggest that ill-qualified candidates for election should appeal for votes in these words:

> Men of Athens, I have never yet learnt anything from anyone, nor when I have been told of any man's ability in speech and in action, have I sought to meet him, nor have I been at pains to find a teacher among the men who know. On the contrary, I have constantly avoided learning anything of anyone, and even the appearance of it. Nevertheless, I shall recommend to your consideration anything that comes into my head.

Here all the emphasis is on the politician's failure to use his social opportunities — not on his failure to read good books. Literature as such was the discovery of a somewhat later age.

The next Greek institution to list was the gymnasium; the place, as it were, of nakedness; the athletic ground where the competitors stripped. This was not the only context in which the Greeks were unclothed. At a banquet they wore little, and the entertainers — boy flute-players, dancing girls, and acrobats — wore nothing at all. The Ionian customs in this respect were

copied by the Etruscans, whose women athletes appeared naked
and whose drinking parties ended in promiscuous love. On this
subject, Charles Seltman observes that:

> The grim thing for a moralist in all this is that apparently the
> Etruscans were none the worse for it. They remained formidable
> and were long feared alike by Roman, Latin and Italiote Greek
> . . . one of Nero's parties was probably very much tamer than a
> Tuscan banquet . . .*

Although the gymnasium came to be more than an athletic
club, the original name needs emphasis. For the Greek attitude
toward nudity was sharply at variance with Asian custom. In
Egyptian or Persian sculpture, the slaves might appear unclothed, and so might captives (and even captive kings) to stress
their humiliation. But the rulers had to wear at least the insignia
of their rank. The Persians were elaborately robed, and Herodotus interrupts his story about Gyges to remark "For with the
Lydians, as with most barbarian races, it is thought highly indecent even for a man to be seen naked." † As for the Jews, they
made it a moral issue from the first. But the Greeks thought
otherwise, and nothing is more significant than the sculpture in
which Alexander is himself represented, wearing nothing what-
soever, least of all the fig leaf to which later moralists attach so
much importance. If Alexander looked and behaved like a
Greek god — as he certainly did — his admirers saw no merit in
concealing the fact. They wanted to place his good looks on
record, just as seen in the gymnasium.

The spectators at the gymnasium came to talk about other
things besides athletics, their discussions gradually turning into
formal lectures and debates. At Athens three gymnasia — the
Academe, Lyceum, and Cynosarges — acquired a sort of univer-

* Charles Seltman, *Wine in the Ancient World* (London, 1957).
† Herodotus, *op. cit.*, p. 17.

sity status, and the number rose eventually to eight. Elsewhere
the gymnasia assumed the combined functions of school and
country club. Important as they had been in Europe, they
gained still further significance in Asia. For it was by their gymnasia that the emigrant Greeks were held together in a strange
land. The gymnasia became centers for many subsidiary associations and interests, serving to educate the young in the Hellenic
way, serving equally to prevent the adult from "going native."
Although under official patronage, they remained private or
municipal institutions, the responsibility of elected officers (the
"gymnasiarch" and "cosmetes"), and the very core of the members' intellectual, athletic, and social life.

Complementary to the gymnasium was the stadium, which
meant then pretty well what it means now. A stade was about
two hundred yards, the race fixed at that distance being the
oldest event and yielding the most coveted prize. All stadia
were copies of Olympia, the scene of the Panhellenic games.
Provision of the basic level stade was the least part of the structure, for seating had to be provided for thousands of spectators
and space found for a whole series of athletic events, most of
them the same as are still held. In later Hellenistic times, the
professional athlete appeared, especially as wrestler or boxer, and
became a popular hero. Even with the abuses that may have
accompanied this trend, the stadium might seem to most people
a harmless institution. But it was more controversial in the Asia
of Alexander's time, being especially disliked by the Jews. As
S. Davis points out:

> The stadium had been regarded as one of the chief symbols of
> the Abomination from the time of the Maccabees, and it was
> even forbidden the Jews to assist in building one. Participation
> in the games was regarded by the Rabbis as sheer idolatry and
> permission to be present was only grudgingly given.
>
> An orthodox Jew would have felt scruples about taking part
> in a course of training such as was to be had in the Greek

Ύυμνασια involving an exhibition of the nude male form and probably worship, or recognition, of the gods of the palaestra.*

Last of all, the Greek city included a theater. This was a tiered outdoor auditorium, usually carved out of a hillside and often affording a view of the mountains or sea. It comprised the theatron, orchestra, and proskenion areas, respectively for the audience, the chorus, and the action of the play. In at least one theater, in Sardinia, there was an effective system of amplifiers. The plays performed varied from the tragic to the satirical and comic. Some, by the great dramatists, are still performed. Many more, no doubt, have been forgotten. It was largely from the theater that the Greek communities took their inspiration, entertainment, and poetry. Plays were much discussed, giving rise to controversy over their meaning and merit. Without a theater, the center of population could hardly even rank as a city. What is especially significant about the Greek theater is the elaboration and permanence of its architectural setting. In part of Asia there were, or were to be, theatrical entertainments of some kind or other: acrobats, juggling, or the shadow play — the floor show, as it were, after the banquet. The Chinese have the theater and the opera, but their actors and actresses have always had the lowest social status. The Japanese have admittedly taken the theater more seriously. But no other people before the Greeks made the theater an essential part of their social life, still less a feature of their city plan. It was vital, they agreed, to their way of living.

Taken together, these institutions, the agora and stoa, the acropolis and council house, gymnasium, stadium, and theater, were the Hellenistic gifts to the world at large. They were all alike in their tendency to detach the individual from his family and tribe, bringing him into an active social life which centered upon a given activity. Moving away from the family circle or

* Davis, *op. cit.*, p. 106.

the harem, the individual took his place, for much of the day,
among like-minded individuals — men interested in politics,
wrestling, racing, philosophy, music, drama, or art. But the
Greeks had, above all, their sense of proportion. Going out of
the home did not mean going into a monastery. Having a business was not inconsistent with a skill at arms. An interest in
sport did not exclude an appreciation of the stage. And it was
the multiplicity of possible interests, the overlapping of different
groups, which made the individual a more distinct person. Of
vast numbers of people in Asia, the biography must have been
of the simplest; born in such a village, cultivating this plot of
earth, married a woman from that family who had so many children, died of this, that, or the other complaint. But even a com-
paratively humble Greek craftsman would have more to say than
that. From a family originally of Corinth, he had learned his
trade as cobbler, gained third prize in throwing the discus, served
in such a campaign and fought in such a battle, moved to Alexandria when it was first founded, taken public office as market
inspector, had been active in a certain prosecution, married a
girl who had been a sculptor's model, had a taste for music but
detested tragedy. And this particular combination of biographi-
cal data would be true of nobody else in the world. It is true
that such individuality was confined to the upper and middle
classes — what we should call the lower class were slaves — but
in the ancient East such middle classes did not exist. They
were, in effect, a Greek invention.

To hellenize the East, introducing all these institutions into
Asia, was a sufficiently ambitious project, one would think, for
even the most imaginative of men. It was a concept, however,
which Alexander's officers could grasp. And they could grasp it
the more readily in that they had been hellenized themselves.
The Athenians had come to regard all non-Hellenes as barbarous
inferiors. Between Greek and barbarian, says Isocrates, there is
no less difference than between man and beast. Macedonians

were necessarily more tolerant than that and were readily convinced that Asians could be assimilated into the Greek world. It was Alexander — and Alexander alone — who saw quite another possibility: the synthesis of the European and Asian ways of life. The contrast between his vision and his generals' common sense is superbly expressed by Freya Stark:

. . . Alexander at the age of twenty-two came to Asia, and the plan of hellenizing the world he brought from his background, his youth, his teachers and — possibly most of all — his father. He transformed the plan, but the essence of it was there already: he seized and developed the impulse of his time. The training of youth, instituted in Athens about 335 B.C. and derived from Plato's Laws spread through the Greek world and into barbarian lands; Alexander's games and competitions in Asia, literary and athletic, developed into festivals held for generations in his honour; and theatres in cities soon began to be built in stone. When the Romans came, a vast network, not pure in race but deeply Greek in feeling, had spread from the Mediterranean to India, and the hellenizing that passed into the Roman world has lived to this day. One may remember the dream of Pyrrhus before his march, when he thought Alexander called to him and offered to assist him. But Alexander lay ill and Pyrrhus asked him how he could do it. "I will do it," he said, "with my name", and his name has done it to our time.

Even if this were all, it would be a record of conquest no other human being has attained before or after. But it is not all. The first part of his plan was in the fashion of his day and of his people, but the second was shared neither by his teachers nor by his friends. It was his own and it steeped him in loneliness. More than two thousand years have had to pass and Alexander's dream of a united world is still a dream . . .*

What dream was this? Its essence was in a prayer:

. . . Alexander 'prayed for all sorts of blessings, and especially for harmony and fellowship between Macedonians and Per-

* Stark, op cit., p. 201.

sians', and 'brought together into one body all men everywhere, uniting and mixing, in a great loving cup, as it were, men's lives, their characters, their marriages, their very habits . . . He bade them all consider as their fatherland the whole inhabited earth, as their stronghold and protection his camp, as akin to them all good men, and as foreigners only the wicked.' *

Alexander's vision leaves the modern reader almost stunned. He conveyed the European message to Asia and realized, as did no one else, that Asia also had its message for Europe. Once on the throne of Darius he looked back on Greece and saw what Cyrus had seen. There was much about Persia he had to admire and much in the Greek world he had to condemn.

Alexander's breadth of sympathy is apparent from his grief at the death of Darius, his kindness to that king's mother, and his distress on finding that Cyrus's tomb had been neglected. From the realization that he had to be Pharaoh in Egypt and the Great King at Susa, he went on to recognize that Oriental monarchy has its merits, especially in ruling an Oriental people. He concluded as rapidly that the only way to blend the opposite traditions in his empire was by marriage. He set the example by marrying first Roxane, a native princess, and second, a daughter of Darius himself. He persuaded ninety of his officers to take Persian wives, gave presents to no less than ten thousand of his soldiers who had done the same, and enlisted thirty thousand Persians in the Macedonian army. So quickly did he pass from the idea of Greek conquest to the idea of a world empire based on a fusion of cultures. As quickly again did he pass from life, leaving behind him an imperishable legend.

Asia has never been purely Asian, save in the Far East, since Alexander's day. His legend went ahead of him, being found today in places he never reached, among peoples of whom he had never heard. Malays give the name Iskandar to their chil-

* *Ibid.*, p. 209.

dren, and even to their cats, little knowing what memory their act enshrines. There are tales still told throughout the world of a man whom all agreed to call "The Great." Great in himself, unexampled in courage and vision, he was also the spearhead of a civilization, which (to quote Freya Stark once more),

> . . . in spite of cruelties and errors can never be superseded, since even the merest trifles it has left us, the siting of its buildings, the stray stones of its walls, the fragments of its marbles, hold that strong thread of immortality we are in danger of forgetting, our only hope and native country in this world.*

* Stark, *op. cit.*, p. 54.

7

CARTHAGE AND ROME

For one dizzy moment, after Alexander's return from India, it might have seemed that the world was one. Of the five known civilizations, four were comprised, more or less, in a single monarchy. It could not last even insofar as it had been really attained, for the Macedonian impetus had finally spent itself at the Battle of the Hydaspes, after which the army would advance no further. This point is reached, as we shall see, in every movement of expansion. Historians are apt to say that the army was exhausted, giving some readers the picture of men who are tired out. There is no ordinary fatigue, however, which cannot be remedied by a week in camp. Exhaustion in this sense means something entirely different. It means that there have been heavy casualties among the best fighting troops. It means that the more fortunate survivors have acquired, and want to enjoy their prestige, their promotion, their girl captives, and their loot. It means that the generals have become elderly and even the unit commanders, middle-aged. It means that the economic system is being strangled by overtaxation. It means, finally, that the whole organization, being committed to teach, has ceased to learn.

Where Alexander was concerned, the economic factor did not apply. He had marched into Asia with supplies for thirty days and more debts than cash, his later operations being financed from the looted treasures of Susa, Persepolis, Pasagadae, and Ecbatana. But all the other factors were operative and the marriage festival at Susa was itself inconsistent with any further conquests. The next phase, as the generals no doubt told each other, would be one of consolidation. At that point Alexander died, and his empire promptly fell apart. Egypt became a monarchy under Ptolemy Soter, Persia fell to Seleucus and Macedonia to Antigonus Gonatas. The dream of unity was over, but the cultural impetus was not yet spent. Hellenization continued in both Egypt and Asia, presenting a first picture of colonialism in the form which has since become familiar. A Greek-speaking military and administrative organization had been superimposed on the Egyptian- and Aramaic-speaking provinces of the Persian empire. This governmental structure rested to some extent upon force but also gained strength from its own innate appeal. Hellenistic influence was strongest, of course, in the cities, but it was fairly widespread wherever there was trade, creating eventually that classical landscape against which the events of the New Testament could be enacted.

Commenting upon the economic results of Alexander's action in spending the Persian hoards of gold, Toutain goes on to describe the general impact of the Greeks:

> Nevertheless, the intelligent use of the public resources would not by itself have been enough to extract the full value of the Eastern countries which had now come into the circle of the Hellenic and Mediterranean world. For that to happen, another leaven was necessary, the human leaven — that is, initiative and method, the signs of a fine, intelligent, voluntary energy. That spirit of initiative and that sense of method were brought into the East by the Greeks. For a long time, travellers, historians and philosophers had observed and pointed out the contrast which existed in this respect between Greeks and Orientals. In his true or fictitious account of the conversation of Xerxes and Demaratos at the beginning of the second Persian War, Herodotus contrasts the inert, cowardly slavery of the Great King's subjects with the Greek's passionate love of freedom and of the free play of his physical, intellectual and moral

forces. Half a century after Herodotus, Hippocrates put down the indolent softness of the Orientals to their climate and declared that the Greeks were destined by the very nature of their country to a hard-working and less routine-ridden life. Aristotle asserts that the Barbarians are born to be slaves.

The contrast between Greek and Oriental may have been accentuated by the manner in which the Persians had tryannized over the East from the sixth century to the fourth. The great characteristic of the Persian rule which had weighed down upon the East for two centuries was that the unity of the Empire was purely mechanical. Nothing was demanded but submission . . . There had never been a power less capable of ruling than the military patriarchal monarchy of the Persians . . . The crowds of Greeks who settled in the East shook the old population out of their barren apathy, and brought in the stead of the tyrannical selfish indifference of the Persian administration, their passion for work, their desire for progress, their thirst for adventure, and their spirit of innovation . . .*

This passage fairly represents the contrast between East and West as it appeared to the Greek authors of the day, and as it has appeared to their readers ever since. Insofar as the picture is accurate, it represents the difference between victors and vanquished, quite irrespective of climate or race. The Greeks of the Hellenistic world felt a superiority which their Asian subjects mostly acknowledged. But the Persians before Thermopylae had felt a superiority which most of the Greeks had been willing to admit. The contrast between East and West was universally recognized, but we must not confuse the generosity of the conquerors with some innate quality of breeding, nor the cringes and subterfuges of the conquered with some innate servility of race. As for the theory that the Persians were unfit to rule, this is obviously baseless. Without the Persian system of communications — to go no deeper than that — the conquest of Alexan-

* Jules Toutain, *op. cit.*, pp. 90–93.

der's world would not have been even technically possible, and
if modern historians can find nothing admirable in Cyrus or
Darius, they differ in this from Alexander himself. The ruins of
Persepolis speak for themselves, and it was Persian horsemanship that the Macedonians had learned while living, in fact,
under Persian rule. As for the Greeks' passionate love of freedom, it rested largely on the institution of slavery. The free play
of the physical, intellectual and moral forces was feasible only
among people whose slaves were doing the actual work.

Innate superiority there was none, but there did exist the current ascendancy of those whose culture had become the fashion.
The tone of the Hellenistic city was set by the gymnasium, the
Greek school and club. It was there, as also in the best seats at
the stadium and theater, that the leading administrators came
together. It was to this society that the ambitious natives sought
admission, for their sons if not for themselves. The Greeks, as
we have seen, had much to give. How far did their influence
extend? How far were they exclusive? How far were they themselves orientalized? So far as is known, race differences tended
to diminish quickly over the countryside, the Greeks being assimilated. In the cities there was something in the nature of a
color bar, as Davis has been able to prove; so far at least as
Egypt is concerned, where the three Greek cities, Naucratis,
Alexandria and Ptolemaïs, had a character of their own.

> Here a conservative policy was followed — the aim being to keep
> the source of Hellenism pure. The members of the citizen body
> were forbidden to contract marriage with natives. Citizenship
> was not made too easy for foreigners to acquire, although there
> were some cases of naturalization. The statutes of the cities
> placed obstacles in the way of mixed marriages and the charter
> of Naucratis refused to recognise marriages between citizen and
> native as lawful. Great importance was attached to purity of
> race, since the citizenship was refused to the illegitimate son of
> a citizen, and in the Roman period Alexandria definitely did not

have connubium with the Egyptians. The same must have been the case in Ptolemais for the names borne by the Ptolemaites . . . always preserve their Hellenic character . . . [Outside the cities the Greeks lose their distinct character.] They read and wrote Greek, but they wrote it more and more incorrectly. In the 2nd and 1st centuries the letters, ordinances, and circulars issued by high officials are drafted in a pretentious, incorrect and hopelessly involved style.*

In the matter of official language some modern parallels may suggest themselves. In general, however, the picture we have is of Greeks holding the higher and more specialized offices, inter-marrying within their own society, preserving their own culture, and being seen at their own club. Around them were the West-ernized natives, making their children chant the Greek tragedies, and seeking an associate membership in the athletic organiza-tion. Around these again were the Asian peoples, still rather im-pressed by Greek architecture and art, and on or beyond the fringe were a few people actively hostile, notably the Jews.

The one class of Greeks who had to accept Oriental supersti-tion from the outset was the class from which their royalty was drawn. Alexander had tried to kill the idea of a color bar at its birth, unsuccessfully even in the cities he had named. But his generals at once discovered what he already knew — that their club memberships would have to lapse. One of them had to become the pharaoh, accepting the marriage of brother and sis-ter which the Greeks themselves disapproved. Another had to be and to look like the successor of Darius. Alexander himself had demanded the prostration before him of all his subjects, Macedonian as well as Persian, and this became of necessity the pattern for his successors on the Persian throne. Alexander came to be deified in his turn, proving that a king must be the sort of being that his subjects have learned to expect. On this pattern of Orientalized rulers and Hellenistic or Hellenized officers, a

* S. Davis, *op. cit.*, p. 54.

Greek empire was maintained from the Nile to the Indus; and nowhere more firmly established than in Bactria, its most easterly province. While its expansion had ceased, its focal points were firmly held.

In such a period as this of European dominance, the logical sequel to the Macedonian effort should have been a third wave of expansion. Another Western people should have annexed the Hellenistic kingdoms, passed through them, and gone further east, reaching the Ganges and making contact with China. But history is not quite as tidy as that. For Alexander's armies, while invading Asia, had not cleared the Asiatics out of Europe. What the modern soldier would describe as "a pocket of resistance" had been left behind. The Phoenicians, spearheading the previous Asian offensive, against which the Greeks reacted so strongly in the Aegean, had made a new base at Carthage from which their further advance had carried them on to Spain. At the very time the Persian attack on Greece began, in 480 B.C., the Carthaginians were attempting to drive the Greeks out of Sicily, being defeated by Gelon on the very day of the Persians' disaster at Salamis. In his drive eastward, Alexander had taken and destroyed their original base at Tyre, but Carthage was still powerful and prosperous. Southern Italy and Sicily might be in Greek hands, but North Africa belonged to the Carthaginians. Westward from Arae Philenorum (near the modern El Agheila), it was theirs indeed by an agreement drawn up c. 500 B.C.; an area from which all trespassers were systematically driven. The result was that the next wave of European expansion, that led by Rome, was initially and inevitably directed against Carthage. By the time the Romans had gone on to absorb the Hellenistic kingdom they too had lost their momentum. They went no further east than Alexander had gone. Indeed, they failed to go as far, being notably less successful than even, say, Antiochus III. Their type of culture spread without much opposition among the barbarian tribes to the westward. In the East, by contrast, when they eventually arrived there, they met with a stiffening resistance; the signs, in fact, of a renascent Asia.

Like the earlier Phoenicians, the people of Carthage were Asian in character and actively opposed to the ideals for which the Greeks stood. Racially akin to the Jews, they were definitely foreign, deliberately different. We know, unfortunately, all too little about them, much of what we know coming from their Greek and Roman enemies. The talk against them centered upon their practice of human sacrifice, their own babies being the victims preferred.

> The whole character of Carthaginian religion was one of the weakness and submission of human beings in the face of the overwhelming and capricious power of the gods and the necessity of appeasing them. The nomenclature of the Carthaginians is expressive of the attitude of dependence; Hasdrubal meant "my help in Baal", Hannibal "favoured by Baal", Hamilcar "servant of Melkart" and most other names borne by them had similar religious connotations . . .
>
> They were always strange to their neighbours who were the more ready to judge them harshly as is the hostile summing up of Plutarch, writing in the second century A.D. but using some earlier writer: "The Carthaginians are a hard and gloomy people, submissive to their rulers and harsh to their subjects, running to extremes of cowardice in times of fear and of cruelty in times of anger; they keep obstinately to their decisions, are austere and care little for amusement or the graces of life.*

So far as cruelty went, the Greeks and Romans were far from blameless. The "exposure" of babies was a common Greek practice, less humane than the sacrifice to Baal. The difference lay, however, in the motive. The Greeks were using a form of birth control, limiting the size of the family and discarding the physically handicapped. They were behaving rationally, even

* B. H. Warmington, *Carthage* (London, 1960), pp. 131–35.

if many would say wrongly. They did not suppose that enthusiastic gods were egging them on. But the Carthaginians had convinced themselves that their gods needed appeasing, for which
purpose only the best babies would do. The effect was not
precisely the same and the ideas were totally different. The
Carthaginian practice sheds light, above all, on their mental
picture of Baal. He is a shade less attractive than the God of
the Old Testament; and as he was made in their own image, his
character can only be theirs. Although not exactly monotheistic,
the Carthaginians were a people to whom their religion evidently
mattered a great deal. Where they resembled the Greeks was in
their taste for ships and horses — a taste which even led them to
put a horse's head on the ship's prow. Their assets included a
great knowledge of seamanship and an almost exclusive access
to the horses of Libya.

Carthage, by 400 B.C., was said to be the richest city in the
world, with a population of well over half a million. Its great
period of growth was under Hanno (538–521 B.C.), the king who
first ordered the exploration of West Africa. Carthage later became a republic, possessing the only non-Greek constitution to
find admirers in Greece. It would seem to have been an oli-
garchy of merchants and stockbreeders. "Obsequiousness to the
powerful, arrogance to the weak and contempt of labor were the
prevailing social attitudes among the financial magnates who
ruled the Carthaginian state . . ." *

> The qualities which they endeavoured to develop in the young
> were, first and foremost a love of undertakings in distant lands,
> smartness if not roguery in business, eagerness to make money,
> and a passionate love of wealth, versatility combined with tenac-
> ity, a political intelligence capable of profiting even by apparently
> unfavourable circumstances . . . The Latin writers may perhaps
> have exaggerated the shortcomings of Punic honesty, *fides
> Punica,* but they did not invent them. The Carthaginians in-

* Ralph Turner, *op. cit.,* I, 494.

spired dislike among the peoples of antiquity as a whole; the Greeks speak of them just as severely as the Romans . . .*

The earliest Carthaginian coins date from the 4th century B.C. and bear the stamp of a horse and palm tree. Ships with a horse's head on the prow were first to be seen at Tyre, but eventually became more typical of Cadiz. These "Hippi" (as they were called) could apparently sail round Africa, for one of these figure-heads was brought to Egypt from a wreck on the East African coast in about 112 B.C., and experts concluded that it was a fragment of a ship from Cadiz.† So the Carthaginians lacked nothing in enterprise. Where they failed most obviously was in imagination. Their art forms that have survived are not negligible, but are only mildly attractive — things made to sell rather than to enjoy.‡

If the Phoenicians had differed sharply from the Greeks, the people of Carthage were still more alien from the people of Rome. In the Punic Wars, the conflict of East and West acquired a new edge. It was no longer a struggle for dominance but for survival. Why was this? Perhaps mainly because the Romans were further from the ancient East. "In a westerly direction," writes V. Gordon Childe, "the rays of the Oriental culture should strike upon the Apennine Peninsula first after Greece." § So indeed they should. But culture in this instance came at secondhand. The Greeks had taken their civilization from Egypt and Mesopotamia, their alphabet from the Phoenicians. The Romans took their civilization from the Greeks, another European people, and were the more remote from Oriental influence. They were a group of barbarian tribes in central Italy, whose original monarchy gave place to a republic in about 509 B.C.

* Jules Toutain, op. cit., p. 188.
† See Cecil Torr, Ancient Ships (Cambridge, 1894), pp. 113–14.
‡ See Donald Harden, The Phoenicians (London, 1962), plates and illus.
§ V. Gordon Childe, The Dawn of European Civilisation (4th ed.; London, 1947), p. 225.

The city of Rome derived its culture from the Greek colonies of southern Italy, the earliest of which date from about 760 B.C. Under aristocratic leadership, the Romans gradually conquered the whole of Italy, including the Greek colonies in the south; a process which strengthened Greek influence on Rome itself. These cities also brought with them their existing feud with the Carthaginians, essentially a struggle for the control of Sicily.

Geographical factors were vital in the conflict which followed. As Childe points out, following Hogben:

> It is possible to sail coastwise from the Aegaean to Italy and Sicily without ever losing sight of land. Progress thence westward meant embarking on the pathless ocean without any guiding point in the heavens like the Pole Star, by which a mariner might set his course. Sicily must have set a bound to a regular intercourse which depended on following the northern shores of the Mediterranean.*

There was no such obstacle in the Phoenician course to the westward, along the African shore. Partly for this reason the men of Carthage had gone faster and further, dispersing their strength among settlements scattered from Malta to Gades and beyond. But opposite Carthage itself was the more concentrated strength of Rome, with Sicily as the obvious steppingstone. In the First Punic War (264–241 B.C.), the Romans, with great difficulty, annexed Sicily. The stage was set for Phase Two, but the Carthaginian army in Spain launched a spoiling attack under the leadership of Hannibal. Among his best troops were the Numidian cavalry led by Maharbal. With 12,000 of these and 90,000 infantry, Hannibal marched overland, and invaded Italy from the north. The campaign lasted no less than fifteen years, but ended with Scipio's invasion of Spain and later of Africa. With his own Numidian cavalry under Masinissa, Scipio

* V. Gordon Childe, *op. cit.*, p. 245.

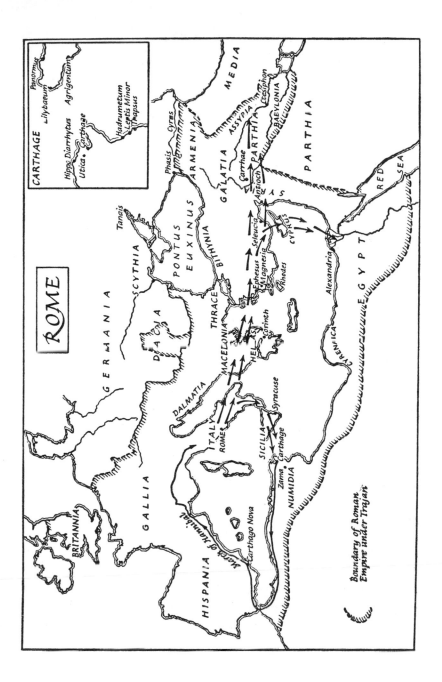

ROME

Boundary of Roman Empire under Trajan

Inset (CARTHAGE): Panormus, Lilybaeum, Agrigentum, Hippo Diarrhytus, Utica, Carthage, Hadrumetum, Leptis Minor, Thapsus

BRITANNIA, GERMANIA, GALLIA, HISPANIA, Carthago Nova, DALMATIA, DACIA, SCYTHIA, Tanais, ITALY, ROME, SICILIA, Syracuse, Carthage, Zama, NUMIDIA, MACEDONIA, HELLAS, Corinth, THRACE, BITHYNIA, PONTUS EUXINUS, Phasis, Cyrus, ARMENIA, GALATIA, Ephesus, Magnesia, Rhodes, Seleucia, CYPRUS, Antioch, SYRIA, Carrhae, ASSYRIA, PARTHIA, MEDIA, BABYLONIA, Ctesiphon, PARTHIA, RED SEA, Alexandria, EGYPT, CYRENAICA

March of Hannibal

finally defeated his great opponent at Zama (202 B.C.) and brought the Second Punic War to an end. Carthage now dwindled in importance, and it was not until 149–146 B.C. that the Third Punic War was waged, ending in the complete destruction of Carthage, its buildings demolished, its site devastated and sown with salt. Rome ruled the western Mediterranean, and controlled the trade route westward from Syracuse; a route which led eastward to Corinth, to Ephesus (replacing Miletus) to Rhodes, to Tanais at the mouth of the Don, to Dioscurias and Phasis at the eastern end of the Euxine, to Seleucia the port of Antioch in Syria, and above all, to Alexandria, which was the gateway to the Red Sea. The whole of this Hellenistic world lay with its momentum lost but its wealth intact, a perfect springboard for the further conquest of Asia. It rested with Rome to establish a new world empire, a European rule extending over what had been the empire of Alexander, but now with the addition of Europe as a whole — Italy, Gaul, and Spain, North Africa up to the Atlantic, and all else that might lie beyond.

More even than the Greeks, the Romans were of Western character. They absorbed the basic Greek institutions, not always with complete comprehension, and then added some contribution of their own. Essential to their way of life was a republican simplicity of dress and manner, combined with an essentially aristocratic constitution. From the Greeks they had taken some elements of democratic practice, public assemblies, elections, and votes. From the Greeks again they had taken their worldly outlook, a concentration on what they could see, to the exclusion of priesthood as a strong element in their society. There was no rank higher than that of citizen, no office that was permanent. With some inspiration perhaps from Sparta, they affected a contempt for the elaborate and artificial in costume, etiquette, food, or speech. Clean-shaven, as from the time of Scipio Africanus, close-cropped, colorlessly garbed, disdainful of mere wealth, ruthless and taciturn, the incorruptible Roman left his mark on the western world. Along with titles and insignia of rank, along with the foppery of gold, jewels, and perfume, the Roman as brusquely dismissed poetry, music, and art. What remained for him was the reputation he could gain on the battlefield, in the law court, in political office, and on the floor of the Senate. His legendary ideal was enshrined in the story of Cincinnatus who saved Rome in its greatest hours of danger and then returned to the plow for his livelihood. A dozen other tight-lipped legends tell of men's courage, integrity, simplicity, and patriotism. While the Romans often failed to live up to their own picture of themselves, it is important to know what that picture was. It was the legend more than the reality that other people were later to imitate.

The appearance of equality at Rome made its impact even at the time. The author of *Maccabees* I, 8, remarks, in describing the Roman Senate, that "None of them did ever put on a diadem, neither did they clothe themselves in purple, to be magnified thereby." This is perfectly true but the senator's toga did have a narrow purple edge, and he knew how to magnify himself in a different way. To come of an ancient family, to have seen active service, to have served as consul — it was these qualifications which gave the senator his influence. Aristocracy at Rome rested thus upon solid achievement, a thorough, if limited, knowledge, a rigorous training, a hard-won experience, and a discipline imposed on themselves and each other by the senatorial families. "I was a friend to my friends," said Darius, but the Roman's loyalty was impersonal. His duty was to the State, to the Senate and People, to an abstract conception of grandeur. As compared with the Greeks, the Romans of the Republican period had the merit of all being on the same side. Their attachments and beliefs, their hopes and fears all centered finally upon Rome, not upon any individual but upon a city.

It was the unity and discipline which made Rome supreme

in Europe. Under Flaminius, the Roman legions intervened in Greece even before the end of the Second Punic War. Later, and inevitably, the conquest began in earnest, Corinth being destroyed at the same time as Carthage, and both Macedonia and Greece were annexed after the Greek defeat in 146 B.C. The attempt to govern the whole Mediterranean area through the political institutions of the city-state broke down immediately. Unpaid public officers, elected for brief periods and theoretically controlled by popular assemblies, were trying to discipline distant provinces by means of a short-service citizen army. The failure of this system was made painfully apparent in 88 B.C. when Mithridates VI of Pontus ordered the massacre of all Romans and Italians in Asia. A hundred thousand died, it is said, on a single day, killed by Asians or by proletarian Greeks. It foreshadowed further Oriental reaction against Rome, with Parthians, Armenians, and Jews in alliance. The first and logical reaction was to reorganize the army. A consul, Marius, transformed it into a paid profession. His place was eventually taken by another general, Sulla, who made himself dictator. During the ensuing scramble for power, Pompey defeated Mithridates of Pontus (66–62 B.C.) and his rival Julius Caesar served successfully in Spain. As their ambitions seemed to lie in opposite directions, there was apparently some possibility of an agreement. With a third general, Crassus, they formed the First Triumvirate in 60 B.C., as a sequel to which Caesar conquered Gaul and Britain. Crassus, for his part, obtained the province of Syria and made this his base for an attempted conquest of what had been Alexander's empire.

The Hellenistic empire, as Alexander had left it, did no longer, of course, exist. It had fallen into three fragments. Of these, the more westerly — Macedonia with Pontus (since Pompey's campaign), and Egypt with Syria — were already within the Roman sphere of influence. There remained the kingdom of the Seleucids, ablest of the Macedonian dynasties. The essence of their inheritance was the great trade route and military highway leading from Seleucia on the Tigris to Bactria and so eastwards.

The Seleucids were masters of the great intercontinental routes crossing Iran in the direction of China and India; they extended and improved them. From the Red Sea to India the routes were protected by military posts; supplies of water were organized in the desert and caravanserais built . . . Although the Seleucids did not control the route passing to the north of the Caspian Sea towards southern Russia, they held the route which terminated on the shores of the Black Sea after crossing the Caspian and following the rivers Cyrus and Phasis . . . They maintained a large fleet on the Persian Gulf which secured the connection with India on the east and the Red Sea on the west.*

Making full use of the Greek overspill of population, they had developed Alexander's policy of urbanization, founding cities both on the trade route and along the Persian Gulf. The ancient Rhagae — now a suburb of Teheran — was significantly re-named Europos. Among the new aristocracy and middle class, Greek was the usual language spoken, and also the language of business and of law. Greek culture did not spread to the Iranian population as a whole, which offered a passive resistance to Hellenism. Eventually, the Seleucid kingdom began to weaken. The first result of this was the revolt which led to the independence of Bactria. The second result was the loss of Parthia, the next province to the west, which fell to an invading group of Scythian horsemen, the Parni tribe. This was soon after 250 B.C. and Seleucus II failed to regain the territory he had lost. His successor Antiochus III was more successful, but incurred the hostility of Rome. He was defeated at Magnesia in 190 B.C., and more of his provinces threw off their allegiance. This gave Mithridates of Parthia his opportunity. Between 160 and 140

* R. Ghirshman, *op. cit.*, pp. 237–38.

B.C. Mithridates conquered Media, Babylonia, and Assyria, defeated Demetrius II, and established his authority from the Euphrates to Herat. The brother of Demetrius, Antiochus VII, made a final effort against the Parthians, gaining initial success but meeting disaster in 129 B.C. That was the end of the Seleucid kingdom. As Ghirshman says, "The frontier of Europe was withdrawn to the Euphrates." * The Parthians staged no immediate movement into Syria — they were busy fending off a new movement of Scythian nomads to the eastward — but Mithridates II consolidated a strong kingdom, taking the title King of Kings.

About 115 B.C. Mithridates received an embassy from the Emperor of China, and the two rulers concluded a treaty designed to facilitate the movement of international commerce in which Iran, as a transit state, formed a vitally important link.†

So the trade between East and West continued. But the midway position was now occupied by a new world power; not a weakened fragment of the Macedonian empire, but a force which would prevent the further eastward expansion of Europe.

On becoming proconsul of Syria, Crassus planned a Roman conquest of Iran in 54 B.C. His own reputation, such as it was, rested upon his success in putting down a slave revolt in Italy. He was better known, in fact, as a financier and land speculator. In Iran he saw a fresh opportunity for plunder and, better still, a chance to rival Pompey and Caesar in military prestige. So far from having bettered Alexander in technique, the Romans still relied mainly upon the tactics which had eventually defeated Carthage; an infantry assault which was little more than a development of the Greek phalanx. Crassus with seven legions and four thousand cavalry (42,000 in all), found himself opposed at Carrhae by a Parthian army which had been organized on Mace-

* Ghirshman, *op. cit.*, p. 248.
† *Ibid.*, p. 250.

donian lines, a balanced force of heavy cavalry, mounted bow-men and infantry. The Romans were not so much defeated as massacred.

According to tradition the head and arm of the ill-fated Crassus was brought to Orodes II when he was watching the Bacchae of Euripides in company with the King of Armenia and the members of his Court.*

It was an instance of the Greek-Iranian alloy being stronger than the pure metal of the West. The surprising sequel to the story has been revealed by Homer H. Dubs. In 38 B.C. a Chinese General, Gan Yen-shun, captured the town of Jzh-jzh on the Talass River in Sogdiana, the headquarters of a rebellious chieftain. Of the prisoners taken, 145 received special treatment. They were settled in a newly founded frontier city called Li-jien, the Chinese name for Rome. There can be little doubt that these soldiers were legionaries, taken prisoner at Carrhae, who had served afterwards in the Parthian armies and then came to enter the service of Jzh-jzh. As Dubs writes in conclusion, "The presence of Romans in ancient China indicates how small the world actually was, even in those days." † Of the second and first centuries B.C., H. G. Wells wrote: "Two great empires now dominated the world, this new Roman Empire and the renascent Empire of China." He went on to describe the limits of their influence, and added, "It was possible then for these two vast systems to flourish in the same world at the same time in almost complete ignorance of each other." Possible it may have been, but the ignorance was less complete than was once assumed. They were connected by the trade route, and the fact that Mith-ridates had talked with ambassadors from China as well as Rome would seem to suggest that more direct contact may have taken

* Ibid., p. 252.
† Homer H. Dubs, A Roman City in Ancient China (London, 1957), p. 23.

place. Roman jugglers reached China if no other free Romans did, and Parthian envoys went both east and west. Indirectly, at least, Rome and China were in touch.

Carrhae brought Roman eastward expansion to an abrupt conclusion. Pompey was eliminated by Caesar at the battle of Pharsalus, his flight to Egypt having the indirect result of bringing that country under more direct Roman control. Caesar was murdered by his republican opponents in 44 B.C. and the subsequent civil war left supreme power in the hands of Caesar's nephew, who came to be called Caesar Augustus. This was the point at which the Roman republic was replaced by the empire. Its eastern limits were represented by Bithynia and Cyrenaica, but its client kingdoms, or satellites, included Armenia, Syria, and Egypt. An uneasy peace lasted between Rome and Parthia until the time of Trajan. During that emperor's reign a determined effort was made to assert Roman authority in the East. Trajan invaded Parthia and captured Ctesiphon, the capital, marching down the Tigris and perhaps planning a further advance into India. It was at this juncture that the Jews of Cyrenaica, Egypt, and Cyprus rose in revolt, the movement spreading to the entire Semitic world. Trajan died on his way back to deal with this new situation and his successor, Hadrian, was glad to accept the Euphrates as his frontier. There was further fighting in this area and Ctesiphon twice more fell into Roman hands (A.D. 165 and A.D. 197). But the Roman impetus had disappeared and these last efforts achieved no permanent result.

8

ROME OF THE EMPERORS

So FAR as the possibility went of Roman authority being extended over Parthia, the Battle of Carrhae had been virtually final. Later campaigns in the area, made feasible by the dissensions within Parthia itself, left no permanent mark. As against that, extensive territories which had been comprised in the Persian and earlier Asian empires — territories which had been more or less Hellenized beforehand — were now under Roman control. North Africa, Egypt, Syria, and Asia Minor were all subject to Roman influence. While this is true, however, the extent of that influence came to be limited by two other tendencies, neither of them new, but both from this time more apparent to the historian. These tendencies can be called cultural inundation and grassroots influence.

To take these in order, it is a commonplace among students of history that the brightest inventions (like the alphabet) can be traced very often to the borderlands between one culture and another — to the borderlands, more especially, between East and West. A given area is conquered and occupied by a people with an Asian background, conquered and occupied later by a people with a European background, and then perhaps again exposed to the same alternation. The obvious analogy is of the flood which causes fertility and the crop which appears after the water has subsided. People of the disputed provinces have been presented with alternating sets of ideas and are compelled finally to form a synthesis or make a choice. They can no longer believe that there is only one possible way of life. After many unhappy experiences — campaigns and massacres, dissensions and disputes — they become more mentally alert and agile than people whose lives have been less disturbed. By the time of Augustus, this mental agility characterized a fair number of people — Armenians, for instance, Greeks, Syrians, and Parthians. The second tendency we must note is the influence of the defeated upon the victors. This may be slight where the conquered peoples were previously uncivilized. The Romans had little to learn, perhaps, from the Britons or Gauls. But the situation is very different where the subject race has a culture of its own, and one not inferior to that of the occupying garrison. In their contacts with the East, the Romans were confronted from the outset with semi-westernized Asians and semi-orientalized Greeks — with people, in fact, like Cleopatra. They were also confronted with people at least as civilized as they were.

A study of these influences must lead us at once to the conclusion that the "purely" European tradition can never have existed anywhere. Insofar, moreover, as it did exist, there were also these tendencies to which it was subject from the start. Ghirshman points out, when dealing with the Seleucid rule of Persia, that cotton, lemons, melons, olives, dates, figs, duck, and oxen all came to Italy at that period from Asia. "The defeated Orient subjugated Europe." * But if the purely European did not exist, and had never existed, the purely Asian was a reality. China might be in contact with the rest of the world but not to the point of being influenced. Chinese influence was felt in the West, as we shall see, but European influence fell short of the Far East at this time, reaching Malaya, perhaps, as its furthest limit. When all this has been said, however, the Roman period remains one of the greatest importance. There was an initial period, fairly brief, during which the Roman ideal made its first impression, a second period during which Rome was influenced by people of very mixed cultural background, and a last period during which a directly

* Ghirshman, op. cit., p. 239.

Asian influence had become dominant. By then Rome was on the defensive and a renascent Asia was moving westward.

One fact apparent from the first is that Rome had no technological advantage over its Asian subjects. As soldiers, the Romans could act with considerable resolution, but they made few discoveries in either technique or tactics. Take steel, for example, a basic material for war. The Greeks used to obtain theirs from Scythia and the Pontic coast. The best steel of the Hellenistic period came from Chalybes, Sinope, Lydia, and Laconia. Nor were the Romans able to improve on these supplies.

> It is well known that in the Roman Empire steel produced by the Seres (Chinese) and the Parthians was regarded as far superior to that made in the Roman Empire and was imported. And in fact we know that both China and India produced excellent steel in ancient times. The primacy probably belonged to India, which was certainly the country of origin of the famous Damascene steel . . .*

So far as weapons went, the Romans had nothing as effective as the Chinese crossbow with its triple compound lever. The only Romans exposed to bolts from the Chinese crossbow were the lost legionaries of Jzh-jzh, who took cover immediately. In a regular battle they would not have stood a chance.

It has been the fashion to allow the Romans a certain supremacy in engineering, but here again the facts are otherwise; nor did the Romans claim as much for themselves.

> According to Roman writers, nothing new was invented. The Romans combined the paved roads of the Carthaginians with the post-system of the Persians. The credit of constructing the first true roadway is given to Carthage . . . Isadorus of Seville . . . describes how the Carthaginians first began to pave roads with

* M. Rostovtzeff, *The Social and Economic History of the Hellenistic World* (Oxford, 1941), II, 1218.

stone, and how first the Romans, then the whole civilized world, took over the idea . . . But paved roads are earlier than this . . .*

Most of the Roman road building was done by Augustus and Tiberius, between 27 B.C. and 37 A.D., but it was largely a development of existing routes. So far as the East was concerned, the Persian road system was already there, and connected, for that matter, with the even more impressive road system of China. Says Ralph Turner on the subject:

> Like agriculture, industry and commerce, transportation reached a new height of development under Rome. But as in the other phases of economic activity, the achievement was largely the result of the systematic use of old means. The great roads which radiated from Rome, bringing the farthermost province within a six weeks' journey of the capital, were developed from the Hellenistic elaboration of the Persian system. The courier service which carried official dispatches followed closely the Persian pattern. Shipping and navigation remained much as they had been in Hellenistic times. Rome added to these means of transportation a police protection, which often broke down, regular posthouses and inns, and travel aids such as guides, guidebooks, and road signs. The mile post and the road sign were Roman inventions . . . However, the Romans' road system was built to serve not an economic but a military purpose . . . In the time of Trajan there were about forty-seven thousand miles of road throughout the empire . . . No roads have surpassed the Roman roads in technical excellence . . .†

Surface and drainage apart, the milestone represents a typically Roman device, an aid in planning the day's march, but marked in such numerals as no mathematician could use to any purpose. The milestone suggests an urge to regulate and organize. It is no symptom of scientific knowledge, least of all when marked

* Astley J. H. Goodwin, *op. cit.*, p. 201.
† Turner, *op. cit.*, II, 912 *et seq.*

XXXVIII or XLIX. Nor is the signpost any proof in itself of engineering skill.

What had the Romans to offer that was specifically European? To what extent, for that matter, did they stabilize the conception of what the European idea was to be? From the Greeks they had taken the concept of the individual. By their stress on "character" — as opposed, say, to education — they made the individual still more distinct. In their sculpture the characteristic form is the portrait bust or scene in high relief. The nude figure has given place to the exact delineation of the human face — the stern, obstinate expression of the Roman aristocrat. Nor is the triumphal procession centered, in art, upon the abstract achievement, but upon the resolute face of the leader. Only in the most formal sense was any credit given to the gods. More credit was due, indeed, to the individual's "genius" or guiding spirit, an extension of his own personality. The victorious general's entry into Rome was a demonstration of what the Roman virtues were taken to be: seriousness, courage, fortitude, and devotion to duty. Woe to the vanquished! The Romans were better at humiliating than they were at converting their opponents. Their destruction of Carthage had been complete.

Above the individual was the abstract State, as we have seen, and the individual's relationship to the State was defined by law. The Greek agora or marketplace, center of public life, became in Rome the forum. In this setting the orator's appeal from the rostrum was not to the rulers, not to the gods, but consistently to the law. The Roman constitution was based on the Twelve Tables, the work not of a god, but of a committee. On these had been built up a superstructure of case law which was destined for eventual codification in the Institutes of Justinian. The Latin tongue has its limitations, but it is admirably fitted for legal argument, being precise, lucid, and terse. As lawgivers, the Romans had a unique contribution to make. Nor were they less distinguished in eloquence, rhetoric being in fact the basis of

their formal education. In Rome, as compared with earlier
civilizations, the rights and duties of the citizen were carefully
defined, defended, and enforced. In support of the law was the
Stoic philosophy which emphasized the dignity of the individual
and his sense of duty, offering no support from the deity and no
hope of reward. Again in support of the law and the republican
virtues was the one literary form in which the Romans may be
said to have gone beyond their teachers — the art of satire. The
contrast between the rigid austerities of Roman theory and the
sordid acquisitiveness of Roman practice provided a situation of
which the great satirists like Juvenal and Martial took full advantage.

According to Roman theory, the individual's duty was to the
State, by which in turn the individual's rights were guaranteed.
His duty was not to the gods, nor to science, nor to art. It is
significant that the Romans used Athens as their university, developing no equivalent of their own. For the scholar's loyalty is
to truth, whereas the Roman's loyalty was to Rome. The Romans with any scientific bent were encouraged to apply their
knowledge in the service of the State, developing the use of the
arch, the bridge, the aqueduct, and the cistern. If their scientific interest were less concrete than that, they could turn their
attention to sanitation and hygiene. Art was not much valued
in itself, being thought unmanly and fit only for the Greeks;
but it could also be used for the public good. The architect and
sculptor could thus provide a dignified setting for the activities
which mattered — the deliberations, the speeches, the proclama-
tions, and triumphs. Among the most typical Roman art forms
is the triumphal arch — commemorative, corinthian or com-
posite, heavy, elaborate, and costly, designed for the glory of
man and the State. As for the typical Greek institutions, the
gymnasium was replaced by the public bath and the athletic
stadium by the chariot racecourse — where horses from North
Africa seem usually to have won. Theaters they had, but they

were overshadowed in importance by the amphitheaters where the games were held; and "games" for the Romans could mean only one thing.

The Roman passion for spectacles in which men fought with beasts, some beasts against others, or the men among themselves, needs explanation. There would seem to have been no Oriental equivalent, nor is there now. In the West, however, the tradition persists in Spain and South America; and indeed, on a make-believe level, in Hollywood. A streak of cruelty in the Roman character was the prime cause, and the games themselves encouraged the instinct which was their origin. Of prime importance was the effect on children. Cruelty apart, however, the games were associated with the Roman rejection of art. Seeking relaxation, the sterner republicans would not turn to poetry, ballet, comedy, or music, the unmanly interests of the few. They would turn more naturally to the racecourse or the gladiators, to gambling or to sex; just as some men today prefer all-in-wrestling to opera. One aspect, however, of the "games" (and one we must not overlook) is their public character. They were a part of the public life of Rome, and attendance at them was a *social* act. The Flavian Amphitheater or Colosseum at Rome was built in 72–80 A.D. for an audience of 50,000. Vespasian could have spent the money on a palace for himself (as a Chinese emperor would have done), but that would not have been in the Roman tradition. The ruins which remain are of the public buildings, and the palaces, before the time of Diocletian, were never of a comparable importance.

Here then are some of the elements which made up the Roman tradition. The total picture is somewhat lacking in charm. What persists, however, is the Roman determination and energy. The road would be pushed on over hill and dale, straight, enduring, and solid. The forum would assume its majestic dignity even if built in a remote province on the fringes of the desert. Whatever the opposition of nature or man, the task would be finished as planned. Without undue economy in money or effort, lives or time, the work would be completed. Of Greek fortification, Freya Stark observes:

> . . . they refuse to be limited to economic terms: they reach their perfection regardless of expense or effort, and a sort of radiance inevitably follows, as if the axle of immortality ran through them. An absence of triviality, a depth and fearlessness triumphant over fashion is reached in all such works — the Greek wall, the Seljuk tower, the wing of the jet fighter, and all the inventions that grasp life so neatly and joyfully that death ceases to matter in the count.
>
> That is excellence for its own sake, which our economic states degrade in favour of minor equalities. Surrounded by second-rate comforts we watch our art and words — our loves themselves — deteriorate and our joy depart. But in all paths that seem permanent, we find this delight as a signpost and what pain goes with it is accepted. 'For this my goddess Mother telleth me, Thetis the silver-footed, that twain fates are bearing me to the issue of death.' *

Not quite as much can be said for the buildings of Rome. Something of the magic has gone. But where perfection has been lost in excessive weight, the passion for excellence is still there. Enough remains to dwarf all that we can build today.

The heavy dignities of Rome were subject, however, as we have seen, to cultural inundation and grassroots influence. Nor were these tendencies confined to their areas of origin. By the very nature of their imperial effort the Romans became dispersed throughout the world. Military and colonial duty, war casualties and economic opportunity drained Rome of its native population, leaving a vacuum into which other peoples were drawn — slaves, migrants, traders, craftsmen, teachers, and priests — groups of mixed origin and alien ways of life. They

* Freya Stark, *op. cit.*, p. 49.

brought with them, among other things, the seven-day week. There is just such a tendency in the London of today, as there was still earlier in Boston and New York. Rome came to be peopled very largely by Levantines, Egyptians, Armenians, and Jews; by astrologers, tipsters, idlers, and crooks.

Even more significant was what the Romans learned while on duty overseas, for the men so influenced were of the highest rank. In Egypt the Roman emperor was pharaoh, in Asia Minor he was the heir to Darius and Xerxes, and these were positions he might well prefer to the republican anomalies of Rome. There the theory lingered that he was First Citizen or commander in chief, deified only with some reluctance. Just as Alexander came to assume the robe of the Persian king, so did his Roman successors. They found, moreover, that the garment seemed to fit and that failure to wear it could lead only to embarrassment. The inconveniences of applying republican ideals to the wrong populace are well illustrated by Gibbon's references to the Emperor Julian. He describes Syrian Antioch in these words:

. . . The warmth of the climate disposed the natives to the most intemperate enjoyment of tranquility and opulence; and the lively licentiousness of the Greeks was blended with the hereditary softness of the Syrians. Fashion was the only law, pleasure the only pursuit, and the splendour of dress and furniture was the only distinction of the citizens of Antioch. The arts of luxury were honoured; the serious and manly virtues were the subject of ridicule, and the contempt for female modesty and reverent age announced the universal corruption of the capitals of the East . . .

He goes on thus to describe the impact made by Julian on the fashionable society of Antioch:

. . . The rustic manners of a prince who disdained such glory, and was insensible of such happiness, soon disgusted the delicacy of his subjects; and the effeminate Orientals could neither imitate nor admire the severe simplicity which Julian always maintained and sometimes affected.*

What Julian eventually discovered had been obvious to others from the beginning, to Pompey and Julius Caesar, to Mark Antony and Cleopatra. Roman austerity made the wrong impression at Alexandria or Antioch. It was easier and pleasanter to assume the public image that the populace would expect. What was more difficult, in practice, was to shed that image after returning to Rome. This became needless in the end, for Rome itself succumbed to Oriental influence. The emperor ended as an Eastern king in all but name.

Symbolic of the decline in Roman austerity was the trade in silk, the thread which connected Rome with China. Silk cultivation was developed in China at some period about 2700 B.C. It reached Egypt and was popularized as a fashion by Cleopatra. Deplored by moralists as indecent and horribly expensive, the silk robe became essential (as one would expect) to the ladies of Rome. Exported from Nanking, the stuff was woven in Persia or Syrian Antioch and reached Rome in the form of cloth, being paid for apparently in gold. The Romans gave the name Cattigara to the one Chinese port of which they had heard, possibly Hangchow, and the Chinese annals record the arrival of a Roman envoy in 166 A.D. This and a later mission would seem to have been unofficial, but some contacts were certainly made and it was many centuries before people in Europe learned how to weave silk for themselves. On the Chinese side there was a name for Rome and indeed for Marcus Antoninus. It took 243 days, however, to travel between Nanking and the coast of Syria, and there were, of course, far closer relationships between Rome and India, more especially after the development of the sea route about the middle of the first century A.D. Roman vessels from

* Edward Gibbon, *The History of the Decline and Fall of the Roman Empire* (1776–1778), Vol. II, Chap. XXIV.

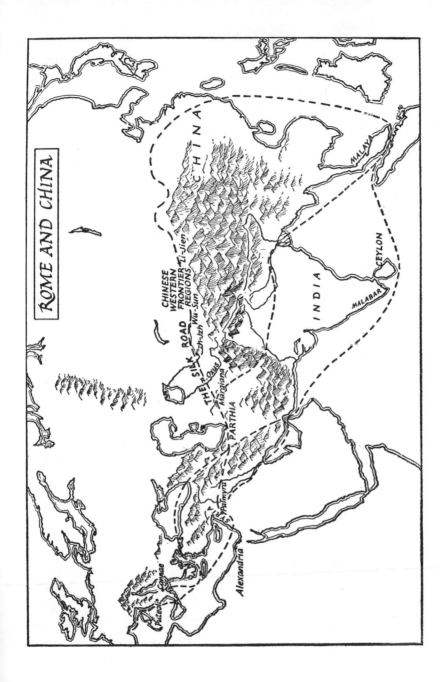

ROME AND CHINA

CHINA

MALAYA

CEYLON

MALABAR

INDIA

CHINESE
WESTERN
FRONTIER
REGIONS

Ti-Jien

Wu-Sun

Szh-Izh

R. Oxus

Margiana

SILK ROAD

THE

PARTHIA

Palmyra

Alexandria

Puteoli Cannae

Alexandria reached Malabar and Ceylon, and Chinese vessels reached southern India by rounding the Malay Peninsula. From Mesopotamia the trade passed through Palmyra in Syria, the luxury goods being landed eventually at Puteoli. Besides silks, the Romans imported cottons, spices, precious stones, fine metal-wares, perfumes, and slaves. In the same way, and by the same routes, they imported some customs, beliefs, and ideas.

To what extent did the Romans use a color bar in self-defense? Was intermarriage allowed between Roman and Asian families? Apparently not. Gibbon tells us that the emperor Constantine specifically warned his son against any sort of mixed marriage.

> . . . A just regard to the purity of descent preserves the harmony of public and private life; but the mixture of foreign blood is the fruitful source of disorder and discord. Such has ever been the opinion and practice of the sage Romans; their jurisprudence proscribed the marriage of a citizen and a stranger; in the days of freedom and virtue, a senator would have scorned to match his daughter with a king; the glory of Mark Antony was sullied by an Egyptian wife, and the emperor Titus was compelled, by popular censure, to dismiss with reluctance the reluctant Berenice.*

Cleopatra was actually a Greek, Berenice an elderly Jewess, mention of whom marks out the limits of Roman tolerance. For the Romans, concerned as they might be over racial purity, were in other respects fairly broadminded. About the Jews they felt quite differently and it is important to know why. Supreme in Europe, they had made their belated effort to conquer the world. Their failure had established the frontiers of the Western world, beyond which lay the Parthians. But for the Semitic Carthaginians, the rest of Alexander's empire might perhaps have been theirs. Carthage had been destroyed, but among the Carthaginian satellites had been the Jews, scattered westward

* *Ibid.*, Vol. VI, Chap. 53.

from Palestine but of Asian origin and sympathies, potential spies and rebels, difficult to assimilate and impossible to trust. The Jew represented then, and has appeared ever since as an enemy agent behind the European lines, tolerated when the East is in retreat but thought dangerous when the movement goes the other way. Anti-Semitism at Alexandria grew during the first century A.D. and led to the sacking of the Jewish quarter in 38 A.D. Complaints and counter-complaints reached Rome, where the emperor Gaius remarked, "After all, those who don't believe in my divinity are more foolish than wicked." The gesture of submission to the deified emperor was used at this time as a political test, like the loyal toast of a later period. The Jews were essentially the people who refused to stand while the national anthem was being played; which again might have been excusable if their loyalty could have been assumed. But no such assumption would have been justified. The Parthians had invaded Syria in 40 B.C., setting up a native king in Jerusalem — one received too willingly by the Jews. Then, under Vespasian, came the Jewish rebellion which Titus suppressed in 70 A.D., scattering the Jews still further. Last of all came the revolt in Cyrenaica and elsewhere which halted Trajan's campaign and led to fresh Parthian efforts. (See page 94.) The Jews had influence in Parthia and a settlement indeed on the banks of the Euphrates. "When you see a Parthian charger tied up to a tombstone in Palestine, the hour of the Messiah will be near." The Jews looked for salvation to the East. At each crisis they were found to be a force in the Asian camp actively hostile to the West. No operational base in Syria could be regarded as secure while the Jews were in the vicinity. They were obstinately and eternally on the other side.

9

THE ORIENTAL WORLD

IN ATTEMPTING to describe the alternate expansion of East and West, the struggle in which first one and then the other side was uppermost, it is never possible to fix a date as representing the turning point, the moment at which advance has turned into withdrawal. If dates can be fixed at all, there must be a series of three: the period at which the civilization under pressure begins to show resentment or resistance; the period at which the ascendant civilization ceases to apply its influence on a big scale; the period at which the counter-movement begins. In practice, moreover, the process is confused — as the tide is apt to be confused — by eddies and currents which conceal the main tendencies. There is never perhaps a moment when the flow becomes the ebb, and yet we must try, as a matter of convenience, to be definite about things really undefined. In attempting to describe the action of the piston it may not be easy to fix the precise moment of time at which its withdrawal has ended, its return stroke begun. All that we can say in the first instance is that the piston is at work; and of this we have reason to be sure.

Asian resistance to Hellenism might be said to have begun in 324 B.C., when Chandragupta Maurya began to unify northern India. This Hindu ruler had met Alexander and was quite hospitable to the Greeks who visited his court, but it was his dynasty that now defended India against further Western penetration. When Seleucus Nicator tried to recover Alexander's Indian provinces, he was defeated decisively in 306 B.C. This did not affect the activities of the Greeks already in India, especially after the Mauryan empire had disintegrated. Greeks from Bactria pushed on through Afghanistan into the Punjab, where they established a kingdom with its capital (it is believed) at Sialkot. Their final effort, under the legendary king Menander, was against the Mauryan capital, in about 150 B.C. The attempt failed and Menander is said to have died in 130 B.C., the Indo-Greeks being driven from the Punjab soon afterwards. Chandra-gupta's empire survived a troubled period and his grandson Asoka (273–232 B.C.) became a convert to Buddhism, the most purely Asian of the great religions. From the date of his conversion (c. 257 B.C.) India's expansion began. Greek influence in Egypt was dwindling as early as 303 B.C. and the Roman influence, as we have seen, was never as great. So the period during which the East recovered was that between 324 and 150 B.C., with 257 B.C. as a useful date to memorize. Roman power was asserted in the nearer East until a far later period, but India was to remain obstinately itself, deriving from the West little more than its coinage and a few ideas in Buddhist art. By 200 A.D., world leadership was passing to the East, where it was to remain for a thousand years.

It would be wrong to see the Western failure in merely military terms. In the long run it was the specifically European ideas that were rejected — almost totally in the East and very largely also in the West. And we are bound to ask, Why? In answering this question, the first point to observe is that the world's basic ideas were formulated in different places but at much the same period. The significant names include Lao-Tze (604–532 B.C.), Zoroaster (570–500 B.C.), Gautama Buddha (567–487 B.C.), Confucius (551–479 B.C.), and Socrates (469–399 B.C.). Among this galaxy of thinkers the Oriental names come first in chronology, but last in order of official acceptance. Socratic ideas had made their conquest of the Greeks by, say, 350 B.C. Zoroastrianism was made an official cult during the Iranian struggle with

Rome "and placed the spiritual forces of the nation" at the State's disposal "for the defense of the Orient." * Buddhism became India's official religion in 257 B.C. and Confucianism was officially adopted in the China of 179–104 B.C. Our conclusion must be that the Oriental alternatives to Hellenism existed before the Greek ideas took their final form, but were adopted afterwards, perhaps in some instances as a gesture of defiance. There was no period, therefore, at which Iranians or Indians had to choose between Greek philosophy and barbarian superstition. The Asian schools of thought were already in existence and might be preferred merely as being Asian. They might also be preferred as offering what the Greek and Roman world conspicuously lacked.

What had Greece to offer? Humanism, individuality, a sense of proportion, a sense of humor, a concept of progress, and all that gave vitality to their public life: the marketplace, the acropolis, the council house, the gymnasium, the stadium, and the theater. The Romans had taken over the Greek institutions and ideas, giving less emphasis to their aesthetic side, but adding a new sense of discipline, law, and order. For active people in a position of responsibility — for Greek diplomatists, physicians, and officers with work to do for a Seleucus or a Ptolemy Philadelphus; for Greek teachers lecturing at Syracuse or Alexandria (like Archimedes, Euclid, Eratosthenes, Apollonius, and Hipparchus); for Roman officers from proconsul to centurion — the Greco-Roman ideas were often enough. There were peoples to civilize, students to teach, bridges to build, and plays to enact; there were also riots to be suppressed, examples to be made, throats to be cut, and work to be done. Life was interesting and varied and the gods had only a minor part to play, worship being perfunctory, formal, and sometimes forgotten. But humanism and individuality, offering so much to the busy administrator, offered nothing whatever to the peasant, the captive, or the slave.

* Ghirshman, *op. cit.*, p. 318.

Marcus Aurelius sought the consolation of philosophy while in the field with his army, but his thoughts were not of a kind likely to comfort the downtrodden and hungry. The Greek and Roman way of life rather assumed the existence of domestic help. It rose beyond the means, indeed, of many of the Greeks themselves. From the sixth century B.C. onward, we read of the Dionysiac cult with its orgiastic practices and its promise of immortality. Of this cult, Professor F. M. Cornford writes, "The supreme means of grace is the sacramental feast in which the soul feeds on the substance of the god who suffered, died and rose again and thereby is assured of ultimate deliverance from the cycle of rebirth." * For the less fortunate people of the Hellenic world, and especially for the women, there existed these cults of Asian origin. They offered a way of escape, a respite from the monotony of life, a hope of eventual happiness.

In Asia, as contrasted with Europe, the proportion was much higher of people for whom life was and is oppressively dreary. Along the great river valleys of India and China, the peasants lived in their villages and raised their crops of rice.

> Peasant self-sufficiency at its best gives everybody something, but it never gives anybody very much . . .
>
> The equality in Asia is . . . an equality in poverty. Agriculture everywhere is a seasonal occupation with days when there is nothing to do except watch the crops and the animals grow. But in Western mixed farming, with its superimposition of the rhythm of animal life upon that of the ripening of the grain, leisure has been reduced to a minimum. In Asia, with its overwhelmingly cereal farming, there are months of utter idleness, with nothing to do but go to a wedding, or lie on a string bed . . . or revive one's local faction fights.†

Zinkin points out that a Javanese holding needs only sixty-five man-days a year, that the Korean farmer works only one hundred

* Bury et al. (eds.), *Cambridge Ancient History* (Cambridge: 1926), IV, 538.
† Maurice Zinkin, *Asia and the West* (London, 1951), p. 10.

days, the Japanese only one hundred and forty, that five months
of idleness is normal in the Deccan, and that one combine har-
vester can do the work of a whole Chinese village.

> . . . In Asia the rule is to divide property between all the sons.
> The equal rights of all heirs explain . . . the extreme lack of
> mobility in oriental society. The sons of the rich and of the
> ruined move, the rest stay in the village, and division amongst
> heirs leaves few who are either rich or ruined.*

This relative idleness might have its advantages for people of
education and energy, or even for people who could use their
leisure in sailing, fishing, or hunting. But the Asian peasant often
lived far from the hills or the sea, the rice fields stretching to
the horizon. He lived, moreover, on a diet lacking in variety and
protein, with insufficient surplus energy for politics or sport.
For the vast majority of Asian peasants, in lands where the peasantry comprised over 90% of the population, life was appallingly
dull. It is one thing to cultivate vines or olives on a hillside in
Delos with a distant glimpse of the wine-dark sea and an awareness of market day tomorrow. It is quite another to grow rice
on the plains round Patna or Hanoi. The difference in background is reflected in political and social life, but above all in
religion. Where life is colorful and varied, religion can be austere
or unimportant. Where life is appallingly monotonous, religion
must be emotional, dramatic, and intense. Without the curry,
boiled rice can be very dull indeed.

Not all Oriental peoples live in the rice fields of the plain.
There were hill towns in northern India, there were even repub-
lics at one time in the Punjab and Indus valley. But any religion which was to have a widespread appeal had to be acceptable
in the plains and among the rice growers. Meeting this need
in India was Hinduism, based upon caste and the doctrine of

* *Ibid.*, p. 22.

reincarnation. Hindu society was divided into four segregated groups: Brahmins, warriors, peasants, and outcasts; priests being drawn from the first of these groups and rulers from the second. But the basic inequalities and rigidities of the system (based as it was on past history and present economy) were explained by the doctrine that the soul is indestructible, passing at death into another and newborn body, the status at birth being fixed as a result of previous behavior. By good conduct the untouchable, the Sudra, can be reborn in a higher caste. By failing in his duty the Brahmin can be reborn as a pariah and indeed as an animal. Good conduct in the Indian sense was not merely ethical, but involved a myriad of prohibitions, rituals, and purifications. The whole social structure was firmly based on the family, the trade, and the village. The same could be said of China, but there the idea of caste was unknown. Against that the life on earth was only a tiny fraction of eternity and death only a prelude to a temporary absence in the spirit world. Moreover, present conduct would govern the circumstance of eventual rebirth — filial piety being more important in this case than ritual purity. In any society permeated by such doctrines as these, religion must be the supreme influence. And, while the individual has the merit of being indestructible, it is only in a very sketchy form; the soul being merely the highest common factor between a number of quite various personalities. In both India and China the gods mattered more than mankind and the community more than the man.

It would be natural to conclude from this brief summary that the Greeks and Romans, absorbed in the visible world, must have had a scientific and technical advantage over their Asian contemporaries. They had, in fact, nothing of the kind. In at least two fields of knowledge the Indians were ahead of them. In mathematics the Indians seem to have been the inventors of what we call "Arabic" numerals, place notation, and the symbol for zero; devices which gave them a lead in arithmetic. The

Brahmin astronomers developed the concepts of "void," "infinity," and "atom," and made some guess at the age of the universe.

> . . . Useful chemical and physical knowledge was almost completely bound up with the technical processes of tanning, dyeing, bleaching, compounding cements, mixing pigments, making soap and glass, and working metals, and was, of course, in the hands of craftsmen, not priests and philosophers. The Indian dyers invented fast colours and discovered indigo, and . . . the Indian ironworkers may have produced the first steel.*

In medical science they were as far ahead, their surgeons being familiar with operations for hernia and cataract, and their text-books listing 121 surgical instruments in use. Technically, the Chinese were still more advanced, and artistically, many Asian peoples have traditions of their own, and can point to monuments as impressive as those of Athens. The truth would seem to be that Asian rulers could muster great abilities about them and that the dullness of life in the villages was a contrast, very often, to the wealth, sophistication, and culture of the court. Indians had their own way of life and good reason to think it superior to that of the Greeks and Romans. Trading contact with the Roman Empire was continuous, the products of East and West were known and those from the East commanded the higher price. To the pressure from the West, the Orient responded in religious terms. First came the so-called mysteries of astrology — ultimately from Babylon — to which we owe the seven-day week. Next there came Buddhism from India, and Mithraism from Persia, followed by Christianity from Palestine. Last of all, defense being followed by infiltration, and that by the counteroffensive, came Islam from Arabia — a movement which almost submerged Europe in its turn.

In the rallying of Asia against Western pressure, Buddhism

* Turner, *op. cit.*, II, 786.

played the central role. Like no other religion before or since, its influence extended to the whole of Asia. It emphasized the exact values which the Romans ignored. It lent new vigor to all that was most attractive in Hinduism. It found its eventual home in the very heart of Asia, the mountain massif between India and China. It gave rise to its own traditions in literature and art. It is gaining converts in the India of today and as many again in the United States. Buddhism has been described as the most scientific of all religions, which is probably true, but it can be taken at different levels. Siddhartha Gautama himself was a nobleman born at Kapilavastu on the Nepalese border in about 567 B.C. He left his wife and family to become a wandering ascetic. Attaining "enlightment," he began to preach and collect followers. His doctrine began with and was based upon the fact of human suffering. The cause of suffering is desire, the motive force for entry into successive lives, and for being thus chained to the revolving wheel of life. Desire has its origin in the illusion that the tangible world is real, which it is not. The remedy is to overcome desire, avoid rebirth, and so achieve Nirvana or absorption into the All. Buddha believed in no personal god, but merely in the possibility — by meditation, not worship — of becoming one with the universe. In its original and agnostic form, Buddhism was a practice and discipline through which inner peace of mind could be attained. Its practice was therefore monastic, only monks and nuns being able to follow the teaching in every way. The full members of the Sangha, or order, thus renounced the world, possessing nothing but their saffron robes, their begging bowls, and staffs. Other Buddhists, not yet ready for this complete renunciation, could follow the Middle Way, a code of belief, conduct, and meditation for the ordinary householder. Some of these Buddhist ideas were of Brahmin origin, but Buddha parted from the Hindus on the question of caste, mainly because the hereditary Brahmin was replaced among Buddhists by the self-appointed monk. Buddha also rejected the popular gods, the priesthood, the mysteries, the sacrifices, and the magic. His original surmise, however, that his teaching might be too profound for his followers, has been more than justified. The Hinayana Buddhists of Ceylon, Burma, Thailand, and Cambodia were to retain something like the original doctrine, but the Mahayana Buddhists of northwest India developed a theistic religion in which Buddha became the incarnation of the Deity; a church, in effect, with its priesthood, its scripture, its ritual and dogma, its processions and incense, its prayer wheels and bells. In this form it spread to China, Tibet, and Japan.

Much of this Buddhist expansion was due to the Mauryan king, Asoka, whose inherited empire stretched from Herat to the Bay of Bengal, and whose conquest of Kalinga in southern India was to prove the turning point in his reign of forty-one years. From that point on, when he realized the suffering his campaign had involved, he became more of a missionary than a conqueror, preaching doctrines of non-violence and moral duty. Ceylon, the next logical objective after Kalinga, was not invaded but merely converted. It may well be that Asoka was a statesman as well as a moralist, using his semi-divine prestige to enforce an ethical system which might hold his empire together. It remains true, nevertheless, that the Buddhist virtues which he attempted to spread by example — simplicity, gentleness, sympathy, vegetarianism, and kindness to animals — were lessons of permanent value and lasting influence. On all his subjects he enjoined obedience to parents, respect for teachers, truthfulness in speech, and courtesy toward relatives. These precepts were generally acceptable, and his rule was tolerant in other respects. Where he came nearest to persecution was in the protection of animals, always a fruitful field for intolerance. The first of the missionary religions, Buddhism was taken by its preacher to places as remote, in the one direction, as Malaya, as far, in the other direction, as Egypt, North Africa, and Greece. Sequel to

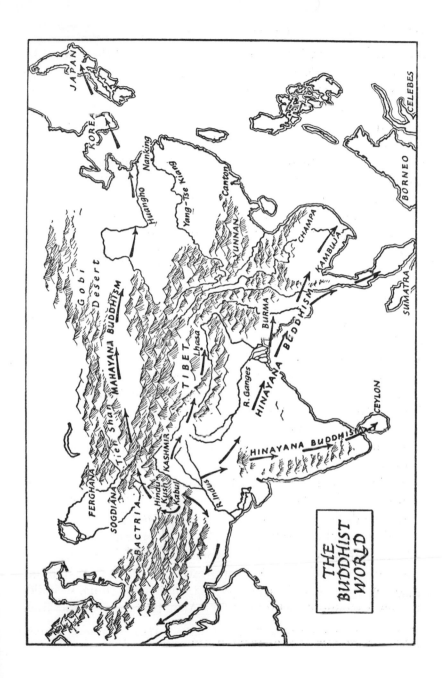

THE BUDDHIST WORLD

the conversion of Ceylon was the growth there of that astonishing civilization which centered upon the city of Anuradhapura. For Asoka's ethical superiority over, say, Cato the Elder was at least matched by his subjects' technical skill. Anuradhapura is believed to have had 6,000,000 inhabitants and a main street sixteen miles long. It had an elaborate water supply and a central monastery with nine floors and a thousand rooms. There was nothing in the West of comparable size and but few scenes, perhaps, of comparable beauty.

No Buddhist missionaries seem to have reached China before A.D. 65, the year in which Dharmaraksa and Kasyapa Matanga, traveling overland, are believed to have founded the White Horse Monastery. The extraordinary feature of this northern route is that it led through Bactria, perhaps the only land to have felt the directly competing influences of Persia, Greece, India, and China. Other missionaries reached southern China by sea at much the same period. It was a period of Indian expansion which brought traders and colonists to Cambodia, Annam, Java, and Sumatra, Srivijaya being the southern center of Buddhist learning, and Tonkin (later, Canton) the point of entry into China. Chinese Buddhists began pilgrimages to India in the fourth century A.D., one such journey being performed by Fahien between 399 and 414 A.D. By the seventh century there were many Chinese students at the Indian University of Nalanda. In 645, Hinan-tsang was received publicly by the emperor on his return. Nor did the Buddhist connection between India and China end until the middle of the eighth century, from which period the contacts were few. Buddhism is practically a dying religion in China, but its great work in all fields of Chinese life still survives. "This work bears testimony to the great effort made by two major countries of Asia, India and China, in building up a common civilization." * At a later period, the Bud-

* Parabodh Chandra Bagchi, *India and China: a Thousand Years of Cultural Relations* (New York, 2nd ed., 1951), p. 119.

dhists lost most of their influence in China just as they had long since become unimportant in India. In the meanwhile, it was Buddhism that gave to the Orient what cultural and religious unity it had.

That Buddhism did not make more progress in China was due to Confucianism and Taoism being established there first; the one being the accepted ethic of the governing class, the other a popular cult of the people at large. China had been unified under a central monarchy in 221–207 B.C., the first emperor Shi Huang Ti, being assisted by Li Ssu. It was Shi Huang Ti's policy to destroy both feudalism and the scholarship associated with it, in which object he succeeded. But Confucianism came into favor again afterwards and remained the basis for Chinese classical education. Thereafter, with few interruptions, China was effectively ruled on more or less Confucian principles which related mainly to political and social duties. The Taoist religion, by contrast, has some resemblance to the cults of India. Lao-tze had taught the relativity of everything in the universe and the futility of interference. The Taoist lets nature take its course, prefers contemplation to action, avoids political office, and tends even to shun society. Taoism apart, the ordinary Chinese were devout ancestor-worshippers, believers also in the transmigration of souls. Buddhism and Taoism had much in common, which led to rivalry. There was little, on the other hand, to prevent the same person professing adherence to three or more religions, and this was often done. All could be regarded as different aspects of truth. It might be added, in conclusion, that the believer in any or all of them was an ideal subject for a Confucian ruler — philosophic, resigned, and obedient. As compared with other countries, China has had, until very recently, an enviable record of stability.

Considered as one of the great civilizations, the Chinese lacks the antiquity which we associate with the Mesopotamian or Egyptian. It has been suggested, indeed, that a basic knowledge of astronomy, mathematics, and medicine could have reached China originally from Mesopotamia. Be that as it may, the Chinese developed their own script at an early period in their history (which begins in about 1500 B.C.), and this was to form an essential feature of their culture. The cuneiform script of the Sumerians comes to light in about 3500 B.C., its two thousand signs being reduced to six hundred by 2900 B.C., not many centuries before Sumer collapsed. The cuneiform pictographs of Mesopotamia appeared first in 3000 B.C., and comprised six hundred characters in their Akkadian form. They began to be superseded by Aramaic (with its twenty-two letters) in 1000 B.C., or thereabouts, and had practically disappeared by 140 B.C. Egyptian hieroglyphics are also pictograms, used first in about 3100 B.C. and practically discarded by 500 B.C. These were successively superseded by the hieratic and demotic scripts, and these again by the Phoenician alphabet as developed by the Greeks and Romans. There is nothing remarkable, therefore, about the Chinese having an ideographic script. It is merely odd that they should have retained it for some two thousand years after its complete disuse in the other regions we have mentioned. It has admittedly had a practical value in extending the same written language to provinces where the spoken languages are different. As against that, however, the process of becoming literate in China is one for which life hardly seems long enough.

One result of a written language in which the scholars need to learn some fifty thousand characters is that years of work are needed to attain mere literacy. Added to that was a system of public examinations in which the emphasis was on a knowledge of the Chinese classics, on literary style, and artistic calligraphy. The candidates for public office had, therefore, to be men of learning but all of the same faculty, trained to express the right sentiments in the right words, illustrating their rightness by the right quotations from the right authors. All this placed a high premium on the value of a classical education, to the virtual ex-

clusion of any other. Nor could the scholar afford to undervalue
a body of knowledge in which he had invested so heavily. No
human being could readily admit to having wasted as much time
as that. So there grew up in China a deep respect for learning,
one which spread from there to Japan. As in all schools of
classic learning, the assumption was that the written word of
an earlier age must be more significant than any verbal observation of the present day. The book or document must matter
more than the man.

It is interesting to note in this connection that the founder
of the Ming Dynasty (1368–1644 A.D.) had actually been a
Buddhist monk. The fact may serve to remind us that a reverence for learning is another feature which links the Indian
civilization with the Chinese. The Brahmin study of the Vedas
was paralleled by the Chinese scholar's devotion to the Analects.
And Buddhism, linking the two systems, added a new scholasticism of its own. Gautama had been concerned only with his
own spiritual experience, which he explained in the simplest
available language. But his followers built up a theological library of formidable dimensions, there being a whole Sanskrit
literature for the erudite to translate into Chinese. Merely to
master the doctrines might involve fifteen year's work and a
single missionary might bring five hundred texts with him. A
commentary on the scriptures could run to two hundred chapters, and to the compilation of bibliographies there was clearly
no end. Deeply rooted in both India and China was this obsession with the written word. The Greeks, by comparison, read
little, and the Romans probably less. It is this contrast which
has led some historians to explain the absence in China of technical progress; mere tools and instruments being beneath the
scholar's notice. The explanation might convince us, if the fact
itself were beyond dispute. But Joseph Needham has shown
that Chinese technology was far in advance of European, especially perhaps from 300 B.C. to 1400 A.D. So he justly concludes

that "all such valuations of East and West are built on insecure foundations." *

Insecure the foundations may be, but disproof of one theory need not prevent our finding another. The western orientalist is often so laden with knowledge as to fear making any generalization of any kind. But some generalizations are, surely, possible. It is known, for example, that the Oriental custom has been (in some lands) for the married son to remain in his father's house and so under parental control. Children born in such a household yield obedience to a variety of older relatives, accustom themselves to hearing a variety of opinions and are taught to observe a ceremonious politeness without which life in so large a family would be impossible. But readiness to accept a number of politely voiced but contradictory opinions has some intellectual disadvantages to balance its practical convenience. The continual quoting of classical authority brings thought to a standstill, for it undermines the ability to choose. China did not lack technical progress but it did fail to develop its science beyond a certain point. And one aspect of that failure is connected, surely, with the Chinese social structure and the individual's subordination to the group. It is here that we must expect to observe a change. The renascence of Asia must mean an end to scholasticism and a turning away from the past. With the development of a readier ability to choose and reject, the Chinese should soon be entering upon a new phase of Asian history and one in which further progress may depend increasingly upon Asia. That the piston of human achievement should again move from East to West becomes more credible when we realize that it has happened before. The wheelbarrow was not the first Chinese invention to reach Europe. It will certainly not be the last.

* Joseph Needham, *Science and Civilisation in China* (Cambridge, 1954), I, 241.

10

THE EAST TRIUMPHANT

So FAR from succumbing to Western influence, India had reacted strongly against it, producing a movement for consolidation and expansion, and fostering a new missionary religion which projected Indian ideas into China, into Egypt, into Southeast Asia. Along with the Buddhist superiority in philosophy and ethics, along with the profundity of Indian thought, went an artistic and technical eminence which historians have only recently begun to recognize. Behind India, moreover, and in close contact, was China, where the people, if less religious, were still more technically proficient. In these two countries linked by Buddhism lay the heart of Asian resistance to the West. But the Indians and Chinese, reacting as they may have done, were mostly remote from European influence. Few had ever come under Roman rule. There were other Asians, however, in far closer proximity: Iranians and Egyptians who had experienced both Greek and Roman conquest; Syrians who had been excluded from colonial society; Jews who would never be admitted to the club; Arabs who had never given their allegiance to any conqueror. Among all these peoples, so much nearer to Rome, the Oriental reaction was the more intense.

The first wave of Oriental influence to reach Europe — a mere ripple as compared with the storms which were to follow — came from Persia. There it was that Zoroaster based a new religion upon one that already existed — a religion concerned as no other had been with the struggle between good and evil. According to Zoroastrian doctrines, the world had been created by

Ahura-Mazda, the Iranian sun god, who was constantly opposed by Aingra-Manu, the god of darkness. The believer's duty was to obey his ruler, work, keep his word, and give to the poor. With the help of the faithful, the god of Light would eventually overcome evil, but only on the Day of Judgment, as from which day the dead would be either admitted to Paradise or relegated to Hell. Zoroastrianism, at one time the officially accepted religion of Persia, never penetrated Europe in its original form. It gave rise instead to Mithraism, a variant of the original cult. Here again, there is the conflict between good and evil, but the virtues now have on their side the god Mithra, the special friend of mankind. He was to be worshipped by initiation and rituals, all so planned as to purify and redeem the soul which could not otherwise be saved. Its sacramental rites centered on Mithra's killing of a sacred bull, and its discipline included rules about continence and fasting. Unlike the original Mazdaist cult which provided a goddess (Anchita, or Artemis), Mithraism offered nothing to women. This did not prevent Mithraism from gaining believers in the Roman army. First learned from prisoners in the time of Pompey, it was the religion of many Roman soldiers in the second century A.D. It undoubtedly served to prepare the way for Christianity.

What is more difficult to establish is the extent to which Buddhism did the same. As Radhakrishnan points out, "Many parables, legends and religious myths and concepts travelled from India, to Syria, Egypt and Palestine." * He goes on as follows:

The influence of Persia and India on the Middle East where Christianity developed is obvious. Buddhist ideas travelled to the shores of the Mediterranean through the Greek cities which lay along the route by means of trade and missions. Alexandria lay open even more than Syria to the ideas of the East. A strange

* Radhakrishnan, *East and West: Some Reflections* (London, 1955), p. 67.

mingling of ideas belonging to the different traditions, Greek, Babylonian, Buddhistic and Zoroastrian, was taking place in the century before the Christian era . . .*

That this is true is obvious from many features in the Christian legend: the Magi from Persia, the parable of the sower (Buddhist), the temptations of Jesus (Zoroastrian), and his renunciation of his family (Hindu). The ethical teaching comes partly from the Essenes (via John the Baptist), who in turn owed something to Buddhism. Hellfire is part of the Mazdaist and Zoroastrian doctrine and the death of Jesus is anticipated by Mithra. From Buddhism, again, was to come the later Christian monasticism.

This is not the place to narrate the events or discuss the validity of the Christian legend. Suffice to say that Jesus was born in about 4 B.C. and appears as a prophet in Judea at the age of thirty or thereabouts, practically nothing being known of his earlier life. Judea was then a Roman province with a procurator responsible to Tiberius. The Jews were restive under this form of rule (see page 107) and would have welcomed the chance to rebel — as they did later — under a sufficiently dynamic leader. Although Jesus had a magnetic personality, and was said to be of royal descent, he emphatically resisted this role. He did not deny, however, that he was the Messiah, the saviour that the Jews had been taught to expect. But he made it clear that his Messianic mission was purely religious. The priests of the day naturally resented his claim to be God's representative, that function being their own. The patriots resented his refusal to join them in planning revolt. In 30 A.D., or thereabouts, the High Priest and Council tried him for blasphemy, condemned him to death, and asked the procurator to confirm the sentence. This he was reluctant to do, but the High Priest next informed him that Jesus claimed the kingship of the Jews. Mindful of Tiberius's

* *Ibid.*, p. 68.

severity in matters of treason, and realizing that the Council could complain to Caesar about his lenience, the procurator confirmed the sentence. Jesus was then executed.

The religious sect founded by Jesus as a heretical branch of Judaism gained many adherents in subsequent years, more especially in Jerusalem. Paul, however, a Hellenized Jew and a Roman citizen, began to make converts in Asia Minor and Greece. Despite some sporadic persecution, Christianity spread throughout the Roman Empire, of which, by 300 A.D., it had become the principal religion. In studying this process the historian is bound to ask, first of all, why this essentially Oriental cult should have spread, not in Asia, but in Europe. Christianity spread to Armenia and Persia, admittedly, and a small Christian sect was established in Malabar; but Christianity moved, in general, toward the Atlantic. Why? Mainly, perhaps, because Zoroastrianism and Buddhism left no room for a new movement. They had absorbed all those to whom that blend of mysticism and ethics would be likely to appeal. Westward the competition was less. The state religion was professed by the upper classes, but had no appeal for the proletarians and slaves. Mithraism was common in the army, but had no place in it for women. There remained the cult of the Egyptian Isis and Osiris, but this offered less than Christianity. For the Christian was offered eternal life as reward for faith alone, with hellfire for his opponents, a battle against evil, membership in a secret society, a sacramental feast, and a sense of brotherhood. By absorbing so many elements from other religions, Christianity had come to offer more than any one of them could offer by itself.

The Christians, drawn from the uprooted and dispossessed masses of the Mediterranean lands, identified suffering with Deity and claimed for the individual, as the individual, in the other world what this world had denied him, namely, peace, joy and worth. Although not so poignant in the other cultures as in the Christian, this feeling arose everywhere from the disorganization of mass life that imperialism brought and found expression in a religion of salvation. The unity of the early Asiatic and European intellectual developments is finally evident in the Saviour-Gods they produced — Christ, the Messiah, Mithra, Krishna, Amitabha, and Omito Fo — who, through the faith of the individual in divine compassion, came to offer men an other-worldly state which is best understood as a compensation for the distresses of worldly life.*

Two other circumstances, less basic, tended to lead the movement in the same direction. Paul and several of the earlier converts were Hellenized Jews, to whom Greek was a first or second language. They were able to preach in Asia Minor as they could never have done beyond the Euphrates. They and their converts must originally have carried less weight than the Jewish-Christian community centered on Jerusalem itself. But there followed the Jewish revolt and the sack of Jerusalem in 70 A.D. The Jews were more dispersed than ever and the church in Jerusalem ceased for a time to exist, giving the more importance to the non-Jewish churches which were unaffected by this event. The speed of these developments owed much to the uncertainty of the times and the decay of the Roman Empire itself. As the military situation deteriorated, as the future seemed to offer less, and as the Roman deities were discredited by their failure to bring victory, people showed more interest in the future life. They could seek in eternity the success they were denied upon earth. Instead of the Rome which had been the political center of their world, they would eventually be able to set up a new Rome, center of a spiritual empire. Their kingdom, they had to conclude, was not of this world, for things on earth were going very badly indeed.

In studying the relationships between East and West, our concern is with civilization and not with the uncivilized. In the early centuries of the Christian era, the movement of barbarian

* Ralph Turner, *op. cit.*, II, 1276.

tribes were of great importance, threatening as they did the civilizations of both Europe and Asia. But although they come incidentally into the story, affecting its outcome, they are not to be considered as protagonists until after they had become civilized. How they were to group themselves, on one side or the other, was to be of vital importance, but they mostly did so group themselves and were influenced in their choice by historical accident or mere proximity. The student of history is bound to wonder where these hordes of barbarians came from and how they had managed to live. The answer must surely be that they were never as numerous as their opponents chose to imagine. What idea we have of their strength is derived from defeated generals whose despatches had to account somehow for the collapse of their own armies. Considering this disintegration, the student is bound to ask whether Oriental infiltration was not in itself a cause of decay and weakness. Many living during the period of decline were apt to assume that it was. They were, however, mistaken, as events were to prove. It was the Oriental element which eventually stiffened the Western resistance. What had undermined the Empire was the complexity of its own administrative machine. It was overtaxation which killed it in the West.

The Romans were not weakened by Oriental vices. They were threatened by Oriental strength. Indirectly, it was the effective rule of the Han Dynasty in China which threw back the Huns and compelled them to move westward, driving before them the Visigoths and Vandals, tribes which constituted the immediate danger. Some climatic change may have given urgency to this movement. Whatever the nature of this drive, however, the pressure mounted along the line of the Rhine and Danube. It became the policy to admit some tribes and use them, retrained and re-equipped, against the rest. There was probably no alternative, but the final product was an army which had ceased to be Roman, a barbarian force within the Empire and so placed in-

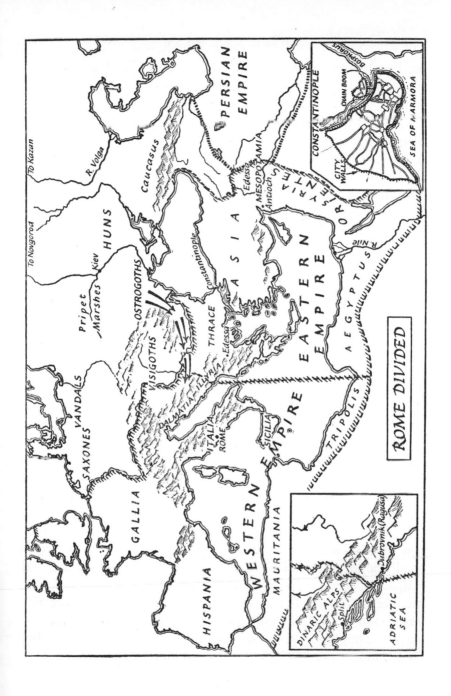

ROME DIVIDED

deed as to control it. Directly, Rome was threatened by the strength of a renascent Persia. Under their Sassanid kings the Iranians were on the move. With Ardashir's accession in 226 A.D., Persia entered upon a new period of expansion. King Shapur first moved eastward to Peshawar, establishing his authority over Bactria, Samarkand, and the Indus Valley. Then he advanced into Syria and attempted to capture Antioch. This first attempt failed, but another campaign, some fifteen years later, ended in victory at Edessa, and the fall of Antioch (260 A.D.). The emperor Valerian and 70,000 legionaries were taken prisoner, providing Shapur with a new supply of technicians. The Iranian threat was a reality.

The Roman Empire, under Valerian's successor, now faced dangers along the whole of a frontier which stretched from northern Britain to the shores of the Caspian, and from there to the mouth of the Nile. Weakest point in this appallingly extended front was the lower Danube. After the loss of Dacia (north of the river) in 275 A.D., the Visigoths were within two hundred miles of the Adriatic and about the same distance from the Bosphorus. A breakthrough at either point would crack the Empire into two fragments. A permanent loss of Syrian Antioch would make the fragments three, with all road communications gone. To end this danger would have meant the reconquest of Dacia and Mesopotamia, but for these operations the available uncommitted troops were insufficient. Chief cause of this was undoubtedly the epidemic which swept the Empire in 250–265 A.D. The population fell from 70–75 million in the first century A.D. to 50 million at the end of the third. The same or a similar epidemic hit China at a rather earlier period, between 105 and 146 A.D., but with less fatal results. This was the background of the barbarian successes in either direction. And, from the Roman point of view, the only answer was to divide the Empire at its weakest point, approximately and appropriately represented by the modern city of Split (north of Dubrovnik), scene of Diocletian's retirement. This final division took place, between the sons of Theodosius, in 395. But New Rome, the eastern capital, had been founded earlier by Constantine, in 324 A.D.

It was Constantine's achievement to give the Empire a new lease of life in its eastward half. Just as the policy in the west had been to admit barbarians and enlist them in the defense against barbarism, so was it Constantine's policy to use Oriental forces to keep the Orient at bay. The move to New Rome, on the site of the old Byzantium, represented a shifting of his headquarters to a strong position near the greatest point of danger. It was Constantine who became a Christian on his deathbed, and Theodosius who made Christianity the official religion of the Empire. When it fell apart, it was the eastern and orientalized half which proved the stronger. This was partly from economic causes, but mainly because the Eastern features of its life — the sacred monarchy, the court's splendor, the mysteries of religion, the intricacies of its art — had a life of their own. Meeting the needs of what was by now a very mixed population, Christianity stood firm against the Persian onset. "The enthusiasm which inspired the troops, and perhaps the emperor himself, sharpened their swords, while it satisfied their conscience." * But Gibbon, deploring the process, looks back nostalgically to the real, to the republican, Rome. In a famous and significant chapter (XVII), he presents his own analysis of the change that had come about:

The manly pride of the Romans, content with substantial power, had left to the vanity of the east the forms and ceremonies of ostentatious greatness. But when they lost even the semblance of those virtues which were derived from their ancient freedom, the simplicity of Roman manners was insensibly corrupted by the stately affectation of the courts of Asia. The distinctions of personal merit and influence, so conspicuous in a republic, so

* Gibbon, op. cit., Ch. XX.

feeble and obscure under a monarchy, were abolished by the despotism of the emperors, who substituted in their room a severe subordination of rank and office, from the titled slaves, who were seated on the steps of the throne, to the meanest instruments of arbitrary power. This multitude of abject dependants was interested in the support of the actual government, from the dread of a revolution, which might at once confound their hopes and intercept the reward of their services. In this divine hierarchy (for such it is frequently styled) every rank was marked with the most scrupulous exactness, and its dignity was displayed in a variety of trifling and solemn ceremonies, which it was a study to learn and a sacrilege to neglect. The purity of the Latin language was debased by adopting, in the intercourse of pride and flattery, a profusion of epithets, which Tully would scarcely have understood, and which Augustus would have rejected with indignation. The principal officers of the empire were saluted, even by the sovereign himself, with the deceitful titles of your Sincerity, your Gravity, your Excellency, your Eminence, your sublime and wonderful Magnitude, your illustrious and magnificent Highness.

He goes on to add:

A people elated by pride, or soured by discontent, are seldom qualified to form a just estimate of their actual situation. The subjects of Constantine were incapable of discerning the decline of genius and manly virtue, which so far degraded them below the dignity of their ancestors; but they could feel and lament the rage of tyranny, the relaxation of discipline and the increase of taxes.

This assessment dates from a later period, to which we shall have to devote attention. But there is a significance in the words used, indicating what Gibbon regarded as Eastern and Western characteristics. For the East, his adjectives are vain, ostentatious, affected, despotic, solemn, arbitrary, abject, proud, flattering, deceitful, servile, and degraded. For the West his adjectives are manly, simple, virtuous, pure, dignified, and free. That Constantinople was the scene of significant change, we need not question. But the later historian's views are apt to be colored by the experience of his own age. The East known to Gibbons' contemporaries was a world in decline and collapse, defeated and cowed. It was in the light of that experience that he could see only corruption in Byzantium. But that impression is not really supported by the facts.

For what actually happened? The western Empire, centered upon a Rome which was at least that much further from Oriental influence, collapsed in utter confusion and ruin, Rome itself being sacked in 455. Of the Roman institutions in the West, it was only the Christian Church which survived. At first it might have seemed that Byzantium would fare no better. The Huns raided up to the walls of Constantinople, destroying as they went. But Constantinople did not fall. The eastern Empire survived and from it the western was even temporarily regained by Justinian (527–565). Attacked again by the Persians, the Byzantines under Heraclius not only drove off their assailants but captured Ctesiphon. Later, it was from Constantinople that Christianity was carried to Russia, where it was firmly established at Novgorod and Kiev; a major achievement which brought that whole vast territory into the Western rather than the Eastern camp. Generally speaking, however, the Byzantines were on the defensive. Their military textbooks are concerned mainly with teaching how to avoid defeat. As Oman says:

> The fact that the main aim of Byzantine strategy was to protect the empire rather than to attack its enemies accounts for its main limitations. But it does not explain the whole of the differences between the military feeling of East and West during the early Middle Ages. Of the spirit of chivalry there was not a spark in the Byzantine, though there was a great deal of professional pride, and a not inconsiderable infusion of religious enthusiasm.*

* Charles Oman, op. cit., I, 204.

With this defensive atmosphere — this emphasis, as it were, on withdrawal exercises — went (and logically) the Byzantine skill in fortification. The great Justinian built or repaired no fewer than seven hundred defensive works. Writes Sidney Toy: "The building activity of the Eastern empire at this time is without parallel." * It may at the time have been without example, but it has certainly inspired imitation. It represents the attitude which, in this century, we have learned to associate with the Maginot Line — with the difference, however, that the Byzantine fortresses were at least completed. For the time being, these virtues and this technical skill sufficed.

Upon the divided and exhausted world which had been the Roman Empire, there now fell the full fury of Islam. First had come Zoroastrianism and Buddhism, affecting only the fringes. Next had come Christianity, which had converted — and to that extent orientalized — the whole of the Empire. Last wave of all rose first in Arabia, and seemed likely to engulf the whole of mankind. So far, in describing the ebb and flow of these world movements, we have had no occasion to mention the Arabs at all. These people, both nomads and town dwellers, had lived from an early period in the Arabian Peninsula, taking no part in the movements we have described. Persians, Greeks, and Romans had occupied Palestine and Syria, guarding the land bridge between Mesopotamia and Egypt, but they had shown little interest in the deserts to the south and east, nor even in the towns of Mecca and Medina, to which the Jews at least had penetrated. The nomad Arabs or Bedouins were wild folk given to much fighting among themselves. They were also believers in their tribal gods, given to sudden enthusiasm and addicted to memorizing their own poetry. Freya Stark ascribes the "Arab elegance" to "the long Bedouin hands and surging movements, and faces furrowed with emotions that belong to the nomad lands, at any rate, of Arabia." She points out the Arab love of

* Sidney Toy, A *History of Fortification* (London, 1955), p. 56.

the abstract and observes that "the Arab, with his tiresomeness, is an artist. To him the unknown world is *real*." * Writes Ibn Khaldûn of Tunis (1332–1406) ". . . Arabs are, withal, the quickest of peoples to follow the call to truth and righteousness. For their natures are relatively simple and free from the distorting effect of bad habits and evil ways!" † But T. E. Lawrence explains that Bedouin movements have their origin in the towns. "Arab movements begin in the desert and usually travel up the shortest way into Syria . . . all prophets go to the desert, yet none of them are ever desert-born. It is the Semetic townsman or villager who receives the revelation." ‡ Such a townsman was Mahomet, born at Mecca in 570 A.D., and living there quietly until the age of forty. It was then revealed to him in a vision that there is only one God, Allah, and that Mahomet himself had been chosen as God's prophet. He began to teach the doctrine of Islam (i.e. submission), adding such further dogma as were revealed to him from time to time by the angel Gabriel. His answers to the questions put to him, with legal judgments on the cases he had to decide, were finally incorporated after his death in the *Koran*. The success of his teaching was considerable, but his opponents drove him and his followers out of Mecca in 622. This "Hegira," or flight, led to his gaining supreme authority at Medina; not, however, until he had crushed some Jewish opposition. With a growing army of Bedouin adherents, Mahomet captured Mecca in 630. He died two years later, leaving his followers in virtual control of Arabia. Finding a new leader (Caliph) in Omar, the Arabs swept northward into Syria and established a new capital at Damascus. The Ommiad Dynasty which they established there (661–750) found itself strategically placed between two crumbling empires, that of

---

* Stark, *op. cit.*, p. 45 *et seq.*
† Ibn Khaldûn, *An Arab Philosophy of History*, trans. by Charles Issawi (London, 1955), p. 57.
‡ T. E. Lawrence, *Oriental Assembly* (London, 1939), p. 87.

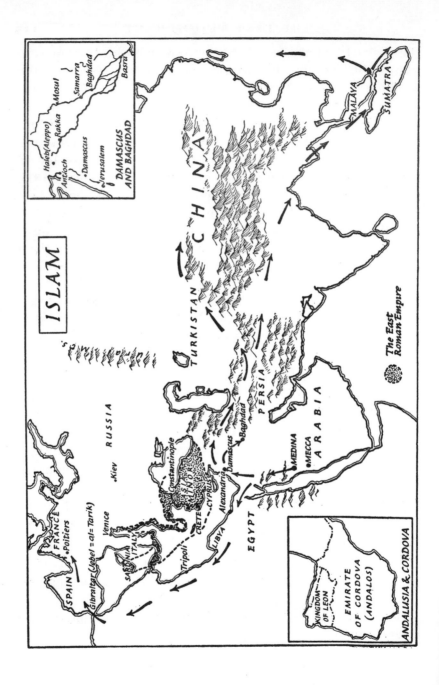

ISLAM

DAMASCUS AND BAGHDAD

Haleb (Aleppo)
Mosul
Samarra
Baghdad
Rakka
Antioch
Damascus
Jerusalem
Basra

CHINA

TURKISTAN

MALAYA

SUMATRA

PERSIA

Baghdad

The East
Roman Empire

RUSSIA

Kiev

Constantinople
ASIA
MINOR
CYPRUS
CRETE
Alexandria
Damascus
LIBYA
Tripoli
EGYPT

MEDINA
MECCA

ARABIA

SPAIN
FRANCE
Poitiers
Gibraltar (Jebel = al-Tarik)
Venice
SARDINIA
ITALY

EMIRATE
OF CORDOVA
(ANDALOS)

KINGDOM
OF LEON

ANDALUSIA & CORDOVA

Persia and that of Rome, exhausted by (among other things) their conflicts with each other. There followed one of the most astonishing campaigns in history, an outburst of energy which led the followers of Islam in both directions. Persia collapsed at once, bringing Islam to the Indus valley and giving that whole empire a new capital at Baghdad (762). To the north, the East Roman Empire stood firm, holding Asia Minor and Crete until the eighth century, the Balkans as far as Venice, southern Italy, Sicily, and Sardinia. Foiled in that direction, the Muslim tide rolled westward, conquering Egypt, Libya, Tripoli, and the whole North African shore as far as the Pillars of Hercules. In 711 the Arabs, with the converted Berbers of Africa, took the rock which they named Jebel-al-Tarik (Gibraltar) and passed onward into Spain, nearly the whole of which they conquered. From there they advanced into France, where they were defeated by Charles Martel near Poitiers in 732. They were finally driven from France in 759 and their frontier stabilized on the line of the Pyrenees.

In accounting for the military success of the Arabs, we must note, first of all, that they were horsemen.

The acquisition of horses by the Arabs in the centuries immediately preceding the birth of Muhammad was one the most momentous events in the history of the world. In the long ages before the coming of the Prophet, the Arab tribes had played no leading part in the struggles for the mastery of Western Asia and Egypt . . . so long as the Arabs fought only on foot or from the backs of camels they never were a real source of danger to the neighbouring lands. All the fervour and fanaticism of the Prophet would have been of little avail, and Islam might never have affected the world as it has done, had it not been that in the period immediately before the birth of Muhammad, their leading men had obtained horses, were engaged in breeding these animals, and had become skilful horsemen. The Prophet himself clearly realised the immense importance of horses to his people, as is plain from various passages in the Koran. He declares that the Almighty created horses from a condensation of the south-west wind and he represents God as thus apostrophising that animal: "Thou shalt be for man a source of happiness and wealth; thy back shalt be a seat of honour and thy belly of riches; every grain of barley given to thee shalt purchase indulgence for the sinner!" Elsewhere, he propounds the comfortable doctrine that the money which one spends on horses in the eyes of God is alms that one makes at one's own cost. "Every grain of barley given to a horse is entered by God in the Register of Good Works." Readers of history will know that it was to their cavalry that the first caliphs owed largely their astonishing conquests.*

Starting thus well mounted, the Arabs who headed westward found still better horses on the way. Remounted in Libya, they pressed on with increased momentum. But they had something besides their horsemanship and their horses. Behind them they had the full force and the technical superiority of a renascent Asia. As A. C. Edwards puts it: "The Oriental renaissance happened to occur at the time when the forces of Islam were overcoming the world." † But it was not, surely, a coincidence. Without that renascence, the Arabs would not have had their astounding success.

Granted, however, that the Arabs had something more than mere fanaticism, it remains difficult to explain their known superiority in war. Their cavalry were equipped with helmet, mail armor, round shield, lance, and sword. Their Ethiopian infantry used only the bow, and often rode pillion with the cavalry. Their tactics clearly involved the combination of archers on foot with mounted archers and cavalry. As in twentieth-century desert warfare, the object was to weaken the enemy's armor, tempt-

* William Ridgeway, *The Origin and Influence of the Thoroughbred Horse* (Cambridge, 1905), p. 213.
† A. J. Arberry, *The Legacy of Persia* (Oxford, 1953), p. 293.

ing him to attack the well placed infantry and lose horses in the process; and then — with the enemy off balance — attack with one's own armor, preserved intact until the proper moment should have arrived. There is no evidence that the Arabs were better horsemen than their opponents and some slight indication that they may have been worse. Their horses were faster and carried less weight, perhaps, than the European horses against which they had to contend. At the Battle of Poitiers, the turning point in the Muslim invasion of Europe, Martel took up a purely defensive position, against which the Arabs seem to have spent themselves. A possible inference from this would be that the previous Arab victories had been gained by maneuver, and especially by inducing the Christians to attack.

It is possible that some Arab successes were due to chain mail, the stirrup, the built-up saddle and the crossbow. The use of chain mail, as opposed to the older pattern of armor, may have reduced the total weight, affording equal protection with less sacrifice in speed. As for the stirrup, it was, says Oman "an invention which had cropped up since the fifth century without one being able to say from whom it had its origin." * Writes Ridgeway on this subject, "stirrups are not mentioned in literature till about A.D. 600." † It is significant that there is no native word in either Greek or Latin for the stirrup. It may be equally significant that its first invention can be traced to Buddhist-influenced China of 420–430 A.D. Commonly in use by 477, and pictorially represented by 523, the stirrup is known to have been copied in Korea and Japan, Turkistan and Persia. It is fairly clear that the Arabs lacked stirrups when they began their great period of conquest in 647. As against that, their first envoys went to China in 651 and could presumably use their eyes. Whether as a result of that or of their campaigns in Persia, the Arabs were using stirrups by 694. These represented a decisive

* Oman, *op. cit.*, p. 137.
† Ridgeway, *op. cit.*, p. 498.

advantage over opponents who rode without them, more especially in allowing the rider to transfer the lance's impact from
himself to the horse. It only needed a built-up saddle to complete the revolution in tactics, giving the armored knight a
longer lance and a virtual supremacy on the battlefield. From
the time of the Arabs' invasion of Spain in 710, their re-equipped
cavalry was having a decisive effect. In the European armies of
the day, infantry still predominated, horses being costly to pro-
cure and maintain. But the Arab conquest of Spain revealed the
need for a complete reorganization, difficult to enforce and almost impossible to finance. Although the Arab advance through
Spain was slowed down by quarrels among the Arabs themselves,
giving the Frankish armies a respite of twenty years, little use was
made of the time. It was not until the Arabs were nearly upon
him that Charles Martel could begin the needed reforms, and
the Battle of Poitiers took place in 733; long before anything
much had been accomplished. The Arabs were beaten off by the
Frankish infantry, using purely defensive tactics, and the tide of
Islam was checked. But Martel's followers were left with no illusions about their opponents' quality in battle. They realized that
they might not be as fortunate again, if not completely re-
equipped. From that date, there began the conversion from infantry to cavalry, which was largely completed by 755. It was
necessary not only to mount the soldiers, but to establish the
whole feudal organization which would serve to maintain them
from childhood in their new, exacting, and strictly professional
role. Charlemagne's army was more than half-feudalized by
807. The superiority of the new armored cavalry was proved
thenceforward in a series of actions, one being the Battle of
Hastings, at which the English still fought as infantry.

What the foot soldier needed was an antitank weapon. The
crossbow, with its high velocity and penetration, had long been
known in China. It came now into use among Saracens and
Christians alike (see pages 97 and 148). It gave any well

disciplined infantry a means of defense and had the further advantage that it could be kept loaded in ambush. It was soon discovered, however, that it could be used by the horseman as well.
This opened up new possibilities. Mounted crossbowmen could
use harassing tactics against their opponents' heavy cavalry, goad-
ing them into exhausting attacks against an enemy able to withdraw in good order and at higher speed. Even in the twentieth
century the Arabs have been able to use such tactics with considerable success. It would be wrong to suppose that the Arabs
had a great technical advantage over all their opponents from
the beginning. It is clear, on the other hand, that they had considerable advantage by the time of the Crusades, no longer in the
use of the stirrup, which was now universal, but in the quality
of their steel and the flexibility of their tactics.

The Arab military success would have been remarkable
enough in itself, but it was paralleled by a naval achievement
which is even more surprising. There had, admittedly, been
Arab seamen from an early period (300 A.D. or earlier), some
of whom even traded to China. Arab merchants at Canton
included, incidentally, the Prophet's uncle. But the Arabs were
mostly landsmen, nevertheless, and brought to this new element
only one skill peculiar to themselves — the art of navigation.
The problem of crossing a trackless desert is much the same as
that of crossing the open sea, but with this difference, that the
caravan leader has a more stable platform from which to follow
the stars. Navigation apart, the Arabs merely absorbed the nautical skill of the Egyptians, Persians, and Greeks, combining the
known techniques, and adding something of their own. In their
westward advance, the vital step was the capture of Alexandria,
with great difficulty, in 641. At the cost of 23,000 casualties, the
Arabs had gained the world's greatest seaport, with docks, quaysides, shipping, and craftsmen. It was there that they fitted out
their ships and it was from there that they captured Crete and
Cyprus. Against Constantinople, however, their efforts failed,

mainly because their opponents knew the secret of "Greek fire," an effective flamethrower, with naphtha, perhaps, as its main ingredient. In North African campaigns, however, their ships kept pace with their cavalry, founding a sea power which was to remain for centuries after their military momentum had been lost.

The first and most obvious result of the Arab conquests was to give Islam control over the world's chief trade route. Preceding powers — Persia, Macedonia, and Rome — had established only a partial control. Persia lacked a permanent foothold in Europe; neither Macedonia nor Rome had much contact with the Far East. But trade in Arab hands could pass without hindrance between Canton and Cordova. They held the whole route from end to end. It was not, admittedly, the only one, for the Byzantine empire could still trade eastward through the Black Sea. But trade north of the Caspian was a laborious and costly enterprise. While it supported the wealth of Constantinople, it can never have been as extensive as the trade carried by the more southerly routes. Islam had spread its power or its influence from China to Andalusia and could draw upon that whole vast territory for its technical inventions and material wealth. Nor was its intellectual inheritance less impressive. By the tenth century, Islam had established a crushing superiority over the West. Spearheaded by Islam, but absorbing also the discoveries of its three component civilizations, the East had come to represent the strength, the progress, and the intellect of the world.

11

THE WEST AT BAY

BY ABOUT 400 A.D., the "Classical" period of European history came to an end. The historian draws a line at that or some other point, turns the page, and heads his new chapter "The Dark Ages." Dark they were, in the sense that we know little about them, but the student, and even the historian, is too apt to regard Europe as the world. For six hundred years, more or less, the Western world was in eclipse; a ruined and depopulated land in which the former Roman provinces gradually turned into medieval principalities and kingdoms. The Roman tradition remained in language and religion, but the population came to absorb numerous elements that had never been civilized. Among the peoples formed of this mixture, camping amid the ruins of former greatness, there developed the mental habit of looking eastward and looking back. In the East lay the civilization of Byzantium, deriving without interruption from Rome. In the past lay the glories of Rome itself, a memory of the time when the West had been supreme. Because of jealousy between the Eastern and Western Churches, the nostalgia for the past proved the stronger sentiment. While it was condemned by some ecclesiastics (like Pope Gregory I), it manifestly gave the prevailing tone to such thought as there was, forming the background to the sort of scholarship that eventually revived. The "classical" or nostalgic type of learning has been a feature of European education ever since. It began to dwindle in importance from the moment when classical achievements had been surpassed.

Granted, however, that men were awestruck by memories of

Rome, to which the Church gave some semblance of continuity, they were more immediately under the influence of the East. To this influence they submitted with some reluctance. For the East they felt what can be described as a superstitious dread. Orientals were possessed of horrible and occult powers, just such advantages, in fact, as all civilized people have over their ignorant neighbors. Traces of this dread survive in Western attitudes toward Asia, and more especially in popular fiction and melodrama. Sinister and inscrutable Chinese figure as the villains in one type of story, hypnotic Hindus as the villains of another. The Yellow Peril is centered upon the Chinese bungalow, and death comes to the man who has rifled the Egyptian tomb. A book remains to be written about European dread of the East, with analysis of all the superstitions which have clouded reality. Failing such a book, we have only the mental image formed by a score of half-remembered novels, motion pictures, and plays. This image plays a real part in foreign affairs. For the moment, however, the fact to note is that the mental attitude involved is a relic of a period when Asian civilization was incontestably superior. Orientals never had the occult powers for which they were given the credit. All they had was a scientific knowledge which surpassed all Western comprehension.

In order to understand this relationship, we have to realize, at the outset, that the Dark Ages were no period of darkness for Asia. They were, on the contrary, a period of exceptional brilliance. By no sort of coincidence, the eclipse of Europe was paralleled by the very brightest period in the history of China. Take the early seventh century as illustrating this contrast. Italy had been invaded by the Lombards and Rome had reached, by about 600, what Gibbon calls "the lowest period of her depression." In describing the misery of the Romans, he says that:

. . . they shut or opened their gates with a trembling hand, beheld from the walls the flames of their houses, and heard the lamentation of their brethren, who were coupled together like dogs and dragged away into distant slavery . . . the campaign of Rome was speedily reduced to the state of a dreary wilderness, in which the land is barren, the waters are impure, and the air is infectious . . . the depopulation was constant and visible, and the gloomy . . . might expect the approaching failure of the human race. Yet the number of citizens still exceeded the measure of subsistence . . .*

Nor was the situation much better in the eastern Empire. There, in 613–19, the provinces of Syria, Egypt, and Asia Minor were conquered by Persian armies and the barbarian Avars raided up to the gates of Constantinople. The situation was saved by Heraclius, but worsened again with the rise of Islam. It was in 622 that Mahomet established his rule at Medina. By 629 he had captured Mecca and soon afterwards declared war on Rome. The great age of Islam had begun at a time when the West, beyond the walls of Byzantium, was scarcely civilized.

What was the situation, by contrast, in China? China's Golden Age, as it has been called, began with the establishment of the T'ang Dynasty in 618. By 623 the separate kingdoms had been subdued and China unified.

Thus, the pageant of the T'angs begins with horsemen — cavalry galloping to Chang-an, bridle to bridle, squadron on squadron, the sun glinting on war-worn armour, on the jewelled scabbards of their leaders, and their nodding plumes. As they approach the triple walls of the capital, horses are reined in and the headlong gallop steadies into the rhythmic trot of many thousands; while from the drum-towers and bell-towers of the watching city, break the clash and clamour of uncontrollable forces, of joy, delight and triumph, and the rapture of sunlight after years of darkness. The great impetus of a young, indomitable leader and his gallant horsemen will surge on through three centuries till its strength is spent, its numbers decimated by

* Gibbon, *op. cit.*, Chap. XLV.

treachery and ambush; finally, a little band of phantoms vanishes into the dust of Chinese chronicle or rides into the twilight tapestries of romance.*

T'ai Tsung began his formal reign in 627 A.D., inaugurating a period of stability which was to last until 906. Never had China been more united or prosperous. Never had it been so civilized and influential. From the Yellow Sea to Turkistan, from Siberia to Cambodia, the Emperor's rule brought enlightenment and peace. Of the period Fenellosa writes:

> . . . Buildings were grander, stuffs and clothing more exquisite, food more plentiful, the people happier, engineering works more stupendous, than in the Han dynasty or in any preceding period of Chinese history. The eastern capital, Loyang . . . now became rebuilt upon a scale which accommodated more than two million people. Great public gardens and museums gave recreation to the people. The private palace gardens were raised on mighty walled terraces, pavilion-crowned, that enjoyed far prospects over lakes and bays . . . Pavilions rose above granite and marble foundations in rainbow tier after tier; great banqueting halls, and blue silk awnings, and heavy portieres, shot with golden thread, adding alike to the exalted coolness and the aesthetic transitions. Indeed, in these great days of early T'ang, China had become the metropolitan garden of Asia, surpassing the splendours of Khan or Caliph at Samarcand and Damascus and Baghdad.†

No historian of art would question the architectural and artistic achievements of the T'ang and later dynasties. No world historian could fail to note the progress of T'ang expansion, the extension of Chinese influence over Tibet, Korea, Manchuria, and Sinkiang, the reaching of its furthest limits in 750 A.D. Mathematicians realize that the Chinese of the third century

* L. Cranmer-Byng, *The Vision of Asia* (London, 1947), p. 141.
† *Ibid.*, p. 144.

THE MIDDLE KINGDOM
CHINA IN 750 A.D.

R. Amur

MANCHURIA

SINKIANG

Peking (Karanbaligh) KOREA

Lan-Chow

Huangho

TIBET

Yang-Tse Kiang Nanking

Lhasa

Brahmaputra

Ganges

JAPAN

Canton

Mekong

CAMBODIA

SIAM

ISLAMIC INFLUENCE

MALAYA

TRADE ROUTE

SUMATRA

A.D. possessed the Pythagorean theorem, an approximate calculation of the ratio between a circle's diameter and circumference, the distinction between odd and even numbers and also between positive and negative, a method of extracting square and cube roots, and some grasp of linear, simultaneous, and quadratic equations. Astronomers are aware that they had by that period computed the distance to, and orbit of, the sun. It is only in recent years, however, that Dr. Joseph Needham has revealed the Chinese achievement in technology. On this subject he writes as follows:

. . . here are a few of the things which may be said about the transmission of mechanical and other techniques. A few fundamental ones diffused in all directions from ancient Mesopotamia, e.g. the wheeled vehicle, the windlass and the pulley . . . The only Persian invention of the first rank was the windmill . . . But China produced a profusion of developments which reached Europe and other regions at times varying between the 1st and the 18th centuries: (a) the square pallet chainpump; (b) the edge runner mill and the application of water power to it; (c) metallurgical blowing machines operated by water power; (d) the rotary fan and winnowing machine; (e) the piston bellows; (f) the horizontal warp-loom (possibly also Indian) and the draw-loom; (g) silk reeling, twisting and doubling machinery; (h) the wheelbarrow; (i) the sailing carriage; (j) the wagon-mill; (k) the two efficient harnesses for draught animals, i.e. the breast-strap or postilion harness, and the collar harness; (l) the cross-bow; (m) the kite; (n) the helicopter top and the Zoetrope; (o) the technique of deep drilling; (p) the mastery of cast iron; (q) the 'Cardan' suspension; (r) the segmental arch bridge; (s) the iron-chain suspension bridge; (t) canal lock-gates; (u) numerous inventions in nautical construction, including water-tight compartments, aerodynamically efficient sails, the fore-and-aft rig, and (v) the stern-post rudder; (w) gunpowder and some of its associated techniques; (x) the magnetic compass, used first for geomancy and then, also by the Chinese, for navigation;

(y) paper, printing, and movable-type printing; and (z) porcelain. I come to a stop, having exhausted the alphabet, but many more instances, even important ones, could be given . . . . . . The feature common to all examples is that firm evidence for their use in China antedates and sometimes long antedates, the best evidence for their appearance in any other part of the world.*

Not all these inventions date from the same period; not all of them may prove to be Chinese; but enough will survive any scrutiny to prove, beyond doubt, that the Chinese have behind them a colossal achievement, much of it dating from the period when Europe produced little or nothing. It would be as easy, however, to draw up a list of the technicalities which the Chinese failed to master; beginning, of course, with anything that could be called orchestral music. Harmony eluded them, successful as they were with porcelain, painting, ivory, and jade.

Between China and Islam there was a closer connection than many people realize. "Seek for learning," said the Prophet, "though it be as far away as China." And that was what the Arabs did, especially in the eighth century, when their ships were a familiar sight in the southern Chinese harbors. With India they were still better acquainted, their conquests there and in Persia giving them access to further knowledge, both theoretical and practical. It was from India that they took their mathematics based on the numerals that we have since called "Arabic." From Persia they took the games of chess and polo, and from Byzantium the techniques of fortification. Neither in science nor in technology did the Arabs invent much of their own, and it might seem odd that these nomads should invent anything. Their own major contributions were in literature and religion. The Arabs had their own tradition of oral poetry and eloquence, based upon a language of extraordinary wealth in

* Joseph Needham, *Science and Civilisation in China* (Cambridge, 1954), I, 240.

expression. Whereas other languages have the same word or sound used with different meanings, the Arabs have scores of different words of which the meaning is approximately the same, giving them, poetically, the sort of advantage which the English have over the French. The essence of Arab culture lay in horsemanship and poetry or that blending of the two which has come to be called chivalry. Included in this concept is the Arab attitude toward women and toward prisoners of war, both an aspect of desert life. On the first point the ideas conveyed in Western fiction are the precise opposite of the truth, which C. S. Jarvis states thus:

> Cases of interference with women are extremely rare in the Arab world, due to the fact that the Bedouin's carefree existence as a gentleman of leisure is based entirely on his women-folk being able to travel about the desert in safety. His laws, therefore, regarding promiscuity are ruthless, as if women were to be subject to attention, welcome or otherwise, from every stray Arab they met, they could not continue to fetch water, plough land, and look after flocks without adequate escort . . . The result is that women can wander at will in the desert without the slightest risk of the loss of their virtue . . .*

The Arab's addiction to idleness, poetry, religion, and war has its logical consequence for his womenfolk. They will have to do much of the work, which would ordinarily spoil their sexual attraction. But the Arab overcomes this difficulty by the institution of polygamy. The youngest or latest wife can be treated differently, as Freya Stark observes:

> . . . In a mixed Muslim place like Iskerundur, the Arab elegance is visible at once, even in the poor Alaonites from across the border; the femininity of the Levant is kept indoors there, but only to be more fit for pleasure; its clothes and easy con-

* Jarvis, *Three Deserts* (London, 1936), p. 143.

tours are made to go to bed with, and the women, when this age
is over, think no more of their appearance and do not, in fact,
try to please in any other way. But while their tide is with
them, the young women's veiling is royal; protected like idols
they breathe security and move with enviable safety in a walled
world, with anything but submission in their seclusion. They
are set apart, yet they remain individual and are not destroyed.*

Here then are two separate ideas. Women are to be kept
within the home, and specially protected when young. At a later
age, they must be able to work and should therefore be free from
molestation; an immunity to be secured by mutual agreement,
custom, and law. It would, of course, be absurd to credit Islam
with the invention of the veil for married women and concubines, for this had been a matter of law in ancient Babylon,
where the veil was specifically denied to prostitutes.† But Mahomet seems to have enforced among his followers an elaboration of earlier customs which formed the basis for "purdah" as
later established. He had eleven wives himself, nine at one time,
but laid down a maximum of four for the guidance of the faithful. With all the disadvantages that we may associate with
"purdah," the Arab women had a privileged position in many
ways. They were treated with a sort of reverence, in short, with
chivalry.

But chivalry has other aspects, all connected with the life of
the desert. Cavalry such as the Arabs used must imply a type
of aristocracy. Against the background of the waterless waste, a
special prestige attaches to the Bedouin who goes furthest into
the desert, the more daring being the best mounted, the more
skillful, and the wealthiest. But where the chief enemy (and
friend) is the desert itself, there is a fellow feeling among the
tribesmen, a readiness to help each other, and a contempt in

* Stark, op. cit., p. 45.
† See H. W. F. Saggs, The Greatness That Was Babylon (London, 1962),
p. 214.

common for those who are running no risk at all. On these
sentiments are based the desert laws of hospitality, the sharing
of provisions or water with a stranger in need.

> The different tribes of the Arab stock have the reputation of
> showing their enemies remarkable clemency after a victorious
> fight . . . The person of the enemy is sacred when disarmed
> or dismounted; and prisoners are neither enslaved nor held to
> other ransom than their mares. This purpose is attained by
> merely dismounting or wounding the enemy. The latter's arms
> and mare become the property of the victor, and he himself is
> then let go . . . It is contrary to the Arab conscience to ex-
> tinguish a kalila (tribe).*

It should, of course, be emphasized that chivalry is a code of
conduct among horsemen, not necessarily extended to the infantry on the other side. But it was something the Arabs had
evolved, and which the Romans and Greeks had conspicuously
lacked. In a sense which was quite new to the world, they were
gentlemen.

Added to their own characteristics, and transforming their attitude in many ways, was their religion. Islam owes much to
Judaism and Christianity and as much again to Persia. The basic
idea of conflict between good and evil, between black and white,
suited the Arab character. So did the Muslim profession of faith,
"There is no God but Allah and Muhammad is the prophet of
Allah," and the concept of brotherhood among the faithful. It
is in this brotherhood, superseding blood ties and theoretically
ending blood feuds, that Islam contains an element of democracy.

> [The rulers of Mecca] . . . jealous of their privilege, watched
> each other with habitual concern for another's pretensions, the
> more so for nature herself had imposed democracy on their desert-

* C. Northcote Parkinson, *The Evolution of Political Thought* (London,
1958), pp. 48–49.

dwelling ancestors in exchange for their survival. A generous hospitality; an equal division of their means of life with way-farers; their conception of every man's right to water, to the serving in case of need and without requirement of cattle and mares, and, above all, to sanctuary — these arise, like their di-rectness of manner and spoken solicitude, out of the nature of desert life, from the narrow margin between them and death, and have their origin long before the revelation of Islam. To break these ancient rules was, for them, to break laws of survival and of Nature herself.*

The deliberate simplicity of the earlier Muslim leaders, whether in dress or speech or dwelling, did not last for long, and provided, in fact, a first source of disagreement among them-selves. But the religion itself remained strong and attracted a fervent loyalty. Some of its rules — the law against eating pork, the law against drinking wine, the law against representing the human form in art — would seem to be accidental borrowings from older forms of belief. Its strength lay in the simplicity of its creed, the brotherhood of its adherents, and the certainty of salvation it offered to the believer. There was only one God, Allah, without the complications of the Christian trinity. There had been other prophets, Moses and Jesus included, but all essen-tial doctrine was comprised in the Koran. There was no priest-hood and no sacrifice. The duties of the Muslim — the prayers, the ritual, the fast — were clearly laid down. One important duty was that of the Holy War against the infidel who had to be converted or subdued. But the captive who accepted the Muslim creed had to be treated thenceforward as a brother. Islam, finally, was precise in defining the price of salvation. Chris-tianity makes an unlimited demand on the believer. Only God can know whether his belief, his love, his devotion and conduct come up to an acceptable standard. But there is no such empha-sis in Islam upon the quality of an adherent's belief. For salva-

* Gerald de Gaury, *Rulers of Mecca* (London, 1951), p. 31.

tion he has only to obey the rules, saying the right prayers, avoiding the sins as defined, and giving in charity up to a stated proportion of his income. For failure in any or all these respects, he can atone by death in battle against the infidel. Nor does the martyr's privilege end there; he can also intercede for seventy of his relatives. It is finally necessary to emphasize that the heaven to be gained is, again, precisely described.

> The Muhammadan Paradise exceeds all others in its presentation of physical pleasures and luxuriant backgrounds. The resurrection is pictured as both corporeal and spiritual, and extended to all created beings, whether angels, genii, men or animals. On Judgement Day, those who are admitted into Paradise will be gathered on the right hand, and those who are destined for perdition on the left.*

Paradise is conceived as a series of gardens, with golden couches, piles of fruit, dark-eyed maidens, shady trees, flowing water, and the wine from which the believer has until then refrained. Hell consists of seven circles, of which the third is reserved for Christians, whose death in battle will merely lead them there the sooner.

But the Muslims, although perfectly convinced of their own salvation, were tolerant, in practice, of other beliefs. In the lands they conquered, they came to liberate rather than oppress. They would allow no Christians or Jews in Arabia itself, but did no more elsewhere than subject them to a special tax.

It has been said that the Arab conquest would have been impossible without the active or passive support of the Syrians and Aramaean peasantry. What they had to offer was, in fact, of value.

> The Arabs gave much to civilisation; a new and fine religious conception; a then quite novel idea of the importance of indi-

* L. Cranmer-Byng, *op. cit.*, p. 83.

vidual behaviour, of personal cleanliness, of good manners and an idealistic treatment of women, which achieved its finest fruits in the chivalry of later ages; and an art convention which, working within the restrictions imposed by religious propriety, produced forms in the realm of decorative work which are acknowledged to be unique. Many of the best ideas of the Arabs — the unity of God; the propriety and necessity of self-indulgence within certain clearly defined limits (as opposed to the ascetic ideal of orthodox Christianity); the essential brotherhood of man, not necessarily conflicting, except in the minds of peasants, with the needed regulations of the everyday world in ranks and classes — came like a breath of fresh desert air upon the pompous, morbid and degraded Christianity of the early middle ages . . .*

To all that was valuable in their creed, the Muslims added a respect for learning. The Prophet himself had been emphatic about this and learning flourished in the wake of the Arab conquest. The very words "algebra" and "chemistry," "zenith" and "zero" are Arabic, and the University of Cairo has some claim to be regarded as the oldest in the world.

When all this has been said, there is something to be placed on the debit side. The Arab was a nomad, not a cultivator, and brought with him not only mental stimulus, but agricultural disaster. As C. S. Jarvis explains:

The Arab is sometimes called the Son of the Desert, but, as Palmer said, this is a misnomer as in most cases he is the Father of the Desert, having created it himself, and the arid waste in which he lives and on which practically nothing will grow is the direct result of his appalling indolence, combined with his simian trait of destroying everything he does not understand . . . In his campaign of destruction, the Arab has been most loyally supported by his animals, the camel and the goat . . .†

* Richard Coke, *The Arab's Place in the Sun* (London, 1929), p. 52.
† Jarvis, *op. cit.*, p. 150.

Is this the sour comment of British officialdom? If so, it is anticipated in the *Prolegomena* of Ibn Khaldûn of Tunis (1332–1406), which reads thus:

> Mark how all the countries of the world which have been con-
> quered and dominated by the Arabs have had their civilisation
> ruined, their populations dispersed, and even the soil itself appar-
> ently transformed. Thus Yemen is in ruins, except for a few dis-
> tricts; similarly Iraq, which was so flourishing under the Per-
> sians, is devastated; so, too, in Syria at the present day. In
> North Africa and the Maghrib . . . ruin and devastation still
> prevail. Yet before that time all the country lying between the
> Sudan and the Mediterranean was the centre of a flourishing
> civilisation, as witnessed by the remains of building and statues
> and the ruins of towns and villages . . . Yet Arabs are withal,
> the quickest of peoples to follow the call to truth and righteous-
> ness. For their natures are relatively simple and free from the
> distorting effect of bad habits and evil ways . . .*

In the ninth century, the merits of Islam were much in evidence, and the longterm devastation had still, perhaps, to be
fully realized. To the Europeans of the day, diminished in
numbers, disunited and ignorant, the Muslims appeared almost
more than human, as cultured in peace as they were terrible in
war. For anything that could be thought progressive or enlightened, men looked to the East as to a civilization that was immensely superior. After centuries during which the balance has
tipped the other way, it is difficult for us to realize how low the
West had sunk. There were signs, it may be, of recovery. As
things were, however, Europe had neither strength nor unity,
neither enterprise nor art. "But behind all this disorder and un-
couthness," writes Pandit Nehru, "you can detect energy at least
and life." † We can detect it now, but it would have been diffi-

* Ibn Khaldûn, *op. cit.*, p. 57.
† Jawaharlal Nehru, *Glimpses of World History* (London, 1942), p. 179.

cult to sense it at the time. For the ruins of Rome still shad-
owed the landscape, making a silent mockery of the hovels in
which men had come to live. What was the West of the present
day as compared with the West in Alexander's time? France
had been saved for Christendom, and so had some fragment of
Spain. The eastern Empire still held some fraction of its former
territory. But all this amounted to very little, and Gibbon is
justified in pointing out that "Like Thebes, or Babylon or Carthage, the name of Rome might have been erased from the earth,
if the city had not been animated by a vital principle, which
again restored her to honour and dominion." * But while the
fact of this is undeniable, we have to remember that this principle also came from the East.

* Gibbon, *op. cit.*, Chap. XLV.

12

THE CRUSADES

THE ONSET of one religion can be resisted only by another. There is a practice in medicine of attempting to prevent disease by artificially inducing a milder attack of the complaint that is especially feared. It was in this fashion that the one Oriental religion tended to exclude the other. Islam could be resisted only in the name of Christ. But while the reaction of the West took this specifically religious form, giving the name of Christendom to the area which was to be defended, the underlying motives went deeper. In all attempts to assess the motives behind historical events, there is an inevitable tendency to exaggerate the influence of the scholar. Philosophers, theologians, and political theorists leave behind them a possibly permanent record of their views, and this is often the only explanation of policy we have to study. Rulers, soldiers, and merchants are far less likely to commit their views to paper. It would be wrong, nevertheless, to conclude that they were speechless or that they looked to the scholars for guidance. They were far more likely to have said, with the astute Ibn Khaldûn, that "Scholars are, of all men, those least fitted for politics and its ways." What their views were we are left to surmise, but that they had other than religious motives for defending Europe is certain. It is at least as evident that the Muslims were not all as fanatically religious as Christian historians have tended to assume. They too had their secular motives, behind which was a belief in the East as such. It was their turn to dominate the world, and this was what they did.

The reaction of the West may be said to have begun in about

1000 A.D. The tide of Muslim conquest in Spain turned with the death of Almanzor in 1002, and there was an almost simultaneous campaign which led eventually to the reconquest of Sicily. But the momentum of Islam was restored by the conversion to that faith of the Seljuk Turks (and later again of the Ottoman Turks), Mongol tribes with a sole interest in war. Freya Stark complains that the Turk "in spite of his strength and self-reliance, is dull," being as different from the Arab as anyone can be: capable, inartistic, matter of fact, and brave. It was the Muslim Turks who reinforced Islam, renewing the old threat in a less attractive form. Their opportunity was the greater in that the Eastern and Western Churches had finally quarreled with each other in 1044, ending all semblance of Christian unity. With the defeat of the Byzantine army in 1071, the West was compelled to rally its forces. Even before that date, the need had become apparent, but the man of the moment was Hildebrand, who became Pope Gregory VII, in 1073. It was his policy to unify Christendom under papal leadership. In that he failed, but his reform of the Church strengthened its authority for the years to come. Henry IV, the German king of his day, attempted to do the same thing on a secular basis, only to fail in his turn. But at last, in 1095, Pope Urban II summoned a Council of the Church at Clermont in Auvergne. On the tenth day of a conference mainly concerned with Church discipline, the Pope suddenly made his appeal for the rescue of Jerusalem. That city had been in Muslim hands for some years, and the real basis of his appeal rested upon the threat to Constantinople itself. With the loss of Anatolia, and the fall of Antioch, the danger had become very real, and the Emperor at Constantinople was appealing for help against the infidel. There was an enthusiastic response, and vast forces eventually took the field, with Jerusalem as their objective. Initially numbering perhaps 300,000, the crusaders marched overland, crossed the Bosphorus, captured Nicaea, captured Antioch (1908), and finally took Jerusalem itself. There they set up a Christian kingdom in the

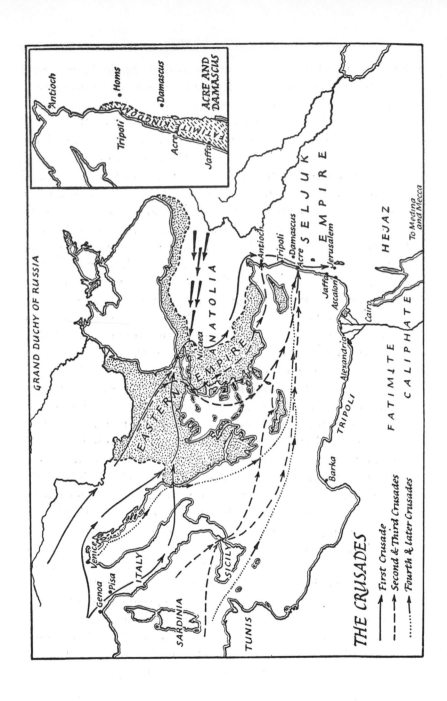

THE CRUSADES

→ First Crusade
⇢ Second & Third Crusades
⋯⋯ Fourth & Later Crusades

GRAND DUCHY OF RUSSIA

EASTERN EMPIRE

ANATOLIA

Nicaea

SELJUK EMPIRE

Antioch

Tripoli
Damascus
Acre
Jerusalem

Jaffa
Accalon

Alexandria

Cairo

TRIPOLI

Barka

FATIMITE

CALIPHATE

HEJAZ

To Medina
and Mecca

Genoa
Pisa
Venice

ITALY

SICILY

SARDINIA

TUNIS

Antioch

Tripoli   Homs

Damascus

ACRE AND
DAMASCUS

KINGDOM

Acre

Jaffa

midst of Islam. Having seen it established, garrisoned, and fortified, the bulk of the crusaders returned, very naturally, to their homes in Europe.

In understanding what they had achieved, the first point to notice is that Constantinople had played a vital part in the whole affair. As against Islam, it had caused the sort of delay that Carthage had imposed on Rome. By it the whole movement had been held up for centuries. More than that, it was from Constantinople that the forces of Europe had passed into Syria, operating thus from a baseline firmly held. The second point to observe is that the capture of Jerusalem was a master stroke of policy, breaking the Muslim world into two halves, and causing that fracture at its weakest point, the land bridge joining Mesopotamia and Egypt. The third point to emphasize is that the Crusades, although representing the unity of Europe against Asia, were purely defensive. They did not herald a major attack on the Orient. The First, and the subsequent or reinforcing Crusades had, as their main result, the rescue of Constantinople. By a vigorous diversion, the Western knights had relieved the pressure on the Eastern Empire, enabling it to survive for another 350 years. They had done very much what the Emperor had asked them to do. The fourth and last point to stress is that the crusaders brought the Christian rulers and their men into close touch with the civilized East. The culture of the Middle Ages is to a large extent what they brought back with them.

In modification of this last statement, it must be conceded that there had been much contact with the East before the First Crusade was launched, especially through Spain and Sicily and the Byzantine dependencies on the Adriatic, of which Venice was to be the most important. But these were indirect influences so far as Europe was concerned. It was the Crusades which brought the semi-barbarous French, German, and English soldiers into a world which was still civilized. Constantinople was, for many, the first real city they had ever seen, and Antioch, perhaps, the second or third. The Kingdom of Jerusalem was lost in 1187, and subsequent operations failed to recover it, but Europeans had in the meanwhile occupied territory which had been Christian, turned Muslim, and then become Christian again. They had been brought into daily conversation with men who knew Persia and India, with others who knew something of China. In fighting the Saracens (or "Easterners"), they came to resemble them. They learned much from both subjects and opponents, and returned home more sophisticated and mature. What they brought with them to Palestine was the concept of European unity, an ideal which had been created by the fear of Islam and which lasted just as long as the threat was real. Symbol of this precarious unity was the crusader's badge. "His cross," Urban II had explained, "is the symbol of your salvation; wear it, a red, a bloody cross, as an external mark on your breasts or shoulders . . ." This the crusaders had done, extinguishing the marks which signified their feudal loyalties. But the crosses changed shape and color, gradually becoming distinct from each other, and assuming their final blazon as the national flags of Europe.

Granted that these banners would finally differ, there was much in medieval Europe which would be the same — the churches, for example, the monasteries and schools. The concepts of empire and papacy were international and so were the customs of knighthood, university, and guild. But practically all that was uniform had an Oriental origin. Christianity is an Eastern religion, its doctrines a variant of Judaism, but its practices derived from Mesopotamia and Persia. Organized monasticism — as distinct from the hermit austerities of the desert — is essentially Buddhist. From Byzantium (at its most Oriental) came the vestments, and from Buddhist China came the bells. Gothic architecture is plainly Islamic, beginning with the First Crusade, and adapting the horseshoe arch from the Muslim mosque. The art of fortification was learned from the Saracens, who had themselves improved somewhat on their Byzantine masters. From Islam came the veil for ladies' use and from China that conical hat, draped in muslin, which was to be the thirteenth-century fashion. From the East generally came the fourposter bed, designed to extend the mosquito net, and from Islam came the first motions of cartography as distinct from the theological map-making in which some monks had specialized.

Saracens and crusaders were eventually armed in similar fashion, and were organized from the start in much the same way. And the European historian has tended to assume that the Muslims had learned from their opponents. The medieval army's strength lay in its armored cavalry, mounted, mail-clad and equipped with helmet, shield, and lance. As each horseman needed attendants, with a pack animal and spare equipment — as each, moreover, was trained from childhood — the army had a feudal basis, the knights being dependent on the areas of land which they held in fief. Their Muslim antagonists had used much the same system from an even earlier period and for exactly the same reasons. In this neither needed to copy the other. But in horsemanship, the East had — and had always had — the advantage. It is doubtful how many of the crusaders were even mounted when their first campaign began. It is fairly certain that their best horses henceforward were those they had captured. And with the horses came the idea of chivalry, first developed among the Arabs. There was little quarter given between Muslim and Christian, but there were courtesies, as between opponents who had come to respect each other. As the fortunes of war fluctuated, each side experienced defeat. Each side also had its victories, with the opportunity each time of studying the captured fortress or equipment. Says Ibn Khaldûn, who should have known, on this subject:

The vanquished always seek to imitate their victors in their dress, insignia, belief and other customs and usages . . . we see the defeated always imitating the victors in their way of dressing, of carrying their arms, in their equipment and in all their mode of living . . .*

What the crusaders immediately learned in this way was the art of making chain mail — light, flexible, and impervious. The Arabs had used it for centuries, an early description reading thus: "Something that keeps the horseman busy; a nuisance for the footman; but in all cases a strong protection." † Its use was confined at first to the leaders, not being generally available until the thirteenth century. An important development was the extension of armor to the horse, which offered a larger target. It was during the First Crusade that the knights of Christendom first encountered, and copied, the wooden crossbow, a weapon of Chinese origin which the Muslims used on horseback. Its special merit lay in its trigger action, which allowed the archer to go into battle with his weapon loaded. It could be shot with accuracy from a horse ridden at the gallop (not the canter), and it was an essential element in Saracen tactics. When first introduced into twelfth-century Europe, its use was banned by the Pope as inhuman. Its limitation lay in the time it took to reload, minutes during which the man "who had shot his bolt" was vulnerable. By about 1370, the steel crossbow appeared, a much more powerful weapon, and one which gave infantry a new importance. Yet a further Arab practice was in the use of the flag and pennon. The lance normally had a strip of cloth tied near the point — initially for safety no doubt, while on the march or in camp. But it was soon found useful in another way. At the siege of Ad Darbul, in the early days of Islam, it was told of one officer: "When he encamped . . . he constructed trenches; lances were set up along the trenches, with flags flying from them and the troops camped according to their flags." ‡

* Ibn Khaldûn, *op. cit.*, p. 53.
† Ahmad Ibn Yahya, *Origin of the Islamic State* (New York, 1916), I, 439.
‡ *Ibid.*, II, 217.

Here was the basis of unit organization and what would eventually become "the company colour." Yet another Arab custom was the wearing of a loose garment over the chain mail to prevent the iron becoming impossibly hot under the sun. Copied by the crusaders, this became the surcoat, marked clearly to show which side the soldier was on. In these and many other ways the crusaders learned about warfare in the desert. With mobile armed columns moving within a framework of fixed defenses held by infantry, they developed the tactics which were revived in the twentieth century. Like these later soldiers, they brought the technique back to Europe. It derived essentially, however, from their time in the East.

The First Crusade was an almost purely land operation, involving a march of 1500–2500 miles, the distance being different for the various national contingents. At this period the shipping for a combined operation was not, presumably, available. Almost the whole of the maritime trade between East and West was in Muslim hands, the Eastern Empire being unable to provide more than a ferry service. Had more shipping existed in Christian ownership, the Byzantines would certainly have offered it, if only to keep the crusaders away from Byzantium. But the capture of ports in Syria altered the whole picture. By 1101 the next wave of crusaders arrived by sea. The ships were those of Genoa, Venice, and Pisa. Bringing reinforcements and supplies, they certainly avoided a return voyage in ballast. Far from that, the merchants were soon established at Tripoli and Antioch, collecting the cargoes for Italy — the silks and spices and ivory which had crossed the desert to Damascus or Homs. It was these merchantmen that cooperated in the capture of the other ports. It was in these again that the exhausted, wounded, and sick men took their passages for Europe. The cultural connection established by the crusaders' experience of the East was maintained and broadened by the trade which had followed in their wake. The Saracens had to trade with their opponents — their goods had no other outlet. The Italians, on their part, might be good Christians, but saw no reason to operate at an actual loss.

Much of the success of the First Crusade was due to a split among the Muslims, which ended in at least temporary agreement against the infidel. Even to maintain a footing in Palestine required, therefore, a series of expeditions, separated in fact by long periods of time. When Jerusalem was lost, in 1187, the leaders of the Third Crusade could achieve no more than the capture of Acre. The Fourth Crusade was finally diverted against Constantinople (1204), the Venetians acquiring a colonial empire in the process. The Fifth Crusade led to Frederic II's feat in securing Jerusalem by negotiation — to be lost again some fifteen years later. By 1250, at latest, the Crusades were over and with them the attempt at European unity. The threat of Islam had more or less vanished (to revive later), and the Crusades had served their purpose. As a spoiling attack they had succeeded. They had proved that the West was beginning to revive. They had also proved that the East was still culturally superior. The capture of Antioch or Acre was the sort of success which made the victors in some sense despondent. In showing their military competence, they came to realize that they were far less civilized than the people whose city they had taken. It is also important to remember that they were finally defeated.

One feature to observe about this crusading period was the severity which was shown toward the potential "fifth column" in Europe. In discovering their own "Western" character, the rulers of the day were quick to eliminate such Asian elements as might appear behind their own lines. Were the Jews of Europe to be regarded as allies? They were not. But how could the soldiers go off to Palestine, leaving wife and children liable to molestation by aliens whose sympathies probably lay with the other side? The best plan, clearly, was to deal with them beforehand. The First Crusade was preceded by the first massacres at Verdun, Treves, Worms, and elsewhere. The Third Crusade was preceded by similar disorders, notably at York in 1189. King

John put financial pressure on the English Jews in 1210, inducing many to leave the country. At the Fourth Lateran Council of 1215, preceding the Fifth Crusade, decrees were passed to make the Jews social outcasts with distinctive clothing and a virtual boycott. This essentially Hindu approach to the problem was rejected by Edward I, who expelled all Jews from England in 1290. Their position would have been happier had the Muslims liked them any better. The result of this treatment was to intensify in them the characteristics to which they owed their unpopularity in the first place. Harsh treatment, writes Ibn Khaldûn, makes men ingrown, corrupt, and mean. "Consider, for instance the Jews, whose characters have degenerated owing to such treatment so that they are renowned, in every age and climate, for their wickedness and slyness."

The Jews were not the only group thought to be in league with the enemy. Manicheism was an offshoot of the Zoroastrian religion, founded by the prophet Mani and driven from the Roman Empire by Christianity. This cult was revived later and its adherents, the Cathari and Albigenses, became numerous in southern France. Here was another pocket of alien influence, against which Pope Innocent III announced a Crusade in 1208. The result was a massacre of heretics, perhaps the first of its kind in history and probably the largest to take place before the twentieth century. Adolf Hitler's prototype was Innocent III, whose slaughter of some hundred thousand deviationists set up a record unbeaten until our own time. But the point which is relevant to the present theme is that all this alien control and heresy hunt coincided with the later period of Asia's ascendancy and was a reaction to it. The movement slackened first in Italy, where the Crusades gave place to a more profitable commerce. It persisted for the longest period in Spain, where war against the infidel occupied the whole of the Middle Ages. It revived as soon as Asia's threat was again perceptible, or before that when the danger was merely to be foreseen.

From 1000 A.D., the West was renascent but still under

Oriental influence, as can be seen most clearly in architecture and art. And perhaps the most important aspect of this influence lay in the caste system which had been set up on the Indian model. The structure of medieval Europe provided a celibate priesthood, monasticism, and hierarchy to which was entrusted the main responsibility for learning, education, science, and art, all more or less harnessed to the cause of religion. On this religious unity depended very plainly the survival of the West. The same structure provided, on its secular side, a feudal hierarchy of emperor, kings, nobles, knights, and peasantry. On this semblance of secular unity depended the success or failure of the Crusades. A parallel structure provided, in the slowly recovering cities, a merchant hierarchy of magistrates, guild officers, masters, and apprentices. The general effect was to keep the available ability in all but watertight compartments. The clergy were literate, but knew little of trade or war. The nobles were bred to arms, disdaining both learning and commerce. The merchants used trade as their own mystery without displaying undue interest in theology or tactics. The completeness of specialization was never quite attained, for there were always a few men who defied classification. But many elements of a caste system were there. The Hindu type of society with its stability, and with its risk of stagnation, had been partially reproduced. Nor was the final result entirely different from the type of society that had evolved in China. In that far more advanced civilization the hereditary feudal element had been eliminated, but there was the same sharp distinction between the scholar, the soldier, and the tradesman. Any emperor or king is the more secure for having no single subject in whom tactical, scientific, and economic abilities are combined. But technical progress — even such brilliant progress as China had made — must be hampered in the end by specialization in this form. It was a specialization from which Europe was to free itself.

In studying the nature of this heavily orientalized Christendom, using the one Eastern faith as a weapon against the next, we have to realize how sharply it differed from the ascendant West of the Classical period. And in nothing was the difference so manifest as in this system of caste. Among the Greeks the priesthood had been relatively unimportant, and much the same people appeared successively as athletes, teachers, tradesmen, and soldiers. The Romans were more specialized in their later periods, but even among them the same man was administrator, lawyer, soldier, and politician. The Roman officer was probably no bookworm, but there was no question of his being actually illiterate; and history seems to indicate that some measure of learning may be useful even in war. The process by which these barriers were broken down in the later Middle Ages was the same that had produced the classical breakthrough: the growth of the city, and indeed of the city-state. Essence of this development was that the city should have a life of its own apart from that of the territory in which it might happen to be or of which it might, in fact, be the capital. It was in the city that the university grew up, to which the noble might eventually send his son. It was in defense of his own city that the merchant became a soldier. It was in the city streets that the priest learned something of commerce and the scholar something of art. It was in the Italian cities more especially that the renascence of Europe began. One European invention or discovery of the Middle Ages, drawn neither from the East nor from classic tradition, was the institution of romantic love between the sexes. So far from being a characteristic of the human species, it did not appear until the eleventh to thirteenth centuries, when it was popularized by the troubadours of Provence, Italy, and Spain. The idea of a passionate and idealized love having a special merit of its own — a right of way, moreover, as against material and social considerations — grew gradually through the following centuries to gain its ultimate sanction in nineteenth-century fiction and twentieth-century cinematography. Love in this sense, little known in India and looked upon with disapproval in China, is an important aspect of European individualism. It had powerful literary expression from 1500 onwards, and added a further element to the dynamic qualities of Western society. The growth of this convention was closely connected with the weakening of the wider clan or family relationships. The boy who left the countryside, seeking his fortune in the city, lost the support of his kinsfolk and reserved all his affection for the girl he would finally marry. A further incentive toward material success was his knowledge that the more attractive girls in a competitive society are reserved for the ablest men. The literary conventions of the novel, derived from and yet influencing the patterns of real life, reveal a close connection between romantic love and social advancement. The growth of this romantic tradition is an important aspect of the European Renascence and one given an increasing emphasis from the eleventh century onward.

But while it is true that we can trace the revival of the West from 1000 A.D., it would be quite wrong to conclude that Asia had ceased to be in the ascendant. The gap between European and Asian accomplishment might be lessening, but it was still there, and in the military sense Islam was to have more than one revival, its threat renewed and its influence reasserted. Its immediate pressure ended abruptly, in about 1250, with the Mongol threat to the Muslim's homeland. These Mongol tribes came from Siberia and swept first into Northern China. Under their leader Jenghiz Khan, the nomads captured Peking and learned something of Chinese technology — gunpowder included. Thus re-equipped and very ably led, the successors of Jenghiz, operating initially from Mongolia, swept across Russia and into Hungary, but then moved eastward again where Kublai Khan made himself Emperor of China in 1280, founding the Yuan Dynasty which lasted until 1368. Another army subdued Persia and Syria, and yet another, in 1505, made a conquest of India. During the

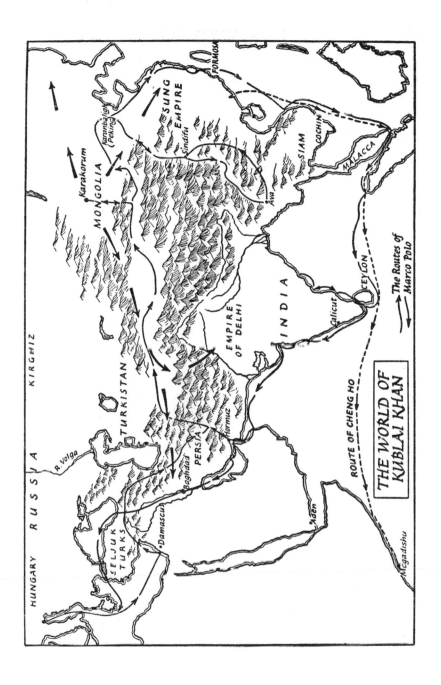

THE WORLD OF KUBLAI KHAN

The Routes of Marco Polo

ROUTE OF CHENG HO

RUSSIA

HUNGARY

KIRGHIZ

R. Volga

SELJUK TURKS

Damascus

Baghdad

PERSIA

Hormuz

TURKISTAN

MONGOLIA

Karakorum

Karambalegh (Peking)

SUNG EMPIRE

Sindafu

Ava

FORMOSA

SIAM

COCHIN

MALACCA

EMPIRE OF DELHI

INDIA

Calicut

CEYLON

Aden

Megadishu

thirteenth century, the Mongols actually drove the Ottoman Turks out of Turkistan. It was this Turkish group, established in Asia Minor, which finally took Constantinople, in 1453, and went on from there to conquer the Balkans, Hungary, Egypt, and North Africa. Being Muslim and fairly recent converts, the Ottoman Turks gave Islam its last burst of energy and fanaticism. Their establishment of what we now call Turkey, with a revived naval activity in the Mediterranean, put Christendom again on the defensive. In doing so, they ended a period of peaceful relationships between East and West which had lasted roughly from 1245 to 1345. For the Mongols or Tartars had so unified and pacified the world of their conquest that travelers could journey safely between Europe and China. There was at one time an Italian archbishop at Peking, Genoese merchants in India, and Franciscan friars in Persia. Of the travelers of this period, one at least has provided us with a vivid account of all he saw. Coming from Venice, Marco Polo had no reason to be ashamed of his own city, but China, he found, was something far greater. As a friar wrote who visited Canton at a later date, it was "a city as big as three Venices . . . and all Italy hath not the amount of craft that this one city hath." There was much to be learned in the Far East, where fourteenth-century Japan was at its zenith of achievement. What the West did learn at this time was the science of navigation, in which China held a considerable lead. Chinese oceanic adventure had been notable from the third century to the tenth, but it dwindled proportionately as the Arabs became more active. From the end of the twelfth century, it revived and there began the last brief period of Chinese supremacy in the Indian Ocean. According to Needham, it brought Chinese vessels to Borneo, the Philippines, Ceylon, Malabar, and even to East Africa. Behind all this activity lie the Chinese triumphs in cartography and mathematics. From the first to the fifth centuries there was considerable progress, but it was after contact with the Arabs, and under the Sung Dynasty (960–1279), that the vital discoveries were made. First of these, in the tenth century, was the magnetic compass. It is first described in a work dating from 1116. From 1137 dates one of the earliest known maps, carved in stone, but by 1155 maps were actually being printed. By 1400 the Chinese maps reflect the information they derived from Arab, Persian, and Turkish contacts. Then, in 1405, Cheng Ho went on his first voyage of discovery. His ostensible mission was to pursue the last emperor of the Yuan Dynasty, who was believed to have fled to the Nanyang (Southeast Asia). With a fleet of sixty-two ships and 37,000 men, Cheng Ho visited Java, Palembang, Siam, Ceylon, Calicut, Cochin, Hormuz, Aden, and Mogadishu. On these and subsequent voyages, Cheng Ho made no profit and incurred heavy losses from sickness. Nothing much came of his efforts. Moreover, there is at least symbolic significance in the fact that he was a eunuch. His achievements were, however, described in accounts published between 1434 and 1451. These were perfectly accessible to Arabs established at Canton, through whom the knowledge gained may have penetrated to Europe.

As navigators, the Arabs were far from negligible themselves, more especially in using astronomic means to fix their latitude. But the tradition was to linger in Europe that the great inventions came from China. Writes Purchas in the *Pilgrimes*:

Others therefore looke further into the East whence the Light of the Sunne and arts have seemed first to arise to our World; and will have Marco Polo the Venetian above three hundred yeares since to have brought it and of Manga (which wee now call China) into Italy. True it is that the most magnified arts have there been borne, Printing, Gunnes, and perhaps this also of the Compasse, which the Portugals at their first entry of the Indian Seas found amongst the Mores, together with Quadrants to observe both the Heavens and Earth.

We have some reason to believe that Purchas was essentially right.

13

RENASCENT EUROPE

THE INFLUENCE of the East, furnishing Europe with its means of resisting further Oriental pressure, came in largely through Venice and Genoa. Other Italian cities played their parts, but the two named were those most ideally placed: Venice, as near Germany as a Mediterranean port could be, and Genoa, placed almost as favorably on the other side of the Italian peninsula. These were the main termini of the trade with Asia, their only rivals being Pisa (until 1284), Florence (through Leghorn after 1421), and Marseilles. The Venetians owed their early prosperity to the Byzantine Empire, of which they once formed a part. The first three Crusades gave them footholds in Sidon (1102), and Tyre (1123), while one result of the Fourth Crusade, for which they had provided the shipping, was to leave them in possession of islands which commanded the Adriatic, the Aegean, the Sea of Marmora, and the Black Sea. Had all the crusaders come from Austria and Germany, Venice might have had something like a monopoly of the Eastern trade. But many of the crusaders came, with Raymond of Toulouse, from France. It was the Genoese who helped him capture Tripoli in Syria. There they gained their own foothold, while also sharing with the Venetians in the trade of Sidon and Tyre. In North Africa, by contrast, they had their own trade, almost unopposed, with Tunis and Tripoli. They had used Sardinia as their steppingstone to the Barbary Coast, building up for themselves a strong trading position in the western Mediterranean and a traditional alliance with Portugal and Spain. But the more

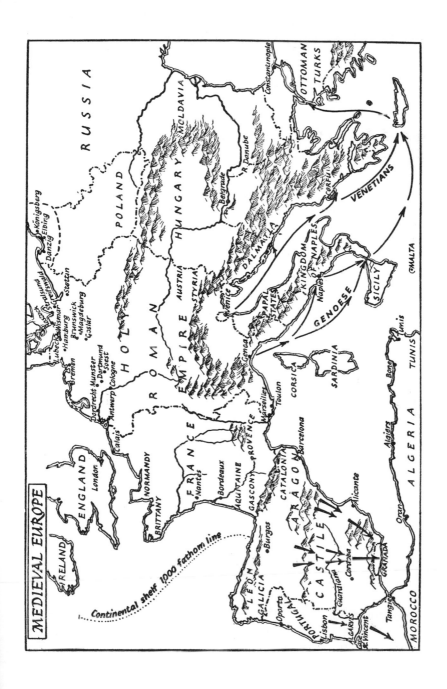

MEDIEVAL EUROPE

valuable trade came directly from the East and especially, at this time, through the Black Sea. Entry into this trade brought the Genoese into direct rivalry with the Venetians. They lost the first round when the Venetians captured Candia in 1206, but they pressed on to form their own trading posts at Galata and Kaffa. Rivalry became intense with almost incessant conflict from 1253 to 1380. It was in 1298 that Marco Polo came to Genoa as a prisoner of war, thereafter dictating his memoirs while in prison. From these and from other sources, the Genoese learned what trade might be possible with China. In a final effort to eliminate their trade rivals, they attacked Venice itself, where they were decisively beaten in 1380. As a result of this setback, the Genoese had to withdraw from the Eastern trade to some extent, and concentrate more on the trade westward, in which they were the specialists, a tendency which was confirmed by the fall of Constantinople in 1453. This left the Venetians with the bigger share of the trade, but it also left them to face the Turks, with whom their losing conflict continued until 1716.

Having learned their navigation, as the Venetians had done, in the East, the Genoese turned their attention to the West. From as early as 1317 a Genoese family, the Pessagni, held Admiral's rank in Portugal. Antonio Uso di Mare explored a part of the West African coast in 1454. And from Genoa, finally, came Christopher Columbus (born 1451), as also, for that matter, John Cabot. It was no accident that these Italian seamen should have entered the service of Spain or England, for Genoa was in no position to help them. Its glory had departed, leaving to others the legacy of its skill in nautical astronomy. Of what did this skill consist? First of all, a merchant of Pisa, Leonardo Fibonacci, had learned, in North Africa, the Indian system of numerals, with the value of the digit or nought depending upon its position in relation to the rest. He explained the system in a work published in 1201, from which date mathematics — including astronomy — became technically feasible.

By 1269 the pivoted compass was in use, and by about 1300 the needle had been attached to the card; nor was it of much value until this had been done. Without the compass, the marine quadrant (or astrolabe) and nocturnal (both for ascertaining latitude) were inaccurate, but these afterwards came into general use. With a table for the sun's declination and a correction for the altitude of the Pole Star, with a log line and hourglass, the fifteenth-century navigator was not ill-equipped. For the Mediterranean, moreover, he had reasonable charts, the portolani, first mentioned in 1270, and based only on estimated distances but accurate, nevertheless, in broad outline, by about 1350. The same relative accuracy was extended to the East in the famous Catalan portolano of 1375. Among Italian seamen the art of navigation was beginning to emerge.

It was in Portugal that the Italian navigators met the mariners of the Atlantic coast. These were pupils of a very different school, men who had learned, not navigation but seamanship. Whereas the Mediterranean sailor specialized in recognizing the outline of every headland from every angle, supplementing this knowledge with chart, compass, and astrolabe, the northern sailor, unable to rely on seeing anything, felt his way with the deep-sea lead. He had little respect for the rowing galley as derived from the ancient world. Of what use was a vessel being rowed at an average of two knots, with four and a half knots as its maximum speed, in tidal waters such as are known to the English or Dutch? In a six-knot tide the seaman needed knowledge and sail area and could regard the oar as a waste of time. Whether in tidal waters or not, the northern ship had to have stout timbers and cordage, canvas to last and anchors to hold. The emphasis was on a different set of qualities in ships and seamen alike. For oceanic voyages, such as the Genoese were dreaming about, the need was to combine the two types of nautical skill in vessels that combined the two traditions of ship design. Nor was that enough in itself. For behind the shipwright and seaman there needed to be a sense of purpose and drive, emotions of gale force pent up for centuries, a whole world of impatience and resentment. It was just this head of steam that the Portuguese and Spanish could provide.

Take Portugal first. It centered originally on Oporto, a port and military frontier post in the war against Islam. The men from this region captured Lisbon from the Moors in 1147, and then pushed slowly southward, driving their opponents ahead of them. By about 1250 they had reached the sea between Cape St. Vincent and the Guadiana. They had a trade agreement with England in 1294 and similar treaties with France and Flanders. A revolution brought a new dynasty to the throne in 1383. John of Aviz (1383–1433) established a strong monarchy, encouraged trade, and clinched the English alliance by marrying Philippa, daughter of John of Gaunt (Duke of Lancaster). His five famous sons were thus half English, being cousins, in fact, of Henry V. Third of these was Henry the Navigator, who became Governor of Algarve in 1418. His province was the southwestern corner of Europe, and he made his headquarters at Sagres (Cape St. Vincent). There, on a desolate promontory, with the Atlantic on three sides, he built himself a palace complete with chapel, observatory, and study. Nearby, at Lagos, was his dockyard and arsenal. A bachelor, abstainer, ascetic, and recluse, he set himself to improve Portuguese shipbuilding, cartography, and navigation. Under his direction, successive voyages of exploration reached Madeira (1418), Cape Bojador (1434), Cape Verde (1445), and Sierra Leone (1455). Henry himself died in 1460, but the work continued, the Cape of Good Hope being located by Diaz in 1486.

On the Portuguese left, in the war against the Moors, was the Christian kingdom of Castile. The Castilians had their first success in 718, and made Burgos their first capital. Pushing southward, they captured Toledo in 1085. On their left again was the kingdom of Aragon, which absorbed Catalonia by marriage, and which reached Alicante in 1179. Alfonso VII of Leon and Castile took Cordoba in 1144, but it was lost again. The struggle against Islam continued, and in 1479 the crown of Castile came to Isabella, who married Ferdinand of Aragon, and the two kingdoms were more or less united. Muslim Spain had by this time dwindled to the one kingdom of Granada, against which the combined Spanish efforts were now unleashed. Granada capitulated in 1492. All Jews were expelled from Castile and Aragon in the same year, giving additional point to the title of "Catholic Monarchs," in which style Pope Alexander VI saluted Isabella and Ferdinand. A reconquest of territory for Christendom, which occupied Portugal for a century and a half, had taken Spain eight hundred years to complete. Such was the momentum of the Crusade that the Spaniards were unable to stop at their newly acquired coastline. With the aid and leadership of Columbus, a Genoese navigator, they broke through the barrier of the Atlantic and, in 1492, discovered the New World. Shortly afterwards (1497), Vasco da Gama rounded the Cape and reached India by sea. With these two events the world may be said to have entered a new phase of history.

The Portuguese and Spanish achievements were, of course, quite different in kind; the former the result of methodical planning, the latter due to a brilliant shot in the dark. They were interdependent, however, Columbus being encouraged by the Portuguese example and Vasco da Gama following in Columbus's wake. For our present purpose, we can treat these discoveries as a single event, its importance generally realized by 1500. For the Spanish, it was an incident in the war against Islam, as Columbus himself made clear in his report which read as follows:

> . . . after your Highnesses had given an end to the war with the Moors who reigned in Europe, and had finished it in the very great city of Granada, where in this present year . . . I saw

the royal banners of your Highnesses placed on the towers of
Alhambra . . . Your Highnesses . . . who are enemies to the
sect of Mahomet and to all idolatries and heresies, resolved . . .
etc. . . . and ordered that I should not go by land to the eastward, as had been customary, but that I should go by way of
the west, whither up to this day, we do not know for certain
that anyone has gone . . .

Thus, after having turned out all the Jews from all your kingdoms and lordships . . . your Highnesses give orders to me . . .

To Ferdinand and Isabella (if not to Columbus), it was all
part of the Crusade.

With that interpretation we need not quarrel. Catholic fanaticism had used Atlantic seamanship and Mediterranean navigation to achieve a startling result. More significant, however, for
the present theme, are two aspects of the central event; the status
of the navigator, and the nature of that movement we describe
as the Renascence. Medieval Europe had something in the
nature of a caste system on Oriental lines; one which tended to
give political and military leadership to the nobility, learning to
the clergy, and financial ability to the merchants. During the
later Middle Ages, this specialization began to crumble. As the
cities became more important, and the universities less ecclesias-
tical in atmosphere, there emerged the type of man in whom
administrative and scholarly interests were combined with business ability and technical skill. Prince Henry the Navigator
came near to being such a man, and Columbus himself came
nearer still. Brought up as a wool corder and weaver, but gaining
some early experience at sea, Columbus became a chartmaker,
taught himself Castilian and Latin, engaged in business as a
merchant, fought in an action between Genoese and French
ships, learned seamanship from the Portuguese, and "read the
canonical offices like a churchman." He ended as a Spanish
nobleman, admiral, governor, and viceroy. What he was not,
and never became, was a nautical astronomer. It was in this

sense that Vasco da Gama was the better navigator, and he
ended, remember, by taking a Moorish pilot.

The process by which the mariner became a scholar and a
gentleman was more gradual than some students have supposed.
As slow was the development of the well read soldier, as exemplified by Shakespeare's welshman in *Henry* V. And slowest
of all, perhaps, was the engineer's and artist's rise to social recognition and knightly rank. But the means of ascent were there.
The language of learning was not impossibly abstruse, the elements of mathematics were not beyond reach, and the gates of
privilege were not barred against ability. The driving force behind the individual's daring and effort was dependent on two
factors: the means available for gaining wealth, and the mecha-
nism by which wealth could be translated into social prestige.
Each European country had a nobility and a gentry held in special respect, and endowed with hereditary responsibilities and
privilege. Each country had, moreover, the legal process of
ennoblement. Nicely adjusted, this could develop all the powers
of the dynamo, at once refusing the easy admission that would
make the entry valueless, and yet yielding to any pressure which
should develop the force required.

In close support of the middle-class aspirant to knightly
honors — the Drake or Shakespeare of the day — was the boatswain or sergeant, a peculiarly European character who combines
handiness and literacy, and who forms the indispensable link
between the officer and his men. No true equivalent could arise
in countries where literacy was the guarded privilege of the few.
It is questionable whether there is a true Asian equivalent now.

Come now to the Renascence. There is a sense in which that
movement made Columbus's discovery possible. There is another and more important sense in which Columbus brought the
movement into being. For 1500, or thereabouts, represents the
moment at which the West began to claim its new ascendancy
over the East. It is a question of whether the claim was alto-

gether justified. Premature or not, it was certainly made. And the symbol of the claim was the discovery of the Indies and the circumnavigation of the world in 1519–22. These voyages raised the morale of the West in exactly the same way as would a successful landing on the moon today. They, the Europeans, had accomplished something which no Asian had even dared attempt. More than that, they had gone beyond the achievements of Greece and Rome. How far they realized the last fact may be open to doubt, but they certainly felt at least more on a level with the heroes of antiquity. Recognizing that the Classical period represented, first and foremost, an age in which Western superiority over the East had been assumed, they sought to revive its literature, science, and art. The Latin phrase, the Greek column, the nude statue, and the revived theater were all so many symbols of that recovered or returning supremacy. Rome was, for various reasons, easier to imitate than Greece, and the emphasis was heavily laid upon its republican virtues and imperial dignity. As time went on, there were men about whose manners and tastes were more Roman than those ever encountered in Rome itself. If most imitations fell short of the original, there were clearly some that went beyond it.

As against that, the Oriental influence upon Europe was far too deep to be erased. Classical palaces might replace medieval castles, but the architecture was more easily altered than the society it was to frame and symbolize. The churches and monasteries, the festivals and fasts, the vestments and regalia, the mysteries and morals — all these remained obstinately medieval. So did the rituals of kingship and lordship, of knighthood and heraldry, of banner and banneret, chivalry and fief. Cities likewise had and kept their own medievalism, and universities as much again. But from 1500 the trend was away from all such things. Cervantes could laugh at knighthood, and Erasmus think the papacy at least mildly amusing. The blazon on the surcoat dwindled to the demure escutcheon on the carriage door.

Universities came to matter less and monasteries ceased to matter at all. Each of the specifically international institutions, formed to unify Christendom against the infidel, began to disappear or weaken, giving place to things more national, secular, and commercial. While this is true, however, many medievalisms survived the Renascence, survived the eighteenth century, and overlapped with the Gothic revival. After years of neglect, they found themselves suddenly in the van of progress. What had been unfashionable was now again the rage.

When the threat of Islam had been real and imminent, the West had formed a kind of unity. From about 1500 all unity gave way to national interests, each king thinking only of himself. One aspect of this new feeling of security was that disintegration of Christendom which we call the Reformation. As a disciplined and centralized organization, the Church had been formed as a bulwark against Islam. As the external threat dwindled, the internal authority was lessened and (in the countries furthest from the Muslims) was entirely lost. It might seem that the total impact of the West should have been lessened by its internal conflict. But it was this rivalry which was to add weight to the whole offensive. As each nation found its moment for expansion, it spent itself in gaining an empire. The next would then pass through the position gained, launching a fresh assault on some further objective, which would become the baseline again for the next advance. The process is a familiar one in war, and there is the further incentive, as between nations, that what one fails to conquer, another will. There had been much of the same pattern in the former movement of expansion. On the other side, there was now a repetition of the parts played on previous occasions by Carthage and Byzantium. The defense of Constantinople had kept the Arabs from advancing up the Danube, compelling them to make their flanking march through Africa. It was now the Turks whose holding action prevented any direct attack on Persia. They were entrenched not only in

Asia Minor, but in North Africa. They had literally taken the place of Carthage. And it was largely because of them that the nations of the West expanded as they did, westward across the Atlantic, and eastward round the Cape.

The story of the Turks is mainly, for our present purpose, that of the Ottoman Navy. After the fall of Constantinople, the Turks broke up the established patterns of trade, and kept the Black Sea for themselves. It was not their object to interrupt all trade between Asia and Europe — nor was there, in fact, more than a temporary disorganization. What they wanted was to secure the trade for themselves, which would mean establishing their own sea power in the Mediterranean. For this they would need a fleet. No such force existed before 1470, in which year Mohammed II began his operations in the Adriatic. Venice collapsed, but the Turks had sturdy opponents in the Knights of St. John, whose headquarters were on the island of Rhodes, and who operated a formidable fleet of their own. The first attack on Rhodes was beaten off in 1480, but the Turks tried again in 1522. After months of fighting, the knights capitulated, leaving the eastern Mediterranean in Turkish hands, but re-establishing themselves (1530) at a new base in Malta. In the western Mediterranean, a similar ascendancy had been established by another Muslim power, that of Algiers. The Moors driven from Spain had there set up another naval base from which the great Admiral Barbarossa operated against the Genoese. Having subdued one corsair base at Tunis (1535), the emperor Charles V attempted to capture Algiers in 1541, but failed, suffering heavy casualties. Then, in 1565, Sultan Suleiman launched an expedition against Malta. But here the Turks were defeated, the knights holding out until a relieving force arrived. Sequel to this success was the concentration of Christian fleets — Papal, Spanish, Venetian, and Genoese — to save Cyprus. In that they failed, but they were afterwards led against the Turks (1571) by Don John of Austria. At Lepanto the Turkish fleet was al-

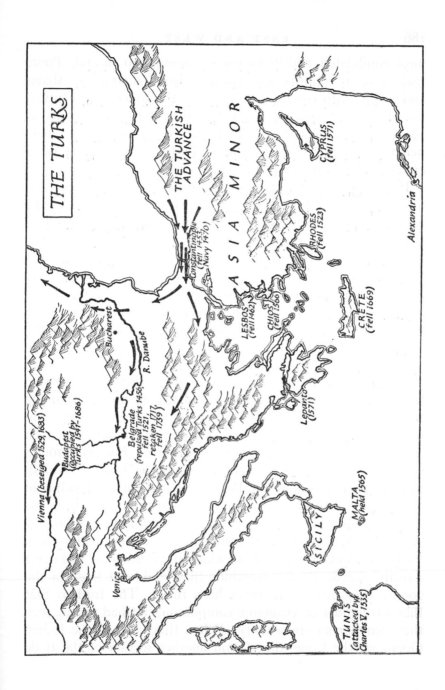

THE TURKS

THE TURKISH ADVANCE

ASIA MINOR

Constantinople (Fell 1453, Navy 1470)

CYPRUS (Fell 1571)

RHODES (Fell 1523)

LESBOS (Fell 1462)

CHIOS (Fell 1560)

CRETE (Fell 1669)

Lepanto (1571)

Bucharest

R. Danube

Belgrade (repulsed Turks 1456, Fell 1521, retaken 1717, Fell 1739)

Budapest (occupied by Turks 1541–1686)

Vienna (besieged 1529, 1683)

Venice

SICILY

MALTA (held 1565)

TUNIS (attacked by Charles V, 1535)

Alexandria

most annihilated, and its supremacy brought to an end. Pirate raids were to continue for centuries, based mainly on Algiers and Tunis, with corsairs still active in the nineteenth century, but these were more of a nuisance than a threat. As late as 1817, a Tunisian corsair appeared anachronistically in the Channel, taking a prize within sight of Dover. This sort of thing ended only with the French conquest of Algeria in 1830.

It is against this background that we must see the expansion of Europe. The European peoples who were placed on the eastern frontiers — the Poles, Hungarians, Austrians, and Italians — spent their renascent energies in containing these last Muslim efforts. They fought for centuries, Vienna being besieged by the Turks as late as 1683. They received little help from the remainder of Christendom and the French even worked against them on occasion. Why was this? Why were the Turks not taken seriously? Why was there no effective call for European unity against Islam? There were two basic reasons why no such appeal could succeed. In the first place, the prize for which they had initially been fighting was no longer there. The Eastern trade — at once the victor's prize and the means of sustaining the conflict — was dwindling in value. The axis of the previous conflicts between East and West had been the trade route, each side seeking to control the bigger share of it. But these routes were now of dwindling importance, not because of Turkish intolerance, but because the Portuguese had cut the pipeline in the middle. The theory was once upheld that the Portuguese were compelled to round Africa because their old trade route had gone with the fall of Constantinople. But this had been a Venetian and Genoese trade in which the Portuguese had never directly shared. It was something they could not lose, for the good reason that it had never been theirs. The truth is that they were under no economic compulsion, but had merely seen their commercial opportunity. When they reached the Indian Ocean via the Cape, they found another section of the trade route over which the Turks and Italians were quarreling. From Malabar to the Red Sea and Persian Gulf, it was in the hands of Egyptians and Arabs. From Malabar to Malacca, it was in the hands of the Indians. From Malacca eastward, it was in the hands of Malays and Chinese. Affonso de Albuquerque saw at once what had to be done. He took Ormuz (1509), Goa (1510), and Malacca (1511). Aden he failed to take, and its capture was in fact needless; the system being improved later, however, by the occupation of Colombo and Macao. From Goa the trade was deflected round the Cape to Lisbon. At other points it continued as before, but now in Portuguese ships or under Portuguese control. The native shipowners were ruined, many of them, and the Arabs largely left India. But at what had been the western end of the trade route, it was the Venetians who were ruined, and the Turks who were driven to piracy. It is true that Venetian trade recovered somewhat from the mid-sixteenth century, but for the moment, the Venetians' trade was gone. Their wealth had dried up at the source. Except in a minor way, they were no longer in business.

But that is not the whole of the truth. For, local conflicts apart, the momentum of the East had been lost. The Ottoman Turks had nothing behind them. It is true that in India and Persia there was a high level of culture. It is true that Chinese civilization had spread even to Korea, Japan, and Malaya. But an Indian scholar has pointed out that Eastern civilization was not as good as it looked and was declining even in 1000 A.D.

Let us have another look and try to see below the surface of things. We find that all is not so well with Asia as a superficial observer might imagine. India and China, the two cradles of ancient civilization, are in trouble. Their troubles are not merely those of invasion from outside, but the more real troubles which sap away the inner life and strength. The Arabs in the west have come to the end of their great days.
. . . Everywhere in Asia the old cultured races seem to be

shrinking. They have lost confidence in themselves, and are on
the defensive. New people arise, strong and full of energy, who
conquer these old races in Asia, and even threaten Europe. But
they do not bring a new wave of civilization with them or a new
impetus for culture. The old races slowly civilize them and assimilate their conquerors.

So we see a great change coming over Asia. While the old civilizations continue and the fine arts flourish and there are refine-
ments in luxury, the pulse of civilization weakens, and the breath
of life seems to grow less and less. For long they are to continue.
There is no definite break or end to them, except in Arabia and
Central Asia when the Mongols came. In China and India,
there is a slow fading off, till the old civilization becomes like a
painted picture, beautiful to look at from a distance, but lifeless;
and if you come near to it, you see that the white ants have been
at it.*

So writes Jawaharlal Nehru, vividly describing a decadence
for which he does not attempt to account. The basic causes
may be biological. The more immediate cause was, of course,
excessive taxation. The Mogul emperors took a third of the gross
produce, and worked on the theory that all land belonged to the
crown; as a result of which vast tracts went out of cultivation.
But what of the symptoms? There was much repetition but
little originality in thought. There was much study of texts,
many efforts to interpret and explain older works of literature.
Works of art were either imitative or grotesque. There grew
up, finally, a defensive outlook, a sort of self-imprisonment
through which stagnation became more stagnant still.

If India's greater days were past, the same can be said of
China. There the Golden Age of the Sung Dynasty, the autumn
period of Chinese culture, ended in 1279. Great painters and
poets were still at work in the south, but revealed their fore-
knowledge of all that was to come.

* Jawaharlal Nehru, *Glimpses of World History* (London, 1942), p. 179.

But no one knew better than these old masters in the art of life that theirs was the end, and not the beginning, of a golden age dying with every sunset, passing with every twilight shiver among the willows, and the tolling of each vesper bell. It was the gla mour of gardens fading on nightfall, the vision that mocked the pale realities of the world.*

The rule of the Mongols had a grandeur of its own, and they at least re-unified the country. They taxed the peasants so heavily, however, that there was a resistance movement. After the revolution, the peasant leader became first emperor of the Ming Dynasty (1368–1644).

. . . for centuries there had been a constant struggle between the Southern or idealist type of mind, and the Northern or practical. So long as the balance between the two was maintained, China flourished. But when in A.D. 1421, the Capital was trans ferred by the Mings from Nanking to Peking and the Northern or Confucian party finally triumphed, decay set in . . .†

The great days for China were over.

If there was an Oriental country which flowered after 1500, it was Persia. The great period for Persian miniatures and bookbinding began in 1397 and reached its highest achievements at Tabriz in 1524–76.

In the second half of the [16th] century there was a marked decline in the production of fine books. The energy and cooperation necessary for the making of one of the great Timurid or early Safarid books seems to have been lacking . . . Seventeenth century painting is . . . dull and repetitive. By the eighteenth century all quality was lost.‡

* L. Cranmer-Byng, *op. cit.*, p. 187.
† *Ibid.*, p. 111.
‡ T. J. Arberry (ed.), *op. cit.*, quoted from D. Barrett, p. 138.

On rather parallel lines, the finest Isfahan carpets date from 1502, one of the more famous being made in 1539. The decline began in 1576, the same designs being used, but the craftsmanship becoming more slovenly and inexpert. Later carpets, after about 1880, are merely copies, treated with wood ash to give the illusion of age. So even Persia, with its national revival under Shah Tahmasp, had expended its energies before 1600. Japan was another Eastern country which flowered rather late, its zenith of achievement being in the fourteenth century, but here again there was decay, manifest at latest in the seventeenth century. More firmly, perhaps, than any other people, did the Japanese attempt to exclude all new ideas. And defensiveness of this kind must reflect, beyond question, a conscious feeling of inferiority. Considered as a whole, the great world of Asia had ceased to expand or develop. It lay as a passive target for the onset of the West.

14

THE WEST GOES EAST

WITH THE REALIZATION that the Atlantic is a highway, not merely a barrier, the West fairly came to life. Whether to the East or West Indies, the route was, in its early stages, very much the same, with Lisbon as the ideal port of departure. It was the moment of opportunity for the Portuguese, one which lasted until 1590. Their period in the East was brilliant while it lasted, but it could not, in the nature of things, last for long. There were too few of them, and their numbers soon began to dwindle, the multiplication of their trading posts being accompanied by an appalling rate of casualties by shipwreck and scurvy. They were not conquerors so much as traders and missionaries, and their empire was overshadowed from the beginning by the power of Spain. But theirs was the first impact made by a renascent Europe upon Asia, and it is they, not the Spanish, who prepared the way for the other nations, partly by a demonstration of how not to do it. Their first successes depended upon the use of cannon and firearms against people who could handle neither. Their seamanship was by no means equal to their commercial ambitions, and it was perhaps as missionaries that they made their deepest impression. But here too their success was very limited indeed.

Bringing with them their atmosphere of fervent Catholicism, their first intention was to crush the Muslims and convert the Hindus and Buddhists to Christianity. In neither plan were they successful. They strengthened Islam insofar as it symbolized resistance to the European — the Malays, for example, turned

Muslim, many of them, as they became aware of the Portuguese approach. And while Hindus would often express a mild interest in Christianity, they were not of the stuff of which Catholics are made. "To the Hindu, God is everywhere, and may be approached through any of His names and attributes, whether as Shiva, Vishnu or Sri Krishna." They would have added Jesus to their pantheon without much argument, but that was not what the Jesuits had in mind. Converts were few, but the Portuguese settled at Goa and Malacca, married Indian, Malay, and Chinese women, and bred a race of Eurasian Catholics — the Goanese seamen and native clerks who are still to be found in Eastern seaports. Whatever the virtues of these native Christians, their basic defect was in their lack of devotion toward a Portugal they had never seen. Their loyalty was to Colombo or Macao, and to their own community, and they were not otherwise to be relied upon as a garrison. Insofar as they came to be absorbed in the local population, they illustrated the weakness in Alexander the Great's idealism (see page 74). The breeding of Greek Persians or Portuguese Malays must depend upon the two races being in roughly equal numbers. A small minority of invaders will be merely absorbed, or remain at best a small minority. One result of the Portuguese invasion of the East was to establish that India was proof against Catholicism and that intermarriage with Asians must produce in the end a progeny which is essentially Asian.

The other result was to prove, during the period of missionary activity in Japan (1549–1638), that there too the Dominicans and Jesuits could not succeed beyond a certain point. The final Japanese reaction was to eject them and exclude all Europeans in the future. Japan was closed, in fact, to all foreign influence for the next two hundred years. For that period, as H. G. Wells points out, "the Japanese were as completely cut off from the rest of the world as though they lived upon another planet." On this same subject, Michael Edwardes writes as follows:

The door was closed. All that a hundred years of contact with the West had given Japan was firearms, tobacco, sponge-cake, venereal disease and some new tortures from the methods of the Inquisition. The memory of the Christian Century was to be a fence against the resumption of relations with the Europeans. Japan had fought her first battle against the West.*

We shall remember, however, that this isolation represented a conscious inferiority, and that its immediate results were disastrous. It was during this period that Russia occupied territories which the Japanese could easily have secured for themselves.

Portugal was absorbed by Spain in 1580, recovering its independence at a later period. But the Spanish made no attempt to sail eastward and use the Portuguese bases as the starting points for their own attack. They were fully committed to exploiting the New World as a basis for developing their position in the Old. They were not, and never really became, a commercial people. With a pastoral and agricultural background, they provided some of the best troops in sixteenth-century Europe; but trade they left very largely to others. Dynastic intermarriage having brought Spain into political association with Austria, Germany, and the Netherlands, it was to these other countries that the Spanish looked for industrial, commercial, and financial cooperation. Most essential to their economy were the Netherlands, the Low Country cities where their wool, shipped from Burgos, was turned into cloth. The fact that the Spanish empire included, for a time, both the Netherlands and Portugal was to prove of great importance. For it gave the Flemish merchants their insight into the Eastern trade. Antwerp was the port of the weaving industry, and this also became the distributing center for spices and silks and ivories. The textile and trading centers of the southern provinces had relied for shipping on the

* Michael Edwardes, *Asia in the European Age: 1498–1955* (London, 1961), p. 44.

Hansa towns of the Baltic, but from about 1425, the Hansa declined and a new shipping industry grew up in the northern provinces, and especially round Amsterdam, Rotterdam, and The Hague. Flemish shipbuilding and shipowning fitted for a time into the Spanish system. So that the Spanish, insofar as they intervened at all in the East, did so merely for the eventual benefit of the Dutch.

Among the other Western nations on the Atlantic coast, the obvious successor to a declining Portugal was, to all appearances, France. The French, like the Spanish, have a Mediterranean as well as an Atlantic shore. But they had at this time many of the assets the Portuguese lacked. They stood opposed to the Spanish empire, disclaiming any part in its crusade against Islam. They had a considerable population, such as Portugal had never had, and some claims to leadership in both arts and arms. But the development of France as a nation came late in the Middle Ages, as the result of English aggression, and came later still to the Atlantic seaports. Normandy fronted on a Channel which the English tended to dominate, and with Calais in English hands until 1558. Havre was not founded until 1517. Brittany, with its ports on the Atlantic, was not united with France until 1491, nor fully annexed until 1532. Gascony and Bordeaux had been an English possession until 1451, not fully absorbed until 1500; and even after that, the *trade* was still carried in English ships. As for Provence and Marseilles, they came to the French crown in 1481; nor was Toulon founded until 1494. Although the Bretons were fairly warlike on their own, France was not unified until about 1500. And French naval enterprise, when it began to develop, was mainly directed toward the Mediterranean. It was only the Turkish alliance that allowed France to attempt its ineffectual blow at England in 1545; and the first French naval victories, against Spain, date from 1635–38. France was generally in no position to exploit the situation in the East.

Of the major countries facing the Atlantic, there was only one left — England. And whereas Great Britain came into existence in 1603, England had been a maritime power since 1204. It was in that year that the Angevin's loss of Normandy made Britain, politically, an island. King John's reaction was to found the naval dockyard at Portsmouth, form the Royal Navy (1204), and entrust the Straits of Dover to the care of the Cinque Ports. These moves were mainly defensive, an acknowledgment of the fact that the French frontier had moved up to the Channel, but he simultaneously began the move westward and outward. For concentrating efforts toward Wales and Ireland, he created the port of Liverpool in 1207. He took a large army to Ireland in 1210, and subdued the Isle of Man at the same time. By 1211, he began a systematic conquest of North Wales, which was resumed by Edward I in 1277. Edward occupied Anglesey, and established the castles and boroughs of Conway, Caernarvon and Beaumaris — all so many steppingstones toward Ireland. The effect of much thirteenth-century effort was to form a strong English bridgehead round Dublin, with trade routes to Pembroke and Bristol, to Chester and Liverpool. Efforts to control Ireland met at first with indifferent success, and were not completed until 1601. It is true that the Elizabethan conquest of Ireland was a defensive move, to prevent its use by the Spanish. But it was also a preliminary to overseas expansion, for which purpose Irish ports, food supplies, and manpower were equally vital. To suppose that English expansion began under Charles I is completely mistaken. There had already been a dress rehearsal, with the Irish reluctantly playing their role as Indians. It was in Ireland that men like Drake and Raleigh gained their notions of Empire. It was there that the problem of how to treat the natives was first seriously discussed; and it is among the tragedies of history that it was never solved. There is nothing in the world as infectious as an Irish accent, which any visitor is liable to pick up in ten days. To become completely Irish in outlook takes a little longer — two generations, perhaps, or possibly three. It has

SCOTLAND

ULSTER

CONNAUGHT
IRELAND
Dublin

ISLE OF
MAN

York · Hull

Conway Liverpool
ANGLESEY Beaumaris (1207)
Caernarvon · Chester

MUNSTER   Waterford
Cork

Welsh
Mountains

Pembroke

Bristol   London

Southampton Portsmouth
Exeter   (1204) CINQUE PORTS
Plymouth

DEFENSE

DEFENSE

Calais · Bruges
FLANDERS

GUERNSEY

JERSEY NORMANDY

R. Seine

BRITTANY

**THE WESTWARD
MOVEMENT**

been the English fate to garrison Ireland with dependable settlers, always as a small minority, and see them become — as
medieval administrators complained — more Irish than the Irish.
It was only after the Reformation that a religious barrier separated the garrison from the populace, the Irish using their Catholicism — whether retained or acquired — as a means of putting their resentment on record. There grew up, thenceforward,
from 1601, the peculiar relationships which existed between the
Protestant settlers and the Catholic peasantry "beyond the Pale";
between the English landlord and the native tenant, between
Dublin Castle and Irish legend. And while the Protestant land-
owners, from the Wellesleys down to Bernard Shaw, were not
precisely English, they were unlikely to make common cause
with the population at large. It was from them that the English
and Scots derived their habits of imperialism, their tradition of
refusing to intermarry and their affectionate regard for people
to whom they flatly denied any status of equality.

For the reasons described, England stood next to Spain in the
race for oceanic expansion. For a time it seemed that the Dutch
could be more formidable than the English, but their effort was
shortlived. There were too few of them. It was they, nevertheless, who first followed in the tracks of the Portuguese. Reaching the Malay Archipelago in 1595, they formed their East India
Company in 1602, and proceeded to annex Bantam, the Moluc-
cas, and Java. Whereas the Portuguese had taken over the
middle section of the trade route, the Dutch — in evicting them
— went on to grasp the far end of it. They completed their
Eastern conquests by the capture of Ceylon and Malacca, trading as far as Formosa and Japan. Having learned something
from the Portuguese mistakes, the Dutch made no effort to
spread Christianity. All they sought was a monopoly of the spice
trade. One effect of their activities, and of their exclusive policy,
was to deflect English effort away from the Spice Islands and
toward India. Much of their success was due to the fact that

seventeenth-century England was absorbed in religious and con-
stitutional quarrels, not fairly ended until 1660. Initially, the
English move eastward had quickly followed the Dutch, their
East India Company being formed in 1599, and its first voyage
launched in 1601. But the efforts thereafter died away, leaving
the English with no more than a footing in the East.

It was only after 1660 that the main conflict with Holland began. By the end of the seventeenth century, the Dutch had lost
their position as a major power, and the United Kingdom, having reached unity at last, was in a position to take its place. For
the period of their effective ascendancy, the British entrusted
their mission to the East India Company, which had its monopoly renewed in 1708 — a monopoly extending to all territories
beyond the Cape of Good Hope. Almost coincident with this
renewal was the union of England and Scotland in 1707, a bar-
gain which gave the Scots their significant share in the Empire,
and the death in the same year of Aurangzeb, which marked the
decline of the Mogul Dynasty in India. From that date, the
native rule began to crumble. As the central government weakened, the Hindus grew restive under Muslim rule. Bahadur Shah
ruled only for five troubled years, leaving a disputed succession.
The death of the ablest claimant left Mohammed Shah (1719–
48) on a tottering throne. There began a period of civil war,
confusion, and defeat, Delhi itself being plundered in 1739.
The provinces became independent and the assassination of
Alamgir II (1759) brought the empire to nothingness. Meanwhile, on the fringes of all this disorder, the British and French
were attempting to trade. Both had factories on the Coromandel
coast, but the British held, in addition, Bombay (ceded by
Portugal in 1660), and Fort William (Calcutta), founded in
1691. One obstacle to trade was the absence of any effective
government with which trade agreements could be made. Another and more formidable obstacle was the lack of any goods to
export. India produced plenty of goods which could find a

market in Europe. These included textiles, indigo, saltpeter, and sugar. But Britain produced little that the Indians wanted or could afford, the difference having to be made up in specie. In such troubled times the "factories" were necessarily fortified and guarded by native troops in the Company's pay. The Company's civilian officers lived a rather collegiate life, studied the local situation, and did what business they could.

The British might have kept their role of merchants had they been the only Europeans there. But France had become a maritime power by 1670, with a fleet of considerable strength and its own East India Company (from 1664). When war between France and England broke out in 1742, the conflict spread of necessity to their possessions in India. Naval and military operations produced no decisive result before the war ended in 1748. But when war was again declared in 1756, the struggle ended in a British victory. At the Battle of Plassey in 1759, Clive defeated the French and their Indian allies, the East India Company thus finding itself the chief military power in India. The result was the treaty of 1765, by which the Company became tax-farmer of the Bengal provinces. While nominally collecting the revenue on behalf of the Mogul and the Nabob, the Company's officers became the effective government, using the money for administration and defense, and also to pay for India's exports. This situation lasted until 1773, when the Company was brought more directly under government control. At the same time the native tax collectors and judges were replaced by British officials. The process had begun by which British administration was to spread to half the subcontinent. British India came thus into being with European superiority as its theoretical basis and a British-officered army as its visible strength. The Company ceased to trade with India except one-sidedly, its actual business being with China, from which country it imported tea. Its authority was gradually extended over the East and consolidated in India. Its activities made Britain the principal power in Asia.

What distinguished the British from previous movements of expansion, whether eastward or westward, was the fact that the whole of the trade route was brought under one system of control. The Arabs had come near to the ideal when their empire extended momentarily from Spain to India, their trade from Cadiz to Canton. But the British authority was more firmly established and stretched further in either direction. In its earlier form, the route went via Capetown, Bombay, Madras, Calcutta, and Penang. To these possessions were added, for greater security, the bases of Ceylon, Malacca, Mauritius, and Singapore; with Hong Kong, Labuan and North Borneo as well. The route round the Cape was in general use until 1869, the year in which the Suez Canal was opened to a traffic which was no longer under sail. This necessitated the strengthening of the other route by the development of other bases at Gibraltar, Malta, Cyprus, Alexandria, and Aden. It involved controlling Egypt and the Sudan. It also meant a tightening of imperial discipline by telegraph and fast ships, with colonial authorities kept more strictly on the leash. India had already been placed directly under the crown, and Queen Victoria proclaimed its empress. After 1870, the tentacles of Empire reached out to Malaya, to Japan, and even into the heart of China, with the white ensign regularly seen at Hankow and Weihaiwei. By 1900 the British seemed to be everywhere, their power firmly based upon India and upon their naval superiority in the Indian Ocean.

It is important to remember, however, that the expansion of Europe was not a purely British phenomenon. The French had their own lines of enterprise, to North Africa, to Madagascar, and Indochina. The Dutch were still in the East Indies, and the latecomers, Italy and Germany, were quick to seize any chance that offered. Even the United States, an extension westward of European and especially British enterprise, began to make its influence felt in the Far East by the mid-nineteenth century. Quite as important, and too little noticed, was the

expansion of Russia. The vacuum caused by the weakness of
Asia, which drew the British by sea, was as effective in drawing
the Russians by land. The Mongol collapse and the empty
spaces of Siberia led the Russians toward the Pacific. What is
still more significant is that their advance exactly paralleled that
of Britain, beginning at the same time and ending literally in
the same year. The year when Gregory Strogonoff entered Asia
(1558), with encouragement from Ivan the Terrible, was the
year in which Elizabeth I came to the throne. Tobolsk was
founded just before the defeat of the Armada, Tomsk just after
the accession of James I. The annexation of western and central
Siberia accompanied the development of New England, as also
the foundation, in 1640, of Madras. The date of the first Navigation Act (1651) is also the date of the first Russian clash with
the Manchus. The fateful year 1707, when the Act of Union
coincided with the death of Aurangzeb, was equally marked by
the annexation of Kamchatka. The Russians reached the Amur
River in the year (1847) that James Brooke was appointed to
public office in Borneo. The whole of Siberia was ceded to
Russia in the year (1858) that the East India Company was
replaced by the Indian Office, and Vladivostok was founded the
year after that. Like the British, the Russians were moving
astride the trade route, which they began to transform in 1891,
just after Cecil Rhodes had become Prime Minister at the Cape.
But the 4000 miles of the Trans-Siberian Railway were not finished until 1905, a year which marked the limit of Russian and
British expansion alike.

From 1472, when Ivan III, Grand Duke of Moscow, married
the niece of the last emperor of Constantinople — from about
the time, in fact, when Columbus first went to sea — the Russians had been pursuing their imperial destiny as the "third
Rome." "The importance of the move is in direct proportion to
the neglect it has received in Western studies." * But another

* Michael Edwardes, *op. cit.*, p. 45.

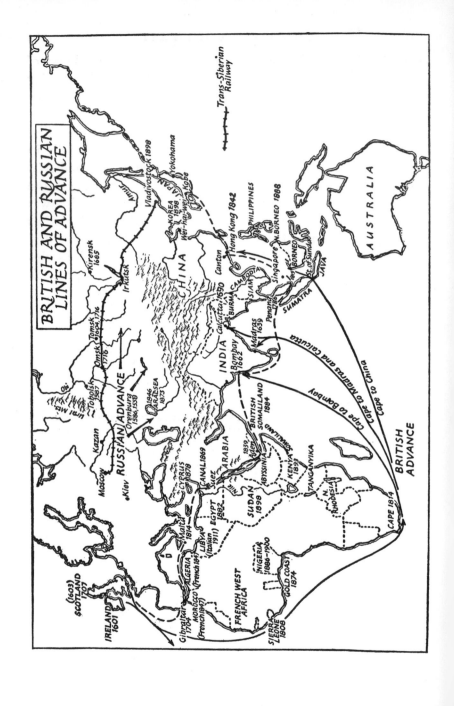

BRITISH AND RUSSIAN
LINES OF ADVANCE

Trans-Siberian
Railway

AUSTRALIA

SCOTLAND
(1603)
1707
IRELAND
1601

Moscow
Kazan
Kiev
Ural Mts.
Tobolsk 1587
Omsk 1716
Tomsk 1604
Kirensk
1665
Irkutsk
Amur
Vladivostok 1898
KOREA
1898
Wei-hai-wei Kobe
JAPAN
Yokohama

RUSSIAN ADVANCE
Orenburg
1586, 1558
1846
ARAL SEA
1873

CHINA
Canton
Hong Kong 1842
PHILIPPINES

Calcutta 1690
BURMA
CAMBODIA
SIAM
N. BORNEO 1888
BORNEO
Penang
1786
Singapore
Madras 1639
Bombay 1662
INDIA

SUMATRA
JAVA
St. of Sunda

Cape to China
Cape to Madras and Calcutta
Cape to Bombay

ARABIA
BRITISH
SOMALILAND
1884
ITALIAN
SOMALILAND

Gibraltar 1704
Malta 1814
ALGERIA
MOROCCO (French 1847)
(French 1911)
LIBYA
(Italian 1911)
EGYPT
1882
CYPRUS
1878
Suez
CANAL 1869
NILE
SUDAN
1898
ABYSSINIA
1859,
1884
KENYA
1893
TANGANYIKA
N.
RHODESIA
CAPE 1814

FRENCH WEST
AFRICA
NIGERIA
1886–1900
GOLD COAST
1874
SIERRA
LEONE
1808

BRITISH
ADVANCE

and earlier author wrote on this subject that "The Cossacks have achieved for Russia what the sea-rovers have done for England." * That is perfectly true, and the story of their move eastward by land, coincident with the British move by sea, should convince us, were we in doubt, that Russia is essentially a Western power. It may suit the Russians to claim, on occasion, a unity with Asia, but the British themselves have claimed as much. It was Disraeli who pointed out, in 1866, that Britain "interferes in Asia because she is really more of an Asiatic than a European power." It is in that sense that the Russians can be regarded as Orientals. Their civilization is Western, however, in character and origin. Whether they like it or not, their fortunes are inextricably bound up with the rise and fall of the West.

Last of all in the story comes the expansion of the United States. Columbus planned his first voyage upon the basis of a completely false assumption about the world's circumference. Learned men had told him in advance that his theory was incorrect, as indeed it was. Instead of reaching China, as he had planned, he merely discovered another continent. Later explorers established the fact that his academic opponents had been, more or less, right. Between them and China there lay a whole continent and, beyond that, an exceptionally wide ocean. The Spanish crossed the Pacific, and in 1564 they founded a settlement in the Philippines, through which they had their own eastern trade. To the existing trade routes, between Asia and Europe, there were added two more: the route between Europe and America, and the route between America and Asia. To the north of Spanish America, the English colonists had the whole continent to cross before they even saw the Pacific. It took them over two centuries, and it was only in 1850 that California became a state in the Union. Perry's fleet broke Japan's isolation in 1853–54, forcing the Japanese to open their ports. The first

* Lancelot Lawton, *Empires of the Far East* (London, 1912), I, 246.

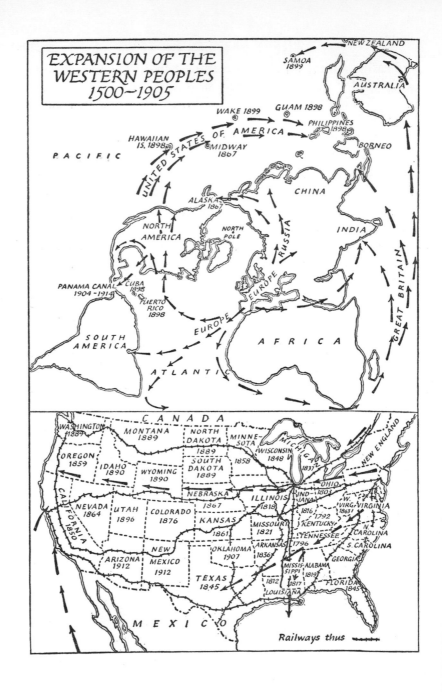

EXPANSION OF THE
WESTERN PEOPLES
1500–1905

NEW ZEALAND

SAMOA 1899

AUSTRALIA

WAKE 1899   GUAM 1898

PHILIPPINES 1898

HAWAIIAN IS. 1898   UNITED STATES OF AMERICA   MIDWAY 1867

BORNEO

PACIFIC

CHINA

ALASKA 1867

INDIA

NORTH AMERICA   NORTH POLE

RUSSIA

GREAT BRITAIN

PANAMA CANAL 1904–1914   CUBA 1898

EUROPE

PUERTO RICO 1898

SOUTH AMERICA

AFRICA

EUROPE

ATLANTIC

CANADA

WASHINGTON 1889   MONTANA 1889   NORTH DAKOTA 1889   MINNE-SOTA   MICHIGAN   NEW ENGLAND

WISCONSIN 1848   1837

OREGON 1859   IDAHO 1890   WYOMING 1890   SOUTH DAKOTA 1889   1858   OHIO

NEBRASKA 1867   ILLINOIS 1818   IND. 1803   W. VIRGINIA 1863

CALIFORNIA 1850   NEVADA 1864   UTAH 1896   COLORADO 1876   KANSAS 1861   MISSOURI 1821   KENTUCKY 1792   N. CAROLINA   VIRG. 1792

TENNESSEE 1796   S. CAROLINA

ARIZONA 1912   NEW MEXICO 1912   OKLAHOMA 1907   ARKANSAS 1836   GEORGIA

MISSIS-SIPPI 1817   ALABAMA 1819

TEXAS 1845   1812   FLORIDA 1845

LOUISIANA

MEXICO

Railways thus ⊢−⊢−⊢

transcontinental railway was completed in 1869, and it was from then that the Americans began to look upon the Chinese and Japanese as possible customers and converts. Result of the Spanish-American War of 1898 was to gain the Philippines for the U.S.A., and so involve the Americans more deeply in the Far East. There was much educational work done by American missionaries in China, but the general trend of events led to a rivalry with Japan. Of the different Western countries bringing pressure to bear on the Far East, the U.S.A., if the latest, was certainly not the least.

This new Western impact from across the Pacific was given additional force with the opening of the Panama Canal in 1914, and the subsequent strengthening of the United States Navy. Vast economic development in the Mississippi Valley demanded an outlet and it was this pent-up flood which broke the barrier of the isthmus and brought the U.S.A. into the Far East with renewed vigor. But the way had already been prepared by the acquisition of island bases, a process which began with the annexation of Midway Island in 1867. The acquisition of the Philippines, in 1898, was accompanied by the simultaneous acquisition of the Hawaiian Islands and Guam. The pattern was completed by the annexation of the Aleutian Islands (Dutch Harbor) in 1900, and Wake Island in the same year. The Panama Canal was already under discussion by that time, and its actual construction began in 1904. All this activity reveals a fairly consistent policy, to which World War I gave additional point. The westward expansion of Europe was continued as a movement across America and afterwards across the Pacific. On the China coast it met with the earlier eastward movement which had reached the same area from the opposite direction. By 1900, the peoples of Europe, or of European origin, had spread over the globe. And by that date they had brought their maximum influence to bear upon the peoples of Asia.

15

THE EAST AT BAY

IN BRINGING Western civilization to Asia, Britain played the
chief part. The Portuguese and Spanish admittedly began the
process. The Dutch, French, and Russians had a significant
influence, and the Americans, coming later on the scene, were
still aggressive after the British impetus had been lost. Nor
were these several influences identical, for the different countries,
representing the same civilization, had a contrasting interest in
its various aspects. The British influence was the most pervasive,
however, and lasted for the longest period. More than that, it
was the most purely Western. While no European country is
free, or has ever been free of Oriental influence, the British had
the least of it during the period that they mattered most. Why
was this? In the first place, they were geographically remote
from Islam. They had never played the defensive role which
had been forced upon the Austrians, Italians, Spanish, and
Portuguese. In the second place, their greatest period of expansion coincided with the most purely Western phase of European
history. Portugal and Spain were more medieval than renascent
when their overseas adventure began. Theirs was a world of
saints and knights errant, castles and monks. But the British assault on the East gathered momentum from 1660 and reached
its climax in 1815. It thus covered the exact period when Europe
was most triumphantly itself.

Insofar as ancient and modern history can be compared, the
British played the Macedonian part. They adopted some of the
purely Greek ideas, which they did not originate, and took them

into the heart of Asia. Nor did they fail to convey their message persuasively, taking the part of Alexander rather than of Rome. In *The Coming Caesars* Amaury de Riencourt shows that it is the United States that has assumed the role of Rome, reiterating a message now somewhat debased.

> Americans hardly ever make basic discoveries but can endlessly adapt, improve and mass produce European discoveries. They *research* endlessly but rarely *contemplate* . . . Europe has produced, at very little financial expense, the great thoughts which have rolled back the frontiers of man's scientific knowledge. At an expense of almost four billion dollars a year, American research exploits Europe's basic discoveries but cannot really progress beyond it in a fundamental way . . . The obstacles being utilitarianism and democracy.*

This comparison with Rome is one that has occurred to many. Fewer perhaps have recalled that the Roman Empire split into two. The European inheritance is, in fact, shared between the United States and Russia, between a new Rome and a new Byzantium.

It was the British, then, who followed Alexander. They did so, moreover, in conscious imitation. When they finally reached the Indus in 1838, during the Afghan expedition, the boast was made that, for the first time since Alexander the Great, the banners of a civilized nation waved along that river. During their greatest period they were classically educated and built in the classic style. Their minds harked back continually to Athens and Sparta, and "literature" to them meant Latin and Greek. Among the Georgian aristocracy, "gothic" was a term of disgust, used later in the sense of "rural" or "quaint." Medieval Europe existed in an age of darkness and barbarity. The elder Mill used the word "civilisation" as a term applicable only to ancient Greece and modern Europe. Edward Gibbon at once typified

* Amaury de Riencourt, *The Coming Caesars* (London, 1958), p. 278.

and influenced the attitude of his day, sharply contrasting republican virtue with imperial decadence. In the minds of Gibbon
and his friends, Parliament had become the Senate, where Latin,
if not spoken, was at least generally understood. No beards were
to be seen and the toga was worn at least on commemorative
statues. Dress became more colorless, for men at least, as the
eighteenth century progressed, and athletics became more promi-
nent in the national life. Horse racing and "Corinthian" boxing
were sports of classic origin, consciously revived. No park was
complete without its Grecian temple, no doorway without its
pillared porch.

   In their attitude toward the East, the English hardened as
time went on. They had appeared first in the guise of merchant,
anxious to conciliate. Then the aristocracy took over, and the
East India Company changed its policy. The change took place
with Pitt's India Act of 1784, which placed the Company under
the government's control. The immediate sequel was the appointment of Lord Cornwallis as Governor-General (1786–
1793), with the general task of ending corruption and setting
up an honest and efficient machinery of government. From the
outset, and until 1813, the directors had expressly forbidden all
missionary efforts — this much they had learned from the Portuguese example. They had added regulations to prevent any
European from settling in India. None could acquire land; no
officer could marry without permission. Partly by law, partly by
social pressure, all intermarriage with the natives was discouraged. Indian mistresses were common, and Eurasian children
came into existence, but these were given no official recognition.
It became the British custom to go East when unmarried, spend
up to ten years in the tropics, and settle eventually in Britain.
Impermanence became the permanent policy. It was from Britain that the wives would come and to Britain that the children
would return. As seen in the East, the British representative,
whether civil or military, would be an eternal alien, never assimilated, never changed. Once the rule against intermarriage, first

learned in Ireland, had been accepted, many social consequences were bound to follow. No father of a family can regularly admit as guests the people he must refuse to accept as relatives by marriage. Nor can he allow them an equal footing in his club, society, or church. In all his relationships with the natives of rank, he must be studiously formal and aloof.

While it is true that the British were predisposed toward such an aloofness, it was India itself that completed their education. For caste, after all, was an Indian, not a British institution. Establishing their authority over a caste-ridden society, they were more or less compelled to turn themselves into another caste. Technically untouchable in the Brahman's eyes, the British retorted by classifying the whole population as untouchable so far as they were concerned. The character of aloof superiority, which the Englishman assumed in India, came back with him to England, strengthening the discipline and rigidities of the class from which he came or to which, more likely, he aspired. The discipline of the garrison spread to the entire European population, over which the Governor's authority was absolute and without appeal. The British ruling caste was to be always on parade, always rightly dressed for the occasion, always quick with the right response in church or council, and always ready to drink the loyal toast. There were gradually established the canons of conduct as providing courage, politeness, and a cold integrity. There came into being a world of noon guns and mess jackets, memsahibs and aides-de-camp, punkahs and visiting cards. It was all overpowering and impressive, and could be very tedious indeed.

In studying this British system of rule we have to remember, first of all, that India had been conquered repeatedly and had always more or less absorbed the invaders. As almost its only wealth was in agriculture, the pattern had been based upon taxes or rent. Alien kings and nobles had drawn their income from areas of land, as was equally the pattern in Britain. There was nothing to prevent the British from setting up a new resident

nobility of their own — one which would have been absorbed
in its turn. What they chose to do was so totally at variance
with all current practice that its artificiality had to be sustained
by highly artificial means. Members of their official garrison had
to be specially recruited and trained, highly organized, suitably
rewarded, and on retirement promptly withdrawn. The training
process began with the formation of the East India College at
Haileybury in 1806.

> Here British youths appointed for Indian administration studied
> Indian languages, learnt something of the history, customs, and
> laws of India, were introduced to Newtonian science, received
> some instruction in the 'political and commercial relations be-
> tween India and Britain,' and through the study of Paley's
> *Moral and Political Philosophy* got special education in the
> principles of moral conduct . . .
>   The Company had created a Civil Service, educated in the
> British manner and likely to conduct itself with 'honour and
> industry.' This Civil Service was indoctrinated into a sense of
> imperial responsibility and ingrained with a sense of Britain's
> imperial greatness. These new officials were to remain English
> in outlook and sentiment when they served in India. They were
> not encouraged to become Indianized, as some earlier English
> visitors to India had been. They would not possess as much sym-
> pathy for the land they ruled as some of their predecessors.
> Theirs was a new imperial spirit. They would demonstrate Brit-
> ish superiority in arms and in character, and while they might
> learn much about India and its culture, they would favour
> British principles and introduce British institutions in adminis-
> tering India.*

Haileybury was the beginning of a system which was to involve
a whole series of boardingschools. For the British Empire involved, as it grew, the officering of many colonies, agencies,

* George D. Bearce, *British Attitudes Towards India: 1784–1858* (Oxford,
1961), p. 39.

regiments, and ships. Parents serving overseas sent their children home at a fairly early age. There were, and are, three reasons for this. In the first place, English children will bully the servants (whether Indian, Chinese, or Malay) and so themselves become intolerable. In the second place, there will be no local school able to provide them with the competition and discipline they need. In the third place, there was the need to provide the next generation of officers. The boy sent to a boardingschool grows up with no special attachment for any one locality. Born in Ceylon or Jamaica, educated at Marlborough or Tonbridge, holidaying with grandparents at Broadstairs or Lyme Regis, trained at Sandhurst, or inspired at Oxford, the resulting officer leaves for Hong Kong or Mombasa without undue reluctance. He is a member of a class, not of any one society.

Created in one sense by the railways — which gave a special advantage to those on a main line — the public-school system was created in another sense by Thomas Arnold, headmaster of Rugby from 1828 to 1842. It was he who gave the British professional class its sense of mission. Matthew Arnold, one of his sons, gave poetic glamour to the same general concept, and W. D. Arnold, Matthew's brother, went to India as an army officer but ended as Commissioner of Education in the Punjab. Mid-Victorian earnestness spread from Rugby to other schools, many of ancient foundation, but most of them with a school chapel dating from about 1880. Essence of the public-school system was its emphasis on leadership and games. To the VI Form was entrusted a special responsibility, to the prefect an all but complete authority outside the classroom. It was this type of discipline which overshadowed the British communities abroad. Minor indiscretions could be dealt with by the president of the club — ("Frankly, Reggie, this is not playing the game. You must apologize at once to the Colonial Secretary."). But something really black could be dealt with only by expulsion. Without preliminary or explanation, H. E. would deliver his

head-magisterial sentence. "Mr. Robtill, there is a ship leaving
for England tomorrow, and you will be on board." It was in this
sort of atmosphere that a code of behavior was, more or less,
maintained. In the Company's service which became the Indian
civil service, the standards of integrity and of ability were very
high indeed. And in the Sudan, after 1906, the standards are
said to have been higher still. Of whatever administrative talent
there was, the best always went overseas, leaving only the dregs
in Whitehall.

What impact did these public-school men — and their wives
— have on the East? First President of the Board of Control
was Henry Dundas, who used his considerable patronage for the
chief purpose of maintaining his political position in Scotland.
The result was to supply the East with a disproportionate share
of Scotsmen, whose influence in turn led to the appointment of
more. It was at that period the Scottish tendency to sentimen-
talize over backward peoples in mountainous regions. Such
racial groups India can provide, and much of the sympathy and
insight available was lavished on them. Some Scotsmen thought
charitably even of the Indians as a whole. Sir Thomas Munro
thus testified before the House of Commons, in 1813, that India
was civilized.

> Indians, he thought, were inferior to Europeans in the higher
> reaches of knowledge, in the theory and practice of good govern-
> ment, and in an educational system which encouraged free
> enquiry and progressive social reform. On the other hand, India
> equalled Europe in many things — manufacturing and agricul-
> tural skill, elementary schools in every village, the treatment of
> women with delicacy and consideration, the practice of charity
> and hospitality, and a general knowledge of what made comforta-
> ble living. If civilisation is to become an article of trade between
> the two countries, he concluded, 'I am convinced that this
> country [Britain] will gain by the import cargo.' *

* Bearce, *op. cit.*, pp. 124–25.

Munro nevertheless looked forward to a future period when Indians would have abandoned "most of their superstitions and prejudices and become sufficiently enlightened to frame a regular government for themselves." Others were less optimistic about this or more concerned with their own interests. The Duke of Wellington said that he had never met a Hindu with a single good quality, and added, for good measure, that he thought the Muslims even worse. There was, he said, "more perjury in the town of Calcutta alone than . . . in all Europe taken together." * Such prejudices aside, British policy generally favored those whose objects were more immediate. These fell into two broad categories, the utilitarian and the evangelical. Both were represented in the Court of Directors and neither would concede much merit to India's institutions or beliefs.

James Mill set the type for the utilitarian, condemning India as the home of despotism, venality, superstition, and indolence. He wanted to ensure the appointment of administrators acquainted with economics and political theory. Just such a man was Thomas Babington Macaulay, whose views on Hindu and Muslim vernacular education were expressed in an oft-quoted minute of 1835.

> The question now before us is simply whether, when it is in our power to teach this language [English], we shall teach languages in which, by universal confession, there are no books on any subject which deserve to be compared to our own; whether, when we can teach European science, we shall teach systems which, by universal confession, whenever they differ from those of Europe, differ for the worse; and whether, when we can patronize social philosophy and true history, we shall countenance, at the public expense, medical doctrines which would disgrace an English farrier — astronomy which would move laughter in the girls at an English boarding-school — history, abounding with kings

* S. J. Owen (ed.), A Selection from the Despatches, Memoranda and other papers relating to India, of the Marquess Wellesley, K.G. (Oxford, 1877), pp. 630, 773.

thirty feet high and reigns thirty thousand years long — and geography made up of seas of treacle and seas of butter.*

Behind Macaulay was the weight of British opinion. The Hindus and Muslims were so many barbarians. In the words of the *Edinburgh Review*:

The spirit of Oriental institutions was unfriendly to the vigorous expansion of thought. In all ages of the world, Asia has been deprived of the light of freedom, and has in consequence incurred the doom of absolute sterility in the higher fruits of manual and mental culture.†

If the utilitarian could find little to admire in India's culture, the missionaries found less still. First admitted to India in 1813, encouraged by Charles Grant, William Wilberforce, and the "Clapham Sect," the evangelical missionaries found a leader in Reginald Heber, bishop of Calcutta from 1823 until his death in 1826. He was among the most sensible and liberal of men, but even he was horrified at some Indian customs. Other missionaries were more tactless and outspoken. They were appalled by idolatry, indecent ceremonies, the pilgrimages to Juggernaut, female infanticide, slavery, the burning of widows (*sati*), and the evils of caste. The East India Company itself was studiously aloof in religious matters, purporting to be neutral, but Lord William Bentinck, Governor-General (1827–1835), abolished *sati* in 1829 and tried to suppress both child-sacrifice and infanticide. That was as far as he dared go, his view being that further progress depended upon economic growth and technological improvement. As a preliminary to this sort of advance, in 1835 he made English, instead of Persian, the official language for purposes of government, diplomacy, and law. A later Governor-

* G. O. Trevelyan, *The Life and Letters of Lord Macaulay* (London, 1931), I, 291.
† Bearce, *op. cit.*, p. 159.

General, Dalhousie, pinned his faith more specifically to railways, steamships, and telegraphs.

The result of westernization under Dalhousie was the Indian Mutiny of 1857, which took place shortly after he left. The immediate occasion was the General Service Enlistment Act of 1856. The emotional background was a vague and incoherent feeling of protest, to be found among Hindus and Muslims alike. It was the Conservatives who supported the rising, caste grievances and a fear of Christianity being foremost in the minds of those immediately involved. General conspiracy there was none, and the leaders of the movement professed aims which, when coherent, were incompatible with each other. The result was a disorganized outburst of hatred which provoked the strongest feelings of resentment on the British side. The revolt was ruthlessly suppressed, the memory of it creating a new barrier of distrust between the rulers and the ruled. The British decided to be more careful in the future, more aware of Indian prejudice and custom. They were more considerate toward the rulers of the native states, who had been loyal during the crisis. Finally, seeking a scapegoat, they abolished the East India Company and made the government of India responsible to a new Secretary of State. Disraeli underlined the change at a later period, when he advised Queen Victoria to assume the title of Empress of India. The British, it would seem, had definitely come to stay.

In the years following the mutiny, the British influence upon India was increased as much by technical progress as by political theory. The opening of the Suez Canal, which meant the coming of the long-distance steamship, cut down the passage time to India. The laying of telegraphic cables was almost simultaneous, bringing the viceroy into daily contact with London. It became more feasible for British officials to return home on leave, more practicable again for Indians to visit England on business. Indian mistresses gave place to British wives, and children, now of more uniform color, were able to travel back and forth. The British regiments of the Indian Army were replaced by line regiments stationed in India for a period and then replaced by others. More Europeans went to India for shorter periods, and moved around India at a greater speed. Indian newspapers could print recent news from the West, and London newspapers became aware of happenings in India. From 1870 the pressure of the West was intensified in a hundred ways, being felt as far afield as Malaya and Hong Kong — as far indeed as Yokohama and Hankow. British imperialism reached a crescendo in the viceroyalty of Lord Curzon (1898–1905). It was this glittering period of confident rule that marked at once the climax and the end.

On their side, the Indians learned from the mutiny that a traditional opposition to the West was no longer possible. Almost unnoticed there was growing up in India a middle class composed of people with professional or technical skill acquired through instruction in the English language. Many were loyal to the British, upon whom they depended for protection and support. Others came to believe that their nationalist aspirations — acquired like their knowledge from British teachers and English literature — could succeed only in a westernized form. By accepting an injection of European ideas they could acquire an immunity against the remainder. When their opposition to the British regime became effective, it was voiced in the English language by lawyers who had qualified at the English bar. Nationalist conferences were possible only through delegates being able to travel on British-built railways and to express their resentment in a common tongue. Without discarding their own culture, and without being converted to Christianity, they assumed a number of Western characteristics. They could play cricket and quote Tennyson. Most westernized of the Indians were the officers of the Indian Army and Navy, but there were physicians and lawyers who ran them close. There were some aspects of British life for which they developed a certain affection. The I.C.S. tie was still worn with pride after the British rule was ended.

The traffic in ideas was never only in the one direction. The British learned a great deal from India, as also indeed from China. It was the returned "nabobs" who in England tended to build big white houses on the tops of hills, copying the stucco-covered mansions of Calcutta or Madras. It was in India that the British learned to play polo and wear pajamas rather than nightshirts. Indian again in background is the hybrid word "Gymnkhana" as used to describe a wonderful mixture of Greek athleticism and Indian horsemanship. It was, above all, from the Indians that the British learned habits of personal cleanliness. The inhabitants of seventeenth- and eighteenth-century Europe had no passion for soap and water, even the most prosperous being often extremely dirty. Medieval theologians had preferred dirt to the immorality they associated with bathing, and the Reformation had not extended to the bathroom. There was normally no bathroom, in fact, to which it could extend. Practices which are, perhaps, mildly offensive in a cold climate are unendurable in the tropics. For good cause, therefore, the European in India learned the value of cold water. It at once lowered the temperature and lessened the smell. They were in a country, moreover, where there was a tradition of cleanliness. Archaeologists tell us that the Harappa people of the Indus valley (c. 2500 B.C.) had the sort of baths we now describe, rather oddly, as Turkish. In their cities practically every house had its bathroom, usually with an adjacent latrine. Tcheon Tz-Kouzn, at Angkor, Cambodia, from 1296 to 1297, wrote of the inhabitants there that they were often ill as a result of bathing (and love-making) too often, scarcely finishing the one thing before they began the other. But the Chinese were themselves a cleanly people; as Marco Polo noted with surprise, "All are in the daily practice of washing their person, and especially before their meals." In more modern times, the better houses in India and

Malaya have as many baths as beds — contrasting with Britain where many comparable homes have no bath at all. Commenting upon this state of affairs an Indian wrote:

> . . . the West among other things has recently imbibed the notion of the necessity for physical cleanliness and health by daily ablution; but not being quite prepared for it the West is placed in some difficulty. In the East, almost every bedroom has a bathroom attached to it. Space being limited in the West, enough bathrooms are not provided even for the well-to-do — not to speak of humbler classes — either in private houses, clubs, hotels or on board ship, with the result that considerable inconvenience is caused to those who have got into the habit of a morning dip or wash. Like the problem of street traffic, the problem of baths is becoming acute.*

Neither problem is much less acute today. Few people realize, however, that Britain would be more backward still but for Indian example. Whether there is much sense in bringing the cold-bath habit from the tropics to a frozen England must be a matter of opinion; a matter, moreover, in which small boys have often differed from those said to be older and wiser. Be that as it may, the provision of a bathroom attached to every bedroom is still remote from British practice; and the inclusion of a bathroom in every house is more the theory than the fact.

It would be wrong to assume, then, that the British learned nothing in India. The fact is that Oriental influence in Europe had never ceased. Lacquer had been introduced in the seventeenth century, and Chinese wallpaper under William III. The making of "china" had spread from Meissen to Worcester, and even Chippendale furniture shows some Chinese influence, as does the British tradition of water-color painting. There was a great vogue for "chinoiserie" in eighteenth-century France, and

* Mannath C. Mallik, *Orient and Occident: A Comparative Study* (London, 1913), p. 51.

English orientalism produced, among other things, the Pavilion at Brighton. But the Oriental was considered generally more quaint than significant, and while the British learned something from Indian shipbuilders, it is clear that the Indians had, in general, more to learn from them. On the one side was a confident assumption of superiority, on the other a rueful admission of ignorance. On both sides there was an awareness of contrast.

> People of different temperaments give different explanations why East and West do not meet in friendly intercourse. The true explanation is that East is down and West is up, and until East goes up the two cannot meet without strain and injury to either or to both . . . the East is now showing signs of coming up again, and it is to be hoped that, as the East moves upwards, the turn of the wheel of fortune will not take the West downwards and leave mankind in as sad a plight as before . . .*

* Mallik, *op. cit.*, p. 3.

16

VICTORIAN VIRTUES

INDIA, Burma, China, Malaya, and Egypt were all more or less westernized during the nineteenth century, and there have been bitter comments about how this came about. The truth is, however, that the Orientals chose to westernize themselves and did so even in countries like Japan or Siam which were and had always been completely independent. By the mid-twentieth century the symbols of voluntary westernization were the clothes, the wristwatch, the fountain pen, and bicycle. But if these were the symbols, what was the reality? What was the body of ideas which the Europeans had to offer? What was it that the Asian had to accept or reject?

The British way of life, as presented for imitation, involved four distinct traditions. In a modified form, the other Europeans and Americans offered very much the same concepts. First and oldest of these traditions was the Greek. The later Europeans, like the earlier, emphasized the role of the individual as distinct from the family or clan. Their custom of monogamy extended the same individuality to women. It was unthinkable to them that a man's wife should be chosen for him by his parents, for the marriage was essentially between two individuals. With the British, this undoubtedly was still further emphasized by their upbringing, by their boarding-school education, by the small numbers of their colonial society, and by the still greater isolation which often characterized a given occupation or post. It was that sense of isolation which tended to demolish any vestigial caste barrier among themselves. The hierarchy might be rigid, but the garrison stood together, and this solidarity was further enhanced by the Greek ideal of complete humanity; the same man being an administrator, scholar, soldier, athlete, and politician. People of different seniority or standing could meet as equals in some unofficial context, in a learned society or on the parade ground. It is this sort of solidarity which made possible the political institutions in which the British professed to believe — the legislature and the city council. On these two levels, and with at least some talk of democracy, the British did practice a government by public discussion. Officials might rule, but they were also compelled to explain. More important than the voting procedure was the Greek idea of public life — the merchant's duty to serve as magistrate or in the Volunteers.

If the British brought with them the idea of the agora and stoa, the place of the individual (not the family) in public life, they were still more eager to introduce the gymnasium and stadium. To the Greek idea of athletics, fully supported, the British added their own cult of organized games: football, cricket, hockey, tennis, and golf. The gymnasium had become the yacht club, the downtown club, or simply the Club, its intellectual side transferred to the Royal Asiatic Society and its artistic urges confined to an annual presentation of light opera by Gilbert and Sullivan. The British, like the Greeks, were reluctant to admit Asians to the club, even as guests, and still more reluctant to elect them as members. Besides the obvious difficulty of having a close social relationship with people who are barred from intermarriage, there was the added problem of Asian family cohesion. Just as the European who marries a Chinese girl will find, to his dismay, that he has married into a Chinese clan, so the club which elects an Asian will often find that it has elected a tribe. The club deals with individuals, while Asian custom involves the kinship group. So the average club was always more or less exclusive, being the model upon which some Asian or Eurasian groups would form their own. In addition to the club, there was always the stadium. In British hands this had become the racecourse, football ground, cricket pitch, and polo club. Spectator sports could be shared by different peoples, not necessarily in the same grandstand. There were also sports in which Europeans and Asians could play against each other.

The British were never very successful in their attempts to introduce the theater. It was not a subject on which they were fanatical, and their Asian subjects were not generally so westernized as to follow without difficulty the dialogue upon which the modern drama depends for its effect. Many Asian cities were provided, at one time or another, with a theater, but usually on the least ambitious scale. Where the British did better was in presenting a tradition of humor which derived through Lucian from Aristophanes. It was a sixteenth-century development, anticipated by Chaucer, but first explained by Sir Thomas Hoby in his translation of Castiglione in 1561, and first exemplified by Shakespeare and, in 1613, by Beaumont and Fletcher. There was a saving touch of laughter among the British, even at their most imperial, and while they could be ruthless on occasion, their sense of humor — their Greek sense of proportion — saved them very often from severities which they might think not merely inhuman but absurd.

Superimposed on their Greek heritage was all that the British derived from Rome. First in this category was their strong sense of duty, unconnected with any religious belief they may have had. Their standards of patriotism, loyalty, and fortitude were relatively high and their reliance was more on character than upon brains. With their idea of duty went their Roman respect for law. In theory at least — and often in practice — they saw government in terms of legal enactment and procedure. They were especially successful in keeping the military power subordinate to the civil, not by treating the soldier as an inferior but by legally defining the bounds of his responsibility. While the British were always more military than they pretended to be — their officers showing a preference for civilian clothes — their army was nonpolitical; and in the territories they left it was a non-political army they left behind them. Like the Romans, they showed a practical interest in engineering and sanitation. Their most important officials, so far as practical results were concerned, were always the city engineer and the municipal officer of health. It was these two who reduced the death rate, upheld the birthrate, and created the world's basic population problems. Always suspicious of religious or political ideals, the British were happier discussing hygiene and drainage, topics on which they felt certain of being right.

Their final gift of Roman origin, but American manufacture, was the cinema — the modern equivalent of the arena. The linguistic difficulties which handicapped the theater were absent in the motion picture, which depended for its appeal on spectacular violence. Stock in trade of the Asian cinema, therefore, is the film in which wisdom and wit are reduced to the minimum. First in popularity came the biblical epic or early Christian horror film, either of which may feature the arena itself, complete with gladiators and lions. Next came the films which involve Tarzan of the Apes, a character who may say practically nothing. Slightly less popular, perhaps, are the "westerns," produced in quantity and at lowest cost. These illustrate the ideals of the West as upheld by cowboys against Indians, a normally childish form of entertainment which lends itself to anti-American propaganda. Variants on this theme are the same stories performed in the costume of some other region or period. Last in this intellectual feast are the films about gangsters and hoodlums, robberies and murders. These are the urbanized "westerns" with cars instead of horses, cops instead of cowboys, and all problems soluble by a blow to the jaw or a bullet through the heart. Motion pictures which fall into these four categories represent — like all-in wrestling — the less obviously cultural aspect of the Roman heritage.

Superimposed again on this Roman tradition was all that the British had learned from the East during the Middle Ages. From the Jews, through Christianity, they had derived the idea of being a Chosen People. This attitude appeared during the last phase of British imperialism (1886–1905) — the age of Joseph Chamberlain, Cecil Rhodes, Lord Cromer, Lord Milner, and Lord Curzon. The concept of an imperial destiny and mission found its expression in a wealth of literature, beginning with the works of Seeley and ending with those of Buchan. Queen Victoria's Diamond Jubilee of 1897 represented perhaps the peak of imperialism, and the role of its prophet fell to Rudyard Kipling, whose literary career began in India in 1885. He lived for a time in the U.S.A., and there reached the conclusion that democracy is inseparable from incompetence. Traveling widely and writing incessantly, he preached a gospel of law, order, duty, restraint, obedience, and discipline. "God of our fathers, known of old," he wrote in 1897, "Lord of our far-flung battle line." By 1899 he wrote of "The White Man's burden"; nor was his attitude essentially different from that of Joseph Chamberlain, Secretary of State for the Colonies in 1895, who claimed that "the British race is the greatest of governing races that the world has ever seen." Behind their confident assumption of responsibility for the welfare of others, lay the doctrines of Christianity in their Protestant form. Any doubt as to whether the British had the right to rule in Asia could be silenced with a word. The natives, after all, were *heathen*.

That God should be on the Christian side was, of course, an Oriental idea. With it came, moreover, some other ideas of Eastern origin. The British had a strict theory of morality where their own women were concerned, and a disapproving attitude toward peoples whose customs might be different. They looked with horror on the use of drugs as opposed to alcohol. From the Arabs they had derived a concept of chivalry — something unknown to the Chinese — which included a formal respect for women and a formal courtesy toward prisoners of war. Their passionate concern about horses can be traced to the same origin, as can also the horses about which they were most deeply concerned. Of Buddhist origin, by contrast, was their eagerness to protect other animals, as generally to alleviate suffering and famine. During the decade 1901–11 the population of India increased by nineteen per cent, largely through saving children from starvation. This sort of achievement was due to a mixture of administrative efficiency and humanitarian sentiment. The Greeks, remember, would have let the children die, arguing that they were too many for the means of subsistence. Of Eastern origin again were the British hospitals, institutions of medieval pattern which can trace their descent from Buddhist monasteries. The last period of Oriental ascendancy had left its mark on the West. Nor had the British failed to learn something from the peoples they were trying to govern.

To support the authority in which they believed, the overseas British developed the special characteristics they had first learned to value in Ireland. These characteristics were discipline, loyalty, courage, awareness of danger, acceptance of responsibility, aloof superiority, rigid honesty in finance, a black-and-white uniformity in dress, speech, and manner, and a readiness to shoot when the need should arise. Looked at from another angle, the same characteristics might look more like subservience to authority, a readiness to tell lies, unimaginative recklessness, overbearing behavior, snobbishness, red tape, dislike of originality, and sheer cruelty toward the least sign of revolt. Much depends, evidently, on the point of view. Behind the reality of the British Empire lay the child's pony and the blooding at the kill, the prefect's cane in the VI Form room, the broken rib on the rugby football field, the pelvis cracked in the point-to-point, the social discipline of the house party, the smashed furniture on the regimental guest night, and the scorn felt for anyone found reading poetry or showing interest in the arts.

Behind the British in their imperial mission, and behind other colonial powers, was also the technical superiority of the West, a purely modern development and one more recent than is often realized. Writes Maurice Zinkin on this subject:

> Eastern influence on the West remained unquestionably stronger than Western influence on the East until about 1700 . . . for 2,000 years Asia had given and Europe had taken. This was a natural arrangement in trade for Europe had nothing to offer. But in other respects, Asia might have done well to borrow. Roman Commercial Law, Newtonian physics, 18th Century chemistry, might have been no small return for Hindu Algebra and Chinese political thought. The proper pride of Asia in its own achievements had degenerated into obscurantist arrogance long before its weakness was finally exposed in the 19th Century . . .*

This argument that the Western intellectual assault began after 1700 could be supported with many examples. As against that, Western *expansion* began in about 1500, unsustained by the technical superiority which was to be the result of seventeenth-century invention. It would appear from this that technical progress is more the result than the cause of expansion. Discoveries in navigation did not precede but followed the great voyages of exploration. If this is so, the European pressure on the East, increasing from 1500 onwards, was based upon a superiority to be explained in other than technical terms. Material explanations break down in the light of well established fact. In terms of shipbuilding, navigation, seamanship, and gun founding, sixteenth-century Asia had an actual advantage, and yet it was the Europeans who discovered India, not the Chinese who discovered Europe.

When we attempt to explain this circumstance, we should remember, first of all, that scientific discovery is of little practical

* Maurice Zinkin, *op. cit.*, p. 40.

value in itself. For results there is needed a society so organized as to make use of any discovery that is made. And the strength of 16th-century Europe lay far more in its organization than in its technique. This is particularly apparent from the history of cannon and firearms, the weapons with which the West established its supremacy. The origin of artillery would seem to be as obscure today as it was when Camden wrote:

> Some [Sir John Harrington] have sayled a long course as far as China, the farthest part of the world, to fetch the invention of guns from thence, but we know the Spanish proverb Long wayes, long lies . . . The best authors consider that Bertholdus Swarte, a Monk, was responsible, and that he produced the first gun.*

This is a subject upon which the best authors are no longer so confident. Some would agree, however, that gunpowder was possibly a Chinese invention and one first heard of in 1260. The earliest Chinese cannon date from 1356. Whereas there were guns used at the Siege of Metz in 1324 and by the English at Crécy in 1346. They are described in documents dating from 1326 onwards, while firearms are mentioned from 1331 onwards. Both were used by the English at sea from the time of the Battle of Sluys in 1340. Henry V used cannon against Harfleur (1415) — a 40-pounder, 30-pounder, and 15-pounder, from which we derive our odd system of scoring at Wimbledon.

The Turks used cannon effectively against Constantinople in 1453, and the Earl of Warwick was as successful against Bamborough Castle in 1464. The Persians were asking the Venetians for gunpowder and artillery in 1471, and a Shah of Gujerat was making a similar application to Egypt in 1511–12. By 1512 the Venetian ambassador reported to the Doge that Henry VIII of England "has enough cannon to conquer Hell." In 1523 Philip

* Charles Ffoulkes, *The Gun-founders of England* (Cambridge, 1937). But see also W. Y. Carman, *A History of Firearms* (London, 1955).

of Hesse flattened Landstuhl Castle in a single day. The Mughal emperor Babur had cannon in 1526, with Hindu artillerymen. From facts such as these one might conclude that guns were never a monopoly of either East or West. Credit for their first effective use may have to be shared between the Turks and the English; the Turkish artillery being the best in 1550, and the English known to be superior by 1580 or thereabouts, at which period the best firearms came from the Netherlands and Spain. So far as mere invention goes, the story is one that ranges from Peking to Woolwich, with no one country standing supreme.

Why, then, was the position so different by 1700? And why, for that matter, were the Portuguese able to obtain a naval superiority in the Indian Ocean by 1509? The answer is to be found surely in the evolution of the literate soldier.

It is the plain fact that the invention of a gun or firearm is less than half the battle. Cannon, to be effective, must be mounted, maintained, cleaned, and polished. Solid shot must be scraped and repainted. Gunpowder must be kept dry and the kegs regularly turned end for end. Breechings and tackles, ramrods and wedges must be checked and inspected. The gun crew must be taught an elaborate and exact drill, every man learning his own task — and the task, incidentally, of every other man. Upon the precision and speed of the drill depends not merely the effectiveness of the fire, but the mere safety of the crew. One mistake in a rigid sequence of events, one failure to ram home the rod, may wreck the gun with the crew under it. Nor is there any less need for precision with small arms. Infantry drill was invented by Maurice of Nassau, the first manual — by Jacob de Gheyn — being published in 1608. Loading and firing a musket might involve a sequence of thirty-seven actions and as many commands.

III. The Musket must lie upon the Left shoulder, and the Left hand upon the Butt end, the Thumb in the Hollow thereof

. . . the Lock must be turn'd a little outwards, so that the under part of the Butt-end comes straight with the middle of the Body . . . etc., etc.

IV. The Match must be in the Left Hand, the one End between the first and second Fingers and the other between the two Last . . . etc.*

Was this sort of thing really needed? It was essential and not least so in the safety precautions. And the precision of the drill depended upon the officers and sergeants learning the manual backwards. From sergeant-major or boatswain upwards, they had to be literate. From lieutenant upwards, they needed a knowledge of mathematics, and the senior officers were expected to be, and often were, men of birth, education, and accomplishment.

In the East these two classes of officer, of the upper- and lower-middle class respectively, did not exist. Nor were they easily created, for the Indian caste system and the Chinese ideograph tended to keep learning and war in separate compartments. In the sixteenth-century the technical gap between East and West was negligible, with the advantage often on the Oriental side. What was different was the social structure, dynamic on the one side and static on the other. As a result of these social forces at work, the technical gap began to widen, so that nineteenth-century Europe was far ahead. Technological progress then modified the social structure, giving social rank to the engineer and requiring literacy of the petty officer or sergeant. The growing complexity of the weapons used led to fresh emphasis on standards of maintenance, creating a new religion for people who had no other. To the artilleryman the gun is sacred, treated with the reverence which the infantryman reserves for the colors. In accusing the Oriental people of idolatry, the British developed an idolatry of their own, expressed in verses such as these:

* Drill of 1690.

The 'Eathen

The 'eathen in 'is blindness
    bows down to wood an' stone
'E don't obey no orders, unless they is 'is own;
'E keeps 'is side-arms awful; 'e leaves 'em all about,
An' then comes up the regiment an' pokes the 'eathen out.
All along o' dirtiness, all along o' mess
All along o' doin' things rather more-or-less . . .*

And the verses, by Rudyard Kipling, end with the moral —

Mind you keep your rifle an' yourself jus' so!

The principles of infantry training were first evolved in Spain, the Netherlands, and Sweden. It was left to the British to make them into a religion.

The contrast in these matters between East and West is evident, even in 1511. It was in that year that Albuquerque captured the city of Malacca. There was nothing technically backward about the Malay capital. Far from that, it was the place where spectacles were manufactured, some of them reaching China in 1410–30 — not so very long after their first appearance in Italy, c. 1300. It was an ideal place for technological experiment, where Indian shipbuilding and Chinese cartography were equally available. As for cannon and firearms, they might well have been invented there, the gunpowder from China being applied to the aboriginal blowpipe, which is, after all, a form of air gun. Be that as it may, the Malays certainly made cannon, a pre-Portuguese cannon mold having been found in Pahang. The Portuguese claim, moreover, to have found numerous firearms in the captured city. As against that, the Portuguese sustained more casualties from blowpipe darts than from anything else. From all this we might fairly conclude that the Malays had cannon, but no *effective* drill for using them. This was cer-

* Kipling, *The Seven Seas* (1896).

tainly true of a later period. In 1871–72 Raja Mahdie's guns in Selaugor were:

> . . . without means of elevating, being either laid upon two parallel timbers placed in the desired direction, or when on a carriage lashed down with rattan in a fixed position. It was the custom of Mahdie's men before firing a gun to assemble round it and pray for a successful result . . .*

But what success could be expected with a gun unable to traverse, elevate, or recoil? The devotional school of gunnery made a nonsense of any gun, however well cast. Nor was there any startling improvement in the twentieth century. During the recent emergency in Malaya, the Singapore police were all armed with rifles. After a few years, the visit of an armorer established the fact that seventy-five per cent of them were unserviceable. The only consolation for their officers lay in the knowledge that their potential opponents were still more indifferently armed. When General Sir Gerald Templer started to recruit his antagonists into the security forces, he issued a warning on the subject in these words: "*Remember that when the surrendered terrorists come to us they know next to nothing about firearms.*" It was a circumstance to which many policemen owed their lives. Good weapons are useless unless properly maintained and correctly handled.

Artillery and firearms, or at least their proper use, were the basis of European authority in Asia. But the same organization of society which created the artillery and mass-produced the rifles (from 1851) could be applied, and was increasingly applied, to the encouragement of science.

In attempting to explain why Chinese mathematics and science failed to develop beyond a certain point, Professor Needham points a contrast with the West:

* C. Northcote Parkinson, *British Intervention in Malaya* (Singapore, 1960), p. 45.

What was it, then, that happened at the Renaissance in Europe whereby mathematised natural science came into being? And why did this not occur in China? If it is difficult enough to find out why modern science developed in one civilisation, it may be even more difficult to find out why it did not develop in another. Yet the study of an absence can throw light upon a presence. The problem of the fruitful union of mathematics with science is, indeed, only another way of stating the whole problem of why it was that modern science developed in Europe at all.*

Needham's tentative suggestion is that Chinese Confucian bureaucracy gave little opportunity to the mathematician or scientist, least of all after 1368. Artisans were separated by an invisible wall from the scholars of literacy training. Merchants were not much esteemed. No technical discovery would give the artisan that higher status in society which was the reward of scholarship. No Indian invention would bring an untouchable into the highest caste. In this respect medieval society was rather similar. The architect, engineer, or navigator was outside the world of learning, reserved for the priesthood; outside the world of command, reserved for the nobility. There grew up, therefore, the fifteenth-century school of engineer-artists "unlectured in Schooles or unlettered in Bookes." Some of these broke into the ranks of the nobility after 1500, Columbus being one of them. With the Reformation, however, learning became available to the layman, producing such scientifically minded scholars as William Gilbert and Francis Bacon, and whereas the European mathematics of 1550 was scarcely superior to that of India and China, the period between that date and 1665 saw the rapid development of algebra, decimals, logarithms and the sliderule, leading through Descartes and Pascal to Newton and the infinitesimal calculus. On the medical side, similarly, there was little future for a profession in which the university-trained physician

* Joseph Needham, *op. cit.*, III, 153 *et seq.*

stood apart from the trade-apprenticed surgeon, neither being socially acceptable to the gentry. Progress began when the physician and surgeon came together, both eligible for knighthood. Background to the demolition of old barriers was provided by the educated merchants who applied new inventions to their trades and so bought their way into the peerage. From the seventeenth-century onwards, the European in the East had behind him a world of experimental science, exemplified by the firearm and cannon, but illustrated further by the steam engine, the railroad, the insurance company, the telegraph, the operating theater, the lighthouse, the quinine dose, and the bank.

Symbols of European influence were the clock and the printing press. The latter, important in itself, was also the foretaste of something else. As Lewis Mumford observes:

> Printing was from the beginning a completely mechanical achievement. Not merely that; it was the type of all future instruments of reproduction: for the printed sheet, even before the military uniform, was the first completely standardized product, manufactured in series, and the movable type themselves were the first example of completely standardized and interchangeable parts . . .*

Although of Chinese and Korean origin, printing did indeed foreshadow a Western mechanical age. Still more significant, however, was the clock. Invented in the Middle Ages, it acquired the balance spring in 1675, was in general use by 1700, and led to John Harrison's chronometer (No. 4) of 1759. It became the inspiration for other machines, like the precision lathe. Apart from that, however, the clock and the watch brought with them a new attitude of mind, a new feeling for punctuality, a new emphasis on the value of time, and a new belief in the possibility of progress. And the clock, remember, was the first instrument of precision, the pattern of many others

* Lewis Mumford, *Technics and Civilization* (London, 1934), p. 133.

to come. The Victorian administrator ruled with the clock before him and his watch in his hand. He grew impatient with people to whom the clockface was meaningless. He thought that time was on his side and he knew that time is money.

When Queen Victoria died, Edward VIII's coronation was fixed for a date in 1902. Among those invited were some Malay princes, who thus saw London for the first time. One of them told Hugh Clifford, who was their escort, that he had understood for the first time why Europeans value time.

> In this country each day is so packed with living that if a man misses so much as a quarter of an hour, never again will he catch up with the minutes which have escaped him. With us life saunters: here it gallops as though it were pursued by devils!

What the Malay would have found still more difficult to understand was the Englishman's feeling that his time in the East was short and that what he did not accomplish soon might never be finished at all.

> Take up the White Man's burden
> The savage wars of peace.
> Fill full the mouths of Famine
> And bid the sickness cease;
> And when your goal is nearest
> The end for others sought,
> Watch Sloth and heathen Folly
> Bring all your hope to nought.*

* Rudyard Kipling, 1899.

17

THE MARCH OF PROGRESS

As the church bells of Christendom struck the hours they gave a new emphasis to both time and eternity. Each passing hour added something more to the record of history. Each hour left the individual with less time in which to gain redemption. And among the different ideas presented to the East by its European invaders, the concept of time — of past, present, and future — was perhaps the most potent. It derived in part from the clock, the calendar and the history book, in part again from the European's longer expectation of life. And our commonest mistake, in analyzing the impact of modern science, is to forget that archaeological and historical science has been quite as important as chemistry or physics. Our current decisions are based on our assumptions about the future, which are conditioned in turn by our beliefs about the past. Commonest among the beliefs once held is that concerning the Golden Age, the discarding of which has brought about the most significant changes of outlook. It is a legend common to Indians, Chinese, and Greeks, and paralleled by the Jewish story of the Garden of Eden.

The Hindu version of the legend has it that men were formerly equal to gods, perfectly virtuous and happy, free from suffering and fear. This age, called Satya Yuga, ended when the hearts of men were assailed by error, virtue being replaced by greed and avarice, anger and sin. The Chinese Golden Age was described by Kwang-Tze, follower of Lao-Tze (604–532 B.C.) in a passage that has been rendered thus:

In the age of perfect virtue, men attached no value to wisdom
. . . They were upright and correct, without knowing that to be
so was Righteousness: they loved one another, without knowing
that to do so was benevolence . . .*

Essential to Confucius was the wisdom of the legendary Sage
Kings, upon whom current rulers were to model themselves.
Nor were the Greeks uninfluenced by the same assumption,
their remote heroes being godlike and their Homeric characters
apt to pick up lumps of rock "beyond the strength, of any two
men bred to-day." How seriously or universally these beliefs
were held may be matter for dispute, but they reveal a climate
of opinion in which "progress" played no part. Ancestors could
be assumed to have been at least as wise as their descendants.
To equal the virtue of a past age was as much as was feasible
and more than was likely. The great days, if there were any,
were definitely in the past.

Least obsessed with this idea were the Indians, not because
they looked to the future, but because they rejected the whole
concept of historical, as opposed to cosmic time. As Amaury
de Riencourt puts it: "Nothing but the immutable and changeless absolute had any metaphysical reality for the Hindu de-
votee"; as a result of which India produced no single historian
before the advent of Islam. The Chinese were more historically
minded, but their search was not for trends in development
but for ethical precepts — for examples of what to imitate or
avoid. It was the Jewish prophets who first looked to the
future, being followed in this by Mithraists, Manicheists and
Christians. Present miseries would be ended not by the efforts
of man, but by the belated intervention of God. It is true that
the expected deliverance was to be an arbitrary and isolated
event, but it was to happen in the visible world. To that extent
they were looking to the future and to a time when things

* C. Northcote Parkinson, *The Evolution of Political Thought* (London,
1958), p. 20.

would be vastly bettered, at least for themselves. To that extent the attitude of Christians and Muslims was both revolutionary and similar. It cannot be said, however, that medieval Christians had much idea of progress. They looked to the fathers of the Church for guidance and to the Apostles for inspiration. Accepting the idea of Christ's return, they would not have argued in any other sense that the world was in any way likely to improve.

From the fourteenth century the medieval outlook began to change. While it might not be possible to improve on the merits of the Early Church, it was feasible, perhaps, to regain the level of civilization achieved by Rome and Greece. This level was apparently regained, and in some ways surpassed, by 1500. It was possible, by then, to conceive of history as revealing progress, perhaps as a revelation of God's wisdom, perhaps even as a measure of man's achievement. If history was thus progressive, showing the superiority of the present over the past, it became reasonable to conclude that the future might be superior again to the present. And, granted that the world was thus changing, it became natural to ask what the future changes might be and whether they could be hastened or modified by plans made in advance. The immediate result of this thinking was the publication of *Utopia* and of similar works — a type of literature peculiar to the Western world of the modern period. Thomas More was stimulated, of course, by the age of discovery, by the knowledge that different peoples might live in very different ways. But he at once exemplified and influenced Renascence thought about the future. It was possible now to believe that history is a tale of progress and that still better times must lie ahead.

For our present purpose the content of utopian literature is of less importance than the fact that it was nearly all published between 1516 and 1905. *Utopia* itself was followed by *Christianopolis* in 1627, and Campanella's *City of the Sun* in 1637. The eighteenth century yields two significant books, *Memoirs of the Year 2500* (1772), by Louis Sébastien Mercier, and *The Description of Spensonia* (1795), by Thomas Spence. But the bulk of these forward-looking books are of the nineteenth century. We can follow the train of progressive thought from F. M. Charles Fourier to Étienne Cabet, from James Silk Buckingham to E. Bulwer-Lytton. *The Happy Colony* (1854), by Robert Pemberton, leads on to *Freeland*, almost the only German utopia, of 1889, and so to William Morris's *News from Nowhere* (1890). The twentieth century offers *Neustria* (1901), by Emile Thirion, *Altneuland* (1903), by Theodor Herzl, *Underground Men* by Gabriel Tarde, and — almost completing the series — *A Modern Utopia* (1905), by H. G. Wells. The only dream to come true, more or less, was Ebenezer Howard's *Garden Cities of Tomorrow* (1902), which foreshadowed such suburbs as Letchworth. The whole series comes virtually to an end with H. G. Wells, after whose later and feebler efforts we have *Brave New World* (1932), by Aldous Huxley and *Nineteen Eighty-Four* (1949), by George Orwell.

For the whole period, therefore, of European expansion, the idea of improving the world, of pressing forward to some utopian objective, was in the air. Everything could be done, and was done, in the name of progress. In addition to his growing technical advantage, the European had the merit of being progressive. In addition to his comparative ignorance, the Oriental had the faults of fatalism and apathy. It was the British mission to change all that. But whereas earlier empire builders had anticipated only a short period of dominance, the later imperialists saw their role as practically permanent. As example of the older type, we might take Sir Stamford Raffles, the founder of Singapore. On the subject of the college he planned for that city — a city only just founded, the basis for a British Malaya not even then conceived — he said in 1822:

If commerce brings wealth to our shores, it is the spirit of literature and philanthropy that teaches us how to employ it for the noblest purposes. It is this which has made Britain go forth among nations, strong in her native light to dispense blessings to all around her. If the time shall come when her Empire shall have passed away, these monuments of her virtue will endure when her triumphs shall have become an empty name. Let it be still the boast of Britain to write her name in characters of light; let her not be remembered as the tempest whose course was desolation, but as the gale of spring, reviving the slumbering seeds of mind, and calling them to life . . .*

These are the words of a remarkable man, foreseeing the end of a rule which he had only just established. Contrast these with the words of another remarkable man, whose work lay afterwards in the same part of the world. Wrote Sir Frederick Weld in 1880:

To teach men to govern themselves, you must throw them on their own resources. We are necessarily doing the very reverse. Moreover, I doubt if Asiatics can ever be taught to govern themselves; it is contrary to the genius of their race, to what we know of their past history, and to tendencies created by their religious systems. What suits them is a mild and equitable despotism; that *we* can give them . . .†

Such contrast as there is between these views is not primarily one of character but of period. As the nineteenth century went on, the European lead had lengthened. In matters military, naval, technical, medical, and industrial, the Asian was being left further and further behind. Raffles could visualize the Malays ruling themselves; he had seen them doing it. Nor had he any great technical advantage over them. Weld's superiority was, by comparison, crushing. What had been happening is well expressed by Mannath C. Mallik:

* C. E. Wurtzburg, *Raffles of the Eastern Isles* (London, 1954), p. 634.
† Lovat, *Life of Sir Frederick Weld*, p. 312.

Europeans even of a friendly type lament the want of manliness in Indian nature and conduct. It would be strange if after so many centuries of coercion by religious, spiritual and political teachers, and of demoralizing social conditions, any manliness should survive, especially as when any sign of it is displayed by individuals, it is discouraged by parents, teachers, spiritual guides and political rulers as impertinence and disloyalty . . .*

What happened in India happened elsewhere. People adjusted themselves to a foreign dominance. So it would be quite wrong to conclude that the Malays had been merely standing still. They had deteriorated, being driven to piracy by their loss of trade and driven to opium by their loss of prestige. Like the Indians and the Chinese, they had begun to feel inferior and impotent. And part of Weld's doubt about their capacity for rule was due to the fact that government itself — in his sense — had become more complex. It was no longer a matter of merely keeping order. It involved agricultural experiment and monetary reform, docking capacities and sanitary rules. Weld was speaking for his generation when he questioned the Asian ability to rule.

Spokesman for almost the same generation was the Rt. Hon. George Nathaniel Curzon, M.P., the future viceroy, who traveled extensively in 1887–88, and again in 1892–93. Observant, scholarly, extremely able, Curzon made none of the usual mistakes. Believing as he did that Britain's power would increase still further and that the British Empire was "under Providence, the greatest instrument for good that he world has seen," he did not underestimate the East, as the following passage shows:

From Asia we have received the architecture of the Moslem — that most spiritual and refined of human conceptions — the porcelain of China, the faience of Persia, Rhodes and Damascus, the infinitely ingenious art of Japan. On her soil were

* Mallik, *op. cit.*, p. 183.

reared the most astonishing of all cities, Babylon; the most princely of palaces, Persepolis; the statcliest of temples, Angkor Wat; the loveliest of tombs, the Taj Mahal . . .*

Admitting all this, and admitting that Asian countries differ from each other, Curzon tried — as perhaps no other author has done — to define what we mean by the word "Oriental." His finding is this:

> . . . in character a general indifference to truth and respect for successful wile, in deportment dignity, in society the rigid maintenance of the family union, in government the mute acquiescence of the governed, in administration and justice the open corruption of administrators and judges, and in everyday life a statuesque and inexhaustible patience, which attaches no value to time, and wages unappeasable warfare against hurry.
> The impact between this solid amalgam of character and habit, and the elastic and insinuating force which we denominate civilization, is a phenomenon which now in many countries I have set myself to examine, and which, I think, surpasses all others in human interest.†

In studying these very interesting comments, we have to observe, first of all, that civilization to Curzon had come to have a special meaning. Raffles could see the Chinese, Indians, and Malays as civilized, which in the ordinary sense they were. But Curzon, while emphasizing that the wise traveler should not mistake what is strange for what is inferior or degraded, reserved the word "civilization" for the West. We have next to observe that, while understanding the differences between one Eastern country and another, he could still enumerate some characteristics common to all. He could perceive the maintenance of the family union through which the Oriental is less

* G. N. Curzon, *Problems of the Far East* (London, 1894), p. 2.
† *Ibid.*, pp. 2–3.

individualized. But he listed the further qualities of untruthful-
ness, cunning, dignity, corruption, patience, and mute obedience
to authority. What he failed to realize is that these are not
specifically Oriental characteristics. They are, purely, the habits
engendered by a feeling of inferiority to an alien but dominant
civilization. The Victorian mistake was to talk of the changeless
East, failing to perceive that its deterioration was in progress
before their eyes. The qualities which Curzon found in the
Indians and Chinese were much the same as could be found in
medieval Europe. The people of that period were habitually
untruthful — hence our habit of making witnesses give evidence
under oath. The country folk always had the peasant cunning
of the poor. The clergy and lawyers, the doctors and teachers
all had that defensive dignity we associate with ignorance. The
lords and lackeys were corrupt, but could normally count on the
patience and dumb submission of the people at large. These
are the qualities engendered by civilization in decline, by the
knowledge that things used to be better, by the conviction that
things elsewhere are better now.

We might fairly conclude that Curzon's observation was
better than his perception, but we should at least remember
how good his observation was. He was able to contrast "the un-
yielding and pitiless clutch of Islam" with "the mild faith of
India overlaid with superstition and decay," and both alongside
"the mixture of ethics and demonology which passes for religion
in China." He was again able to contrast the street life of
Peking, "a phantasmagoria of excruciating incident too bewilder-
ing to grasp, too aggressive to acquiesce in, too absorbing to
escape" with the atmosphere of the Forbidden City, where
"everything is clandestine, veiled and sealed." He looked on
the Chinese with some respect:

> the frugal, hard-limbed, indomitable, ungracious race, who op-
> pose to all overtures from the outside the sullen resistance of a

national character self-confident and stolid, a religious and moral code of incredible and all-absorbing rigour, and a governing system that has not varied for ages and is still wrapped in the mantle of a superb and paralysing conceit.*

His diagnosis of China's decay lies in those last words, but he went on to ask more specifically what hindered China's recovery:

The answer lies in the immemorial curse of Oriental Countries, the trail of the serpent that is found everywhere from Stanboul to Peking — the vicious incubus of officialdom, paramount, selfish, domineering, and corrupt. Distrust of private enterprise is rooted in the mind trained up to believe that the Government is everything and the individual nothing . . .†

In reality, therefore, the institution of which China is most proud, viz. a lettered bureaucracy, is the source of her greatest weakness. Educated upon a system which has not varied for ages, stuffed with senseless and impracticable precepts, discharging the ceremonial duties of his office with a mechanical and servile accuracy, the victim of incredible superstitions and sorceries, but arrogant with a pride beyond human conception, furnished with an insufficient salary, and therefore compelled to peculate and plunder, the Chinese mandarin is China's worst enemy. All private enterprise is killed by official strangulation, all public spirit is extinguished by official greed. Nor, as it is the ambition and is within the scope of everybody, whatever his class, to become an official himself, is there any order to which we can look for successful protest. The entire governing class, itself recruited from the mass of the people, is interested in the preservation of the *status quo*. The forces ordinarily enlisted on the side of change, those of the *literati* or student class are more reactionary in China than any other, seeing that, unlike Russia — where they are trampled upon and ignored — and unlike

* *Ibid.*, p. 221.
† *Ibid.*, pp. 337–38.

India — where they complain of inadequate range for their ambition — they already, by virtue of their degrees, hold the keys of power. Neither can it be supposed that, with a people so obstinate and so vain, there is the smallest inclination among the lower strata of society to move where their leaders decline to advance. Both find an equal charm in stagnation.*

Curzon's gifts as a prophet were less remarkable than his powers of observation, for he could see no likelihood of Chinese aggression, e.g. against Russian Turkistan:

. . . The idea of her marching through Tibet, and across the Himalayas, to recover Nepal from Great Britain, is scarcely less fantastic . . .

To an even more nebulous future, into which not even the charms of an unfettered imagination will seduce us, belongs the epoch when, according to Mr. C. H. Pearson [Author of *National Life and Character: A Forecast*] Chinese gentlemen will throng the salons of Paris and the clubs of Pall Mall; when a Chinese patron of the turf will lead back to the weighing-room a winner of the English Derby; and when the problem of superfluous womenkind will be solved by the apparition at Christian altars of eligible Chinese husbands . . .†

In many respects, Mr. C. H. Pearson's nebulous future would seem to have arrived, and sooner than Lord Curzon had thought possible. But Curzon's historical sense was no better than his foresight, for he failed to see the wider significance of his own observations. All that he said about the decadent China of 1893 was almost equally applicable to the decadent Mughal Empire of 1707, and to the equally decadent Roman Empire of, say, 200 A.D. That it should apply, almost word for word, to the Britain of 1963 — as to the United States of 1993 — is something he could hardly have foreseen. From our present stand-

* *Ibid.*, p. 259.
† *Ibid.*, p. 406.

point it is easier to see that he was describing not merely China but *any* civilization in a state of decay. Bureaucracy — complete with its mantle of a superb and paralyzing conceit — is one of the symptoms. Overtaxation is another, with gambling as its counterpart, and superstition as its sequel. To Curzon's just criticism, a Chinese philosopher should ideally have replied, "Ask not for whom the bell tolls. It tolls for thee."

When viceroy of India (1898–1905), Lord Curzon exemplified British imperialism at its best. He galvanized the government departments into action and did much on behalf of the peasants. He did all he could for archaeology and art, the discovery of the ancient Indus civilization (in 1925), being indirectly the result of the work he began. "Curzon could not conceive that Indians could take over their country in a foreseeable future," writes Percival Spear, "but he was convinced that he must work to the limit for their good." Work he certainly did, and in so doing created the "Congress" opposition to British rule. "The breach between the government and the new intelligentsia was wide and deep." Reading this, it would be natural to suspect that Lord Curzon had been a tyrant whose troops had mown down Indian rioters, and whose prison doors had slammed on Indian politicians. But this would be quite untrue. He was among the ablest of administrators, and yet it was he who aroused the greatest opposition.

Why was this? What was his crime against humanity? His existence was the crime, and this is what we have to understand. His inhumanity was in being, as it might seem, more than human. Their civilization's decay, followed by years of alien rule, had left the Indians with no capacity for leadership. They have little enough even now. No one had asked their opinion about anything since the century began. They had been subjected, instead, to an increasingly benevolent rule — "a mild and equitable despotism," as Weld put it. There had been rare moments of panic violence as at the time of the Mutiny, leaving behind some traces of mutual distrust. But the occasional volley, like the bribe accepted by the European of Clive's day, was at least understandable — a human reaction, a yielding to anger or avarice. What was past endurance was the later philanthropy. "You must understand," said the British ruler, "that I plan everything for the benefit of the people. Other people can say what they like but, personally, I think the Bengalis (or Sikhs or Pathans, as the case might be) are terribly good chaps!" To his subjects, he added, "You won't understand everything I do — some of the things I have to consider are a bit complex, actually — but you must realize that I know what is best for you. It's simply your welfare that I care about." Cynics will deny that British officials were as altruistic as they pretended to be. They will hint that they were serving their own, or their own country's interests, as many undoubtedly were. But what if they were genuine lovers of India, loyal to the precepts of Christ or Jeremy Bentham? What if they really cared, as some unquestionably must have done? Their crime, in that case, was past all forgiveness.

Look at it from the Indian point of view. Here is an alien ruler who is busied with railways and famine relief, education and hygiene. He knows more about finance and irrigation, more about commerce and law, than anyone else in the district. He played cricket for Oxford, and won the Military Cross in the last war. He is energetic, kindly, humorous and efficient, knowing every yard of the territory he has to administer. "Ah, but he doesn't know the people as an Indian would!" Suppose the answer to that is that his grandfather and father both served in India, he himself being born there, that he speaks Hindi and Urdu with equal fluency, and that he has actually written a book about the Sikh religion. To this the Indian critic might reply, "All very well, but his motives are doubtful. He does his work for money and would never be paid so well in England." Comes now the final parry and thrust. "For money? My dear fellow, he doesn't need *money*. He has an estate in Norfolk. He married into a wealthy family, for that matter. There is no need for him to work at all." With this final revelation the Indian is left with a hopeless feeling of inferiority. He cannot claim to be as efficient. How could he be? He has never had a position of responsibility. He cannot claim to be as energetic. How could he be energetic on the diet to which he is restricted? He may have no ground for thinking himself equal to this European in any single respect, not even in knowledge of the vernacular, not even in benevolence toward the people. He *has* to treat the Englishman as his superior, and he hates himself for it.

All the circumstances in the above case are imaginary, and there have been examples enough to the contrary. There have been Englishmen that the Indian could comfortably despise — ignorant, drunken, and venal. Such bitterness as many Indians still feel against the West can be traced to personal humiliations they have suffered, especially in being treated like servants by people whose own social status in England is far inferior to their own. The British could not avoid a tone of patronage even toward Indians they liked, even toward Indians, like Gandhi, whom they felt compelled to admire. But the fact remains that it was the knowledgeable, efficient, and polite Europeans who did the serious damage, simply because he left the Oriental nothing to do and no basis, therefore, for self-respect. Of all superior Englishmen, Curzon was the ideal type; and it was his rule that represented the last straw. The Indians did not hate him, and it would not have mattered so much if they had. They hated themselves, and that is where the real trouble begins. For the man who has inspired those feelings can do nothing about it. Indeed, his efforts to be more friendly will only make matters worse. His crime is not in what he does, but in the competent way he sets about it. His crime is in being what he is.

248 EAST AND WEST

There are critics of colonialism who will reject this interpretation as a covert defense of Britain. They will point to British economic exploitation of the East, to the ruin of local textiles, and the cultivation of opium. They will tell of misunderstanding and bloodshed, oppression and injustice and looting. But the plain fact is that the sacrilege of which they complain was even more characteristic of countries, like Turkey or Siam, which were never conquered at all. And the unpopularity of the European reached its peak, not in places where the British had ruled, but in Japan, where they had never appeared save as allies and friends. In the pamphlet issued to the Japanese troops invading Malaya, the following passage occurs:

> In the Japan of recent years where no one who cannot read English can proceed to higher education, and where English is widely used in all first class hotels, trains and steamships, we have unthinkingly come to accept Europeans as superior and to despise the Chinese and the peoples of the South.
> This is like spitting into our own eyes. Bearing in mind that we Japanese, as an Eastern people, have ourselves for long been classed alongside the Chinese and the Indian as an inferior race and treated as such, we must at the very least, when in Asia, beat these Westerners to submission, that they may change their arrogant and ill-mannered attitude.*

And yet, what positive harm had the British done to Japan? They had thought the Japanese mildly amusing as caricatured in The Mikado of 1885. They had collected Japanese woodcuts and sent missionaries to preach Christianity. They had trained the Japanese Navy and attended performances of Madam Butterfly. It was not they who insisted upon the Japanese westernizing their economy and their forces. It was not they who made the Japanese learn English or put their schoolgirls

* Masanobu Tsuji, trans. by M. E. Lake, Singapore: The Japanese Version (London, 1962), p. 306.

into Edwardian sailor suits. All this the Japanese had done of their own free will. They had taken to wearing bowler hats, just as Gandhi in his younger days had worn a top hat and frock coat. They had thought themselves inferior and reacted in just such a way as to seem as inferior as they felt. But it was their own choice. And their emotion, after the Omoto-Kyo sect had done its work, convincing them of Japan's world-conquering destiny, was one of bitter contempt — not for the British, but for themselves. It is this self-hatred which can make a people — any people, East or West — behave with surprising violence. They can gain the momentary reputation of being very tiresome indeed.

18

THE TURNING POINT

AT WHAT POINT in modern history did the tide turn against the West? There is, of course, no such point, no single moment. But two dates emerge, marking the early stages in a movement which has still to be completed. And the first of these dates might well be 1845, fixing the period at which Europe began to lose confidence in its mission. This wavering appears first in architecture, taking the form of an abrupt collapse in the established tradition of design. The classical style of eighteenth-century architecture was maintained into the nineteenth century, with Georgian giving place to Regency and that again to Early Victorian. There had been minor eccentricities, Chinese pavilions and artificial "ruins," but they were of marginal interest. The builder had normally to exercise his talents within the boundaries of an accepted routine. But, after about 1845, the known methods ceased to work. The classic proportions were lost as rooms gained a new height — Anglo-Indian influence providing space for an imaginary punkah. The magic had gone out of the formula and buildings varied from the mediocre to the drab. With all its own inspiration lost, the established school of Italianate Victorian went down beneath the onset of the Gothic revival.

The Greek and Roman tradition represented, remember, the assertion of the more purely Western aesthetic, contrasting scornfully with the world of Asia. The medieval tradition had represented something quite different, the frank admission that wisdom comes from the East. It was toward the East that the

churches were orientated. It was from the East that their doctrines and rituals had come. And now, after 1840, the movement began for a return to the Middle Ages, to the last period
of Oriental dominance. Augustus Welby Pugin entered the
Church of Rome in 1837; his masterpiece — the first monastery
to be built in England for three centuries — being consecrated
in 1844. In 1840, Charles Barry began the construction, in
Gothic style, of the present Houses of Parliament. In 1845,
John Henry Newman was received into the Catholic Church,
leaving his Tractarian followers at least near to the Catholicism
from which most of them actually recoiled. Ruskin published
his *Seven Lamps of Architecture* in 1849. By 1850 the trend
was well established, leading eventually to much that was sensible in domestic architecture. It also led, and logically, to
buildings of a specifically Oriental style — to Islamic railway
stations in India and Malaya, to Moorish arcades and bazaars
in England itself. In all the ferment of this period the important event that attracted least attention was the publication
of the *Communist Manifesto* in 1848. But this too fitted into
the pattern of the time.

The European loss of direction, in 1845 or thereabouts, was
followed, as one would expect, by the beginnings of revolt in
Asia; and whatever previous discontent there may have been,
1850 remains about the earliest date to which it can be assigned. It was in that year that the Taiping Rebellion took
place in China. Directed against the Ch'ing Dynasty, the revolt
was also one against missionary and foreign influence. It was
suppressed by "Chinese" Gordon, one of the more formidable
evangelists of the day. It had scarcely ended when the Indian
Mutiny began.

The Indian Mutiny was preceded, however, by Commodore
Perry's visits to Japan in 1853–54, which were the prelude to
the astonishing process of Japan's renascence. From the time
of the Meiji restoration of 1868 and the overthrow of the

Tokugawa Sbogunate, the Japanese westernized and industrialized their country. By the end of the century, Japan was a world
power and the only Asian country of which this could be said.
The Boxer Rising of 1900 showed that there was feeling against
the West in China, already a victim of Japanese aggression in
1894–95. But this first demonstration of Japan's strength was
a mere rehearsal for the expected clash with Russia. The Russian advance across Asia had brought them (see page 201) to
Manchuria. For the Tsar of Russia it was important to establish a naval predominance in the Far East. For Japan, such a
Russian achievement would have been fatal. Without declar-
ing war, the Japanese attacked Port Arthur in 1904. The Russians' countermove was to bring their Baltic fleet round to the
Far East. It was destroyed on arrival by Admiral Togo at the
Battle of Tsushima. With that fatal blow, accompanied by the
fall of Port Arthur and military defeat at Mukden, the Russians
had to make peace, leaving both Manchuria and Korea to
Japan. For Russia the year of disaster was 1905.

There is an interesting book by Maurice Paleologue, called
*The Turning Point: Three Critical Years, 1904–1906,** in which
he shows that the First World War had become a certainty by
the time of Théophile Delcassé's resignation in June, 1905. He
also remarks that Nicholas II was urged to war with Japan by
the German Emperor, who told him "God has ordained you to
defend Christian civilisation against the Yellow Peril and bring
about the triumph of the cross of the Saviour on the shores of
the Pacific Ocean." † It is not clear that Nicholas II saw the
problem in exactly that light. But the years 1904–6 were certainly crucial in the relationship between East and West, and
particularly so where Britain was concerned. For Britain had
entered into an alliance with Japan in January, 1902 — mainly
to prevent an understanding between Russia and Japan at

* Maurice Paleologue, *The Turning Point*, trans. by F. Appleby Holt (London, 1935).
† *Ibid.*, p. 36.

Britain's expense — but also as a result of the Germans building their high seas fleet. Authorized in 1898, the German Navy was already a force to be reckoned with in 1903. At this juncture Britain needed two fleets, one to face Germany in the North Sea, the other to defend British interests in the Far East. But these two fleets did not exist, both political and technical considerations preventing their ever being built; and it is proper to ask at this point what these considerations were.

In a book already quoted, written in about 1894, the Rt. Hon. George Nathaniel Curzon foretold the increase of British influence in the Far East, provided only that British sea power were maintained. Explaining this proviso, he added this footnote:

> I introduce this qualification because the naval strength of Great Britain in the Far East, i.e. in the waters between Singapore and Vladivostok, when compared with the combined fleets of France and Russia can scarcely be said to possess that incontestable predominance without which security cannot be predicated. In April 1894 the British squadron in the Far East consisted of 2 ironclads aggregating 11,150 tons, 20 unarmoured vessels, comprising 7 cruisers and seven gunboats; and six torpedo-boats . . .*

If not incontestably superior to the next two fleets in the Far East, the British had at that time nine ironclads and cruisers against a Franco-Russian equivalent of four. Their force was one, in short, of a respectable size. By 1905 the position has entirely altered, with the Russians replaced by the victorious Japanese and the high seas fleet constituting a new threat in home waters. In that year the British Far East fleet was withdrawn, leaving British interests to be protected by the Japanese. This fleet was never replaced, and into the vacuum its departure created were drawn the competing influences of Japan and the U.S.A.

In theory there was nothing to stop the British from build-

---

* Curzon, *op. cit.*, p. 426.

ing another Far East fleet, but the Conservatives, who might just possibly have done so, were defeated in the general election of 1905. The government which took office early in 1906 had been elected by a Liberal-Labour alliance. Its leader, Sir Henry Campbell Bannerman, was a moderate, but with the fiery David Lloyd George as one of his ministers. And when Campbell Bannerman died in 1908, to be succeeded by Asquith, it was Lloyd George who became Chancellor of the Exchequer. In his speech made when presenting the budget of 1909, he said that his additional taxes were to wage implacable warfare against poverty and squalor. These taxes were, in fact, highly significant, comprising both a new super-tax, and far heavier death duties. As the revolutionary H.M.S. *Dreadnought* had been launched in 1906, starting an armament race in which Britain had only the smallest lead, some increase in taxation might have been thought inevitable. But it was not on the Navy that the money was to be spent. More of it was to go for old age pensions, which were quite expensive in theory and far more expensive in practice. And the most significant thing about this socialist legislation was — for our present purpose — its looking to the past. Spent on education or health, the money would have done something for the rising generation. Spent on armaments, it might have averted the First World War or at least shortened its duration. Instead, its purpose was more sentimental — the care of the old. Only in a country with a slackened momentum could such an emphasis have been possible.

In the long run, the incidence of the rising taxes would have been enough in itself to bring the British Empire to a standstill. The comforts of the welfare state would discourage ordinary people from going overseas. The dwindling reward for outstanding effort would discourage the enterprise of the empire builder and capitalist. But a high taxation, although lethal in its results (as previously shown in Mogul India, and Imperial Rome), is almost certainly the symptom, not the cause, of a more basic

failure. Britain was not the only European country to reveal a
new interest in social welfare. The trend toward socialism was
almost equally apparent in France, where there was a socialist
prime minister in 1906. The German socialists held eighty one
seats in the reichstag by 1903, and there was a roughly equivalent
movement in the U.S.A. Nor was the British withdrawal from the
Far East a purely naval phenomenon. It affected colonial
policy, not only in India, but — still more significantly — in
the very latest territories acquired on the very furthest frontier.
And here too the story brings us back to the year 1905.

Of the more extensive territories under British control — as
distinct from isolated bases like Hong Kong, or trading communities such as existed in Shanghai — the last to be acquired
were in Malaya. To the original outposts, the Straits settlements, consisting of Singapore, Penang, and Malacca, there
had been added the greater part of the Malay Peninsula. The
states first brought under British protection were reorganized as
the Federated Malay States in 1895–96. North of these lay
the other Malay states, all more or less subject to Siamese over-
lordship. Beyond these again lay the natural frontier, the
Isthmus of Kra. This might be compared to the line along
which the tired Romans fixed their northern frontier in Britain.
Unwilling to take much more trouble with the wretched country, they fixed their boundary at Solway Firth in 122 A.D. It
was on a line easy to patrol, but there existed a still shorter
line, that of the Forth and Clyde, to which they advanced their
frontier at a later date. To have stopped short of occupying
the whole island could have been regarded at the time as a symptom of fatigue. But to have called off the hunt while de-
ployed between Scarborough and Whitehaven, would have been
regarded as a symptom of collapse. And this was, roughly, what
happened in the Malay Peninsula. The neck of the Peninsula
reaches its narrowest point near the southern boundary of the
Tenasserim provinces. Perhaps the shortest distance would fol-

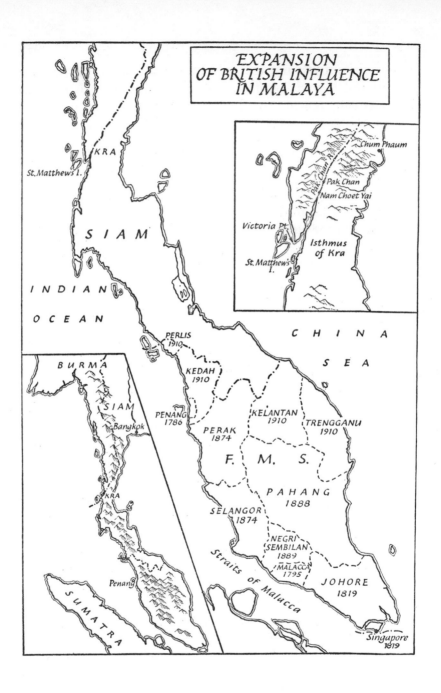

EXPANSION
OF BRITISH INFLUENCE
IN MALAYA

Chum Phaum

Pak Chan

Nam Choet Yai

Victoria Pt.

St. Matthew's I.

Isthmus
of Kra

K R A

St. Matthews I.

S I A M

I N D I A N

O C E A N

C H I N A

S E A

PERLIS
1910

KEDAH
1910

BURMA

S I A M

Bangkok

PENANG
1786

PERAK
1874

KELANTAN
1910

TRENGGANU
1910

F. M. S.

PAHANG
1888

SELANGOR
1874

NEGRI
SEMBILAN
1889

MALACCA
1795

JOHORE
1819

K R A

Penang

Straits of Malacca

S U M A T R A

Singapore
1819

low the 10th parallel, but the line of the Pak Chan and Chinpohun rivers makes the more natural line. It was toward that natural frontier that the British were moving from about 1874.

The current genius among the British builders of Empire was Sir Frank Swettenham, who had a hand in every stroke of expansion from 1871 onwards. He rose rapidly in the Malayan Civil Service, and was finally appointed Governor and High Commissioner in 1901. It was the summit of his ambition and the climax of a brilliant career. More than that, it gave him the opportunity to round off the Empire he had done so much to create. Behind him at the Colonial Office was Joseph Chamberlain, Britain's greatest Secretary of State for the Colonies. In front of him lay the northerly Malay states, Kelantan and Trengganu, and beyond them the natural frontiers. The result of British diplomacy was the treaty of 1902, which brought Kelantan and Trengganu under a measure of British influence. The agreement was obviously unsatisfactory, and it must have been assumed that Swettenham would bring more pressure to bear. Instead, he suddenly resigned in 1903, leaving his work unfinished. With the reasons for his departure we need not concern ourselves, but the results were disastrous to the forward movement with which he had been associated. By 1909 the Siamese had admittedly placed Kedah and Perlis, as well as Kelantan and Trengganu, under British protection. But there the matter ended, leaving Malaya with an unmarked, unsurveyed, and rambling frontier, impossible to defend and difficult even to locate. This was the first British handicap during the campaign of 1941, and a perpetual liability during the emergency which began in 1948. Nor will Malaya have any measure of security until this frontier has been rectified. That the British should have called a halt in 1906 was perhaps inevitable, but their effort had virtually died away in 1903.

A wavering of British determination, which might pass unnoticed in Paris or Berlin, was instantly sensed in Shanghai and

Hong Kong. China itself has been ruled since early times by that form of government which is coming to be described as a meritocracy, one feature of which is the complete separation of the governing from the governed. Under such a bureaucratic rule, the people at large become expert in the interpretation of evidence which may seem to reveal a government policy not otherwise explained. They automatically reject the press release, while studying carefully what the officials actually do. Nor have they become less cynical under British colonial influence or rule. They ignore the speeches, and count the warships in the harbor. Among people with this keen sense for realities, the disappearance of the British Far East fleet could not pass unnoticed; nor, for that matter, could they fail to remark the resignation of a Curzon or a Swettenham. They had noticed, moreover, that Britain's last deliberate acquisition, Weihaiwei, at the tip of the Shantung Peninsula, occupied in 1898, had never been actually fortified. What, they asked each other, if the British were going to writhdraw?

The Chinese, who formed over half the population of British Malaya and nearly the whole population of Singapore, had mostly come from Kwangtung or Fukien provinces, driven out by unemployment and water shortage. Their migration had been illegal in the first place under the Manchu penal code, but they had come originally, like the British, with the intention of returning eventually to their homeland. Failure to do so would mean a drastic break in the continuity of family life. So the womenfolk were left behind, partly to perform the religious duties to their husband's dead ancestors, partly to care for the parents still living. In this they were assisted by remittances from their menfolk overseas. The successful migrant would return to China without attracting official notice; the less prosperous would return in a coffin, equally ending in the village from which he had come. Between 1880 and 1900, the migration changed in character, the women now tending to accompany their husbands. Of these migrants, male and female, many still returned to China. Others, however, did not, and Malaya gradually acquired a resident and balanced Chinese population, with an increasing proportion of these actually born in the country. Although many of them had maintained close contact with China, others looked back with a certain resentment. Under the Manchu rule (essentially alien), they had been desperately poor, suffering the extortions of the minor officials until forced to emigrate; but this was itself illegal, exposing them to a possible charge of piracy should they return. They had some reason to look with gratitude toward the British, to whose protection they owed such prosperity as had come their way.

Dr. Wang Gung Wu of the University of Malaya made a study in 1953 of the attitudes to be discovered among the Straits Chinese at the turn of the century. English education and example were having an effect on them, he points out, so that they made a voluntary contribution to assist the British against the Boers. More than that, they organized the Straits Chinese British Association in 1900. Fervent in their loyalty, as was shown at the time of Edward VII's coronation, some of them formed the Chinese Company of the Singapore Volunteers. Others were active in the Chinese Y.M.C.A. After the Chinese defeat in 1895, with subsequent humiliation at the hands of the European powers, there was no authority in China for which the overseas (or Nanyang) Chinese could feel much respect. Attempts were being made to depose the emperor — attempts which were applauded by some and condemned by others — but perhaps the majority of the Chinese regarded the whole situation as hopeless. There was a moment, in fact, when the Straits Chinese might conceivably have transferred their loyalties to Britain. The moment passed, however, and the arrival of Sun Yat-sen in 1906 was decisive, tipping the scales the other way. Straits Chinese interest began to center once more on China, a trend still further confirmed during Sun Yat-sen's visit

in 1908. Largely through his efforts, and with appreciable help
from the Straits Chinese, the Manchu Dynasty was overturned
in 1911, with Sun Yat-sen as President of the Republic which
took its place. The Chinese renascence had begun, and the
overseas Chinese began to take a new pride in their country of
origin.

That the Chinese should have chosen to be themselves may
not seem in any way unreasonable. What is significant is the
period at which this change of attitude took place. For, however prone they may be to sentiment about the homeland, they
have no urge to support the losing side. Their conclusion in
1906 that Britain was past its zenith can be regarded as a fairly
objective assessment of strength, and one which events were to
justify. First result of the British withdrawal was the Battle of
Coronel in 1914, second was the loss of H.M.S. *Pegasus,* and
third was the cruise of the *Emden,* which culminated in the
raids on Madras and Penang. The logical sequel to this last
event was the mutiny of Indian troops at Singapore, in Feb-
ruary, 1915. It was suppressed with some difficulty, the available security forces including 190 Japanese special constables,
raised by the Japanese consul in Singapore, and a landing party
from the Japanese cruiser *Otawa,* the second warship to arrive
on the scene. There was a period, indeed, during the First
World War, when the Japanese Navy was more in evidence
than the British in Malayan waters; a period even when they
had their own signal station ashore. All this foreshadowed their
later appearance there, no longer as allies.

As the old imperialists disappeared from the British scene —
Rhodes died in 1902, Joseph Chamberlain resigned in 1903,
Alfred Milner left South Africa in 1905, Lord Cromer left
Egypt in 1907 — their places were taken by people to whom the
Empire meant a great deal less. Simultaneously, Asia began its
systematic rejection of Western values. It must be understood,
however, that this rejection was never complete. The Asian
leaders realized that Western techniques were essential to the

exclusion of Western ideas. More than that, it might be necessary to accept some ideas before rejecting the rest. Sun Yatsen preached revolution in a European tropical suit and pith helmet. His "Republic" was an essentially Western institution. He knew, moreover, that European uniform is the key to success in war. Those who discard everything British on principle would never discard the Sam Browne belt and cross-strap, for this is everywhere the symbol of authority. Foremost in their rejection of the West were the Japanese, who were also the most thorough in westernization in so far as it was clearly unavoidable. By 1905, their year of victory, they knew exactly how far they meant to go. And the point where they stopped dead was in their refusal to give the individual his Western individuality. They could not and do not see that the separate ego has the importance assigned to it by Christian doctrine and Western political theory.

Mr. Sumi Myakawa, a Japanese who visited England as recently as 1908, explained the position in simple language when he wrote: "This mode of living is the most fundamental cause of difference between Oriental and Occidental civilisation, and I think the most powerful one of all causes. The advantages of the English custom of a separate home are — it is easy to live, do what you like according to your own taste, and you can carry your home to any part of the world you wish, thus helping colonisation. Again, this custom makes people work and get money to have a proper home. I tried the English way of living, but after a few years I began to think, 'I do not want to live exactly like this.' In the separate home there is too much individualism, too much egotism. I am afraid you are losing respect due to old parents, also the mutual help to your family." Mr. Myakawa would appear to forget that unless the Japanese are prepared to establish "separate homes" they cannot hope to realise their cherished dream of Empire. The emancipation of women is destined to strike deep at the root of a system that has ceased to help and now only hinders true progression.

That emancipation cannot possibly be achieved without disturbing the foundation of filial piety and of loyalty. Individualism will assert itself . . .*

The author of this interesting comment emphasizes that, whereas Christianity teaches the value of life, Buddhism teaches that life has no value. He does not see a lack of comprehension between East and West, but rather a sharp difference of opinion, and one mainly affecting the position of women. He says that the Japanese will be looked upon as an inferior race as long as they allow children to marry, as long as they keep concubines and treat their women as slaves, as long, finally, as they are ready, some of them, to sell their daughters as prostitutes. As against that, he is uneasily aware that the Japanese can no longer be ignored:

Asia is no longer slumbering. In the vast territories that stretch from Peking to Teheran signs are manifest that the real awakening is at hand. Nor is it an awakening that will pass with the hour. It is an awakening that means that the East is standing upon the threshold of a new era, one that may be destined to witness a re-shaping of the map of the world. In other words, after centuries of dull sleep the East is now undergoing the process of re-vitalisation. And Japan leads the van in the march of Asia towards the attainment of her ideal, the recognition of equality with the nations of the West. The civilisation of Japan may be superficial, but it is essentially a militant civilisation. The danger to the West lies in the existence of a state of indifference which may find unpreparedness when the time arrives for the inevitable conflict with the nations of the East . . . unless the West awakens to the imminence of danger, the predominance of the white over the yellow races will cease . . . There will be keen commercial strife. By countries now prospering under alien guidance demands for self-government and eventually for autonomy will be insisted upon. And unless the

* Lancelot Lawton, *Empires of the Far East* (London, 1912), I, 701.

Powers are virile enough to combat such movements they will lose their possessions one by one . . . Japan has been the guiding star of the East. The knowledge she is imparting to others may not be of the deepest kind, for she herself is as yet groping in a darkness only illuminated by a few shafts of the light of true civilisation. But this knowledge will be sufficient to inspire effort and to raise ambition. At least it will tend to give to peoples fresh from the sleep of ages that burning desire to fight and conquer in all fields of human activity. Time and experience will do the rest.*

These are prophetic words, of which the general truth is apparent. Where the author is mistaken is in supposing that there is only one civilization and that any alternative offered must be superficial. Where he is again mistaken is in assuming that the Japanese demand only equality with the West. In point of fact, the Japanese in 1915 — the rescuers of Singapore from its mutinous sepoys — were already asking much more.

We are only aiming at making the Emperor of Japan ruler and governor of the whole world, as he is the only ruler in the world who retains the spiritual mission inherited from the remotest ancestors in the divine world.†

Even this diffident claim goes a little beyond the demand for equal status. As for Lawton's dictum that the Japanese will be thought inferior so long as they ill-treat their women, he forgot that the Japanese might already think the British inferior for the opposite reason, that they could not keep their women in order. He could hardly have foreseen, in this context, what the Japanese would think of the Americans. As for the shallowness of Japanese civilization, there are few more embarrassing experiences than attending an American motion picture about

* *Ibid.*, II, 800.
† Nehru, *op. cit.*, 835.

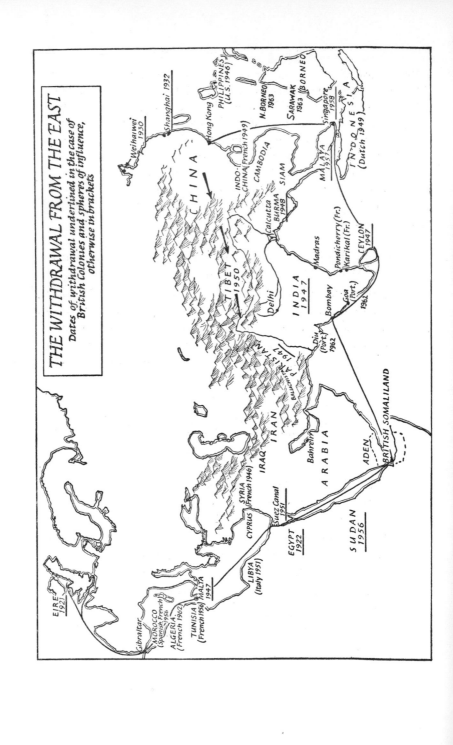

THE WITHDRAWAL FROM THE EAST

Dates of withdrawal underlined in the case of
British Colonies and spheres of influence,
otherwise in brackets

Japan. The contrast between Japanese and American manners becomes almost too painful to watch, and it is precisely the contrast between the highly civilized and the unbearably crude.

Having said so much about the turning point, we must avoid any exaggeration of the speed with which events actually move. To say that the ascendancy of the West has been on the decrease since about 1905 is not the same thing as saying that the East has reached a position of equality. No such parity has been gained, nor could the trend of events suggest that it is even imminent. The torch of Western supremacy has been passed from Britain to the U.S.A., much as it passed long ago from Macedonia to Rome. It is no longer, perhaps, the pure flame that it once was. In all the arts our greatest achievements lie unquestionably in the past. But Asian leaders who conclude from this that the West is already finished are likely to be disappointed. While the East is progressing fast, the West is not standing still. The technical gap remains and is likely to remain for years to come. What has disappeared is the established prestige of the West, the veneration for the white man as such. Britain lost that forever with the fall of Singapore in 1941, when 120,000 Commonwealth troops collapsed before the attack of 60,000 Japanese. Then followed the disintegration of 1947, the abandonment of Turkey and Greece, the withdrawal from Cairo, and the independence hastily conceded to Pakistan, India, Ceylon, and Burma. The Americans lost it afterwards in Korea, where their armies were fought to a standstill by the Chinese. While still powerful, the Americans lack the will to accept, in full, the leadership which has fallen to them. They shrink from assuming the responsibility which Britain has relinquished. "History makes it quite plain," writes Amaury de Riencourt, "that as the dominant West becomes more unsure of itself, the Orient slowly regains a new self-assurance."

World War II accelerated the most important event of our

time; the gradual falling away of the Orient, with its determined rejection of European values and economic domination . . . In all respects, this evolution is similar in scope and significance to the rise of the Parthian power in the Orient two thousand years ago, its rejection of Greek culture at the time when Rome was driven to assume leadership of the classical world.*

It remains to analyze the motives and nature of this new rejection of the West. What Western values does the East refuse? What philosophy does the East maintain? In the name of what religion is its attack to be launched? These are the questions we must seek to answer. In the meanwhile, one other question must inevitably be asked: "When will the East draw level with the West? From what date will its coming ascendancy begin?" This is the sort of fact which becomes apparent only in retrospect, all guesses beforehand being wild indeed. Should we see 2000 A.D. as the end of our Western era? One guess on this subject was made in a letter written by Henry Adams to Henry Osborn long before Spengler's time:

At the present rate of progress since 1600, it will not need another century or half century to tip thought upside down. Law in that case would disappear as theory or *a priori* principle and give place to force. Morality would become police. Explosives would reach cosmic violence. Disintegration would overcome integration.

This forecast dates, oddly enough, from 1905. It points to a collapse before 2000, and perhaps we should agree that, the pace having quickened, 1984 might be nearer the mark. And George Orwell, remember, was born in 1905.

* Amaury de Riencourt, *op. cit.*, pp. 213, 296.

19

THE RENASCENCE OF ASIA

IN HIS valuable book *Americans and Chinese*, France L. K. Hsu concludes that:

> The Western world is today the arbiter of mankind's fate. It is paradoxical but true that the reaction against Western physical domination has gone far to complete the conquest of the world by Western culture. To ensure its own survival the rest of the world has been obliged to imitate the West. It is Western methods, beliefs and goals that have been accepted and utilized to combat Western control.[*]

This is perfectly true and perfectly normal. Europe used an Oriental religion, Christianity, as a means of averting Oriental conquest in the name of Islam. Oriental people had previously used Western ideas in self-defense. It is a first and inevitable gesture of self-preservation. After this first precaution it becomes essential to decide how far the process can be allowed to go. A line must be drawn somewhere. If some techniques and ideas must be accepted as a measure of defense, others must be rejected as a method of preserving cultural identity. The first problem for renascent Asia has been to fix the point of refusal.

How was this problem faced by Mahatma Gandhi, leader of India's revival? Maurice Zinkin defines this with some precision:

> Mahatma Gandhi describes in his Autobiography how, as a student, he attempted to become completely an English gentle-

[*] Francis L. K. Hsu, *Americans and Chinese: Two Ways of Life* (New York, 1953), 441.

man: he even wore a top hat and frock coat. But English gentlemen are not merely always courteous and considerate; they
also drink whisky and eat beef, and the Mahatma could not
imitate them in this. He therefore stated a synthesis. He rejected the respect for wealth and force which runs through so
much that is bad in our Western civilisation, but he accepted
the democracy, the eagerness to take action to relieve the suffering of the poor, the respect for the individual conscience, and
the willingness to let each group get its own way which consti-
tute so much of the good. What he accepted he married to certain aspects of his own tradition — the emphasis on moral force,
the admiration for withdrawal from worldly desires, non-violence, the realisation that in India the poor meant above all the
villager. Out of the combination of these concepts he produced
the Congress Movement.*

This is a fair description of what Gandhi thought was happening, and the author comments favorably on Britain's success
in transmitting, and India's success in absorbing, the essentials
of Western liberalism. But the practice has differed from the
theory. Britain's first gift to India and Pakistan was a westernized élite from which its leaders — Gandhi, Nehru, Jinnah, and
Ayub Khan — have all been drawn. Britain's second gift comprised the Indian armed services, organized in an almost overpowering atmosphere of Aldershot and Camberley. As armies
go, those of India and Pakistan have been so far remarkably
non-political. British soldiers have thus made a deeper impression than British politicians. The third British gift was the English language, the common tongue in which the Congress members could discuss their grievances against Britain. This language
has been of practical convenience, but it has also produced an
Indian literature of its own, and one through which Indian
ideas can reach the rest of the world. Authors like K. D. Sethna,

* Zinkin, *op. cit.*, p. 89.

and followers generally of Sri Aurobindo, see merits in the language for its own sake. The English tongue has done much, and will do more, to influence Indian thought. "Far and wide," writes Sethna, "by means of English, the Indian genius will spread the word born from the occult immensities that are the luminous source and support and goal of its unique history." *
Be that as it may, the English language has been an important factor in India's progress.

More important perhaps than any of these things has been the impact of Western medical science. By forcing down the death rate, the physicians and sanitary engineers have provided India with a larger population than its traditional economy could possibly support. The scientific industrialism that is needed to equip armies must also be applied to agriculture and textiles. Mahatma Gandhi's ideals — involving a contented peasantry, with subsistence farming and homespun cotton — are being swept away by the tide of events. What he advised is not even possible. And industrialism brings with it a whole sequence of changes — in social structure, in costume, and in diet. The wristwatch, the bicycle, and the fountain or ball-point pen are the symbols of progress; with time as a new factor in life, with semi-literacy as a normal accomplishment, with mobility (beyond the confines of the village) as a new source of independence for the young. Still more basic is the change in the status of women. The factory for them means ultimately the substitution of overalls and jeans for the sari, as also the elimination of those Indian meals that take so many hours to prepare. It means the crumbling of parental authority, and the scattering of relatives between one place and another.

While introducing its own evils, the factory must tend to eliminate some of the customs which the West has found most alien. The Muslim attitude to women could survive the preach-

* K. D. Sethna, *The Indian Spirit and the World's Future* (Pondicherry, 1953), p. 76.

ings of the missionary. It cannot survive the routine of the
factory floor and pay check. Women operatives cannot remain
in purdah. Typists cannot wear the veil. Patients on the operating table may not be able to wear anything. As for multiple
wives and concubines, they will not be available; nor would
they be reasonably economic even if they could be found. This
does not mean the end of Islam, for its teachers adjust their
religion to the changed circumstances. Monogamy is becoming
usual among Moslems, and theologians are asking each other
whether the Prophet really intended it to be otherwise. The
passages in scripture which enjoin the use of the veil are being
re-interpreted. It can be shown, with some ingenuity, that
something else was meant, and that the rules about seclusion
are not to be applied in all circumstances. Granted, however,
that Islamic doctrines can be adjusted to the world in which
people have to live, the whole social structure must be affected
by the change. Seclusion can hardly be forced on a woman who
has already taken a university degree. The injunction "abide
in your own homes" is as little applicable to the teacher or the
nurse. While the Western concept of romantic love may have
its influence on the East, the impact of the factory must be far
more immediate and far more effective. Many institutions it
will destroy completely.*

Nor is the situation very different in China. There too the
treatment of women had been distinctive and in some ways
disastrous. At the higher levels of society, there had been the
harem system, with its usual atmosphere of secrecy and intrigue.
And where women had influence it was usually productive of
the worst results.

Confucius ignored women as he ignored Heaven. Both appeared to be beyond his understanding, and therefore, he wisely

* See V. R. and L. Bevan Jones, *Woman in Islam* (Lucknow, 1941), pp. 208–
32.

left them alone. Only here and there do we get any indication
of a cautious masculine mind on subjects he knew little about.
'Girls and servants,' said Confucius, 'are the most difficult people to handle. If you treat them familiarly, they become dis-
respectful; if you keep them at a distance, they resent it.'*

One knows what he meant. It is broadly true, however, that
the Chinese attitude to women was unsound. But whatever
the justice or folly of their tradition, it could not be reconciled
with an industrialized society. Much the same factors as in
India — medicine, hygiene, military technique, and industry —
have in China produced much the same results. Up to a certain
point — and especially where the Oriental attitude to women
is concerned — westernization has been at once widespread and
inevitable.

Unavoidable in some degree, westernization has gone further,
in some places, than seems consistent with common sense; and
this is especially true of countries which have never been brought
under European control. Kemal Atatürk and his Persian or
Afghan imitators did more to westernize people than any colonial government would ever have dared. Only "westernized
Oriental man" could actually impose bowler hats and jazz dance
bands. But whether the westernization has been indigenous
or alien, it is equally coming to an end. As L. Cranmer-Byng
puts it, "The voices of the West are beginning to die away,"
and the languid drawl of the B.B.C. critic "trails off into a
confused murmur and a babble of books essential to leisure." †
Critics of the West have begun to comment upon the Western
traffic jams and squalor, clutter, and destruction. Still more to
the point, Western teaching has lost its authority, and Western
thinkers their confidence. Philosophers exaggerate the influence
of organized thought, but it is a symptom (if not the cause) of
the way people feel. If this is so, the wavering of the Western

* L. Cranmer-Byng, op. cit., p. 157.
† Ibid., p. 23.

thinkers is significant. Still more significant, however, is the
Western collapse in architecture and art. For the West no
longer believes in itself.

Having accepted from the West all that they must accept,
and having sensed the confusion among Western cultural
groups, the peoples of the East have called a halt. They have
rejected, or are on the point of rejecting, the Western values
associated with individualism, Christianity, and democracy.
These ideas, so central to Western ideology, are all unacceptable in the East. Take individualism first, from which the others
spring. The widespread Oriental custom is for married sons to
live with their parents, not leaving the home but adding to it.
People thus remain members of a family group, never becoming
individuals in the Western sense. Oriental wisdom consists in
multiplying and mingling relationships, sharing each other's
lives and so expanding the self to include all. Its final achievement is to be able to claim "There is nothing that I am not,
and nothing that is not I." Buddhism represents this assertion
in its most extreme form, involving the negation of individuality. Preparation for such a group life is provided by a childhood
in which children come emphatically last. They are made to
realize that they are subordinate to many elders, not merely to
their parents, and matter less than any of them. Living in a
group where many ideas are expressed, the child does not readily
adopt a personal and exclusive belief in any one viewpoint. The
group ideal is more one of harmony and compromise, all harsh
disagreements being regarded as impolite. And although there
have been changes in social structure, individualism remains,
for the Oriental, an anti-social characteristic. More than that,
the most highly educated Orientals have come to see in individualism the source of many Western failings and neuroses.
They are quite definitely against it.

What of Christianity? This came nearest to success in India
before 1857. There was then a period when many Europeans in
India were themselves Christians, and able to recommend a

faith in which they genuinely believed. But Hinduism recovered as the century went on, its adherents revealing a mild and tolerant interest in a cult which they had ceased to fear. More tolerant still, the Chinese have often added effigies of Jesus Christ and Mahomet to those of Buddha and Confucius, finding nothing incongruous in these additions to a fairly crowded pantheon. As K. M. Pannikkar points out, "The doctrine of the monopoly of truth and revelation is altogether alien to the Asian mind." * Of India and China, this would seem to be generally true. What success Christianity has had in the East has been notable mainly in Japan. But there, as in India and China, the religion of Christ has been fatally associated with Western ascendancy. The result of this in China was that the Boxer Rising of 1900 was directed against the Christian missionaries; and so was an anti-Christian Association formed in 1922. A religion so individualistic would have had only a limited appeal in any case, but its intolerance has combined with its political associations to eliminate its influence in the East.

That democracy is a dying creed is less generally recognized. Many Americans feel certain of Asian sympathy, provided only that Americans prove true to their own ideals. Papers read in the course of an "Asian Year" at Cleveland, Ohio, were afterwards published under the title *The East and West Must Meet*.† One of these, by John D. Rockefeller III, illustrates this sort of American confidence; based, of course, on a complete incomprehension.

> Asia today is looking to us to reaffirm our respected humanitarian and democratic heritage, not alone by words but also by action. Our history as the first of all the peoples of the world to throw off colonialism inspires Asia. Yet when our actions seem to belie our history, Asia is understandably puzzled, disappointed, and disillusioned.

* K. M. Pannikkar, *Asia and Western Dominance* (London, 1953), p. 445.
† Benjamin H. Brown (ed.), *The East and West Must Meet: A Symposium* (Michigan, 1959).

When our actions confirm our history, the heart of Asia feels a glow of kinship. When we gave independence to the Philippines we fulfilled our national image in the eyes of Asia. Asia cheered when we led the United Nations to the prompt defence of the independence of South Korea. When we went counter to our traditional allies in last year's Suez dispute, Asia regarded our stand as a forthright appreciation of our opposition to colonialism. Each of these actions lifted the hopes and spirit of Asia.

But Asia at other times is confused and puzzled. The people of Asia are unable to understand what seemed to be our defence of colonial domination in Indo-China, and Asians are disappointed in our apparent lack of sympathy for the Algerian struggle for independence. They are deeply disillusioned by our acts of racial discrimination within our own borders. They wonder how we could declare all men to be equal 180 years ago in Philadelphia when this year in Little Rock we must have armed troops escort children to school. Asians, we must understand, equate racial segregation with colonialism. To most Asians, colonialism is nothing more than exploitation of the non-white by the white.*

Much in the above passage is too naïve to deceive a schoolboy, but, factual errors apart, the central theme is totally wrong. The peoples of Asia are not enthusiastic democrats, nor do they complain that American democracy is a sham. Granted that they think it bogus, the fact is that they would like it no better for being genuine. Referring to the Western type of utopia, S. K. Maitra writes indignantly, "It is an insult to humanity to suggest, as the Western humanists do, that man can ever be satisfied with the picture of ideal human society that they present to us. God forbid that mankind should ever descend so low as to accept it as its ultimate goal!" †

The error about Asian democracy springs from the fact that

* *Ibid.*, p. 89.
† S. K. Maitra, *The Meeting of the East and the West in Sri Auribindo's Philosophy* (Pondicherry, 1956), p. 55.

Asian leaders resent being treated as inferiors, and talk glibly therefore about human equality. It does not follow that they will concede the same equality to other people, and in fact they seldom do. In the exuberance of expansion which follows the removal of colonial paternalism and patronage, the more backward peoples — like the Red Indians in America — are apt to fare very ill. In a period of expansion, the cry is not for equality, but for leadership and enterprise. And democracy has become popularly associated with the last phase of Western withdrawal. Like any other gifts from the Greeks, it is thoroughly suspect, a wooden horse which may contain the means of disruption. How can democracy survive in Japan, for example, where its origin dates from the period of American occupation? Quite apart from any such association of ideas, however, democracy is impossible without a previous consolidation under some other form of rule. It presupposes a frontier already fixed and a population already defined. It is impracticable to count votes until it is known which votes are to count. The problems which arise in connection with Kashmir, Indochina, Sumatra, Brunei, West India, and Taiwan admit of no democratic solution. We may question, moreover, whether democracy would be welcomed even in the few areas to which it is technically applicable. Among Indian metaphysicians all talk of inalienable rights must pass as childish twaddle, scarcely deserving an answer. And Gandhi, the founder of modern India, was himself no strong believer in the Western ballot box. When opposed or outvoted, his remedy was to embark on a fast unto death. Nothing could have been less democratic or more effective. But the procedure illustrates a fundamental difference between existing types of society. Saints have no such influence in the West.

Does the rejection of Western ideas mean that the East can revert entirely to its own traditions? We have seen already that this is impossible and that technical trends cannot be reversed.

This is obvious, above all, in architecture and art. The tremendous achievements of Islamic architecture date from a fairly distant past. It was admittedly Akbar (1542–1605) who built that masterpiece, Fatehpur Sikri, near Agra, of which Edmond Taylor writes:

> Every excellence of man's environment has its specialised setting in stone, the place is a visual organ, and not a visual one alone, for there are latticed tower-chambers turned to the wind, cloisters of silence, walls of redundant echo, fountain courts for the enjoyment of splash and murmur as well as of light and shade upon dancing water; there are marble solariums for the enjoyment of reverberant heat and vaults of coolness; there are even very precise architectural expressions of the less remote abstractions of peace as repose, of dignity as balance, of introspection as enclosure, incompletely veiling visual infinity. As in most masterpieces of Islamic art, space, light, shadow, wind temperature, and water are structural elements of the edifice, this art being really a kind of landscaping in stone . . .*

But no such masterpiece has been built since 1700. And Osbert Sitwell says of Moorish or Turkish architecture that it often begins in a promising manner but seldom reaches the first floor without a "powerful blunder of some sort or other." This is the approximate truth, and the story of art has been one of a decline which Western influence has turned into a collapse. Marco Pallis complains that almost every art in the Orient has died in the course of two generations. Kashmir shawls, for example, have been ruined by chemical dyes and time-saving techniques.

> The colour-sense of the people, formerly unerring, once having been disturbed, deadly logic subconsciously working in the artist, would have taught him next to alter the designs also, to save

* Edmond Taylor, *Richer by Asia* (Boston, 1947), p. 176.

labour and thought. Patterns would have become bigger or more repetitive or more obviously striving after self-advertisement. The result would have been the same in the end — extinction. There seems to be no trifling with the artistic ideal. To recover the sense of craftsmanship, one must retrace one's steps right back to the point where the traditional and anti-traditional ways parted . . .*

But whoever heard of such steps being successfully retraced? How could anyone revive an art based upon metaphysical ideas in which people no longer believe? On this same general theme, Freya Stark remarks that educated Europeans fear to recommend their own art, doubting whether it is any better than the dead imitations which it has tended to supersede.

This feeling is dimly at the root of what the Arab and other nations continue to think of as a grudging attitude towards their own modernity. They prevent us, if they can, from taking even a picture of their old world; nor will they believe that their own tradition already possesses what anything copied from aliens can only acquire by a long process of adoption and change. A doubt has come upon us, whether what we offer is really worth such sacrifice . . .†

This process at work in the East, by which cheap products drive out good craftsmanship, is the symbol of a mental process which it would be as impossible to reverse. The old arts could not be revived even were the shoddy manufacture unobtainable. In its most crude, materialistic, and Western sense, progress has become unavoidable.

Asians cannot return to their traditional ways of life, nor would they if they could. For they know that their moment is coming for economic, political, intellectual, and cultural ex-

* Marco Pallis, *Peaks and Lamas* (London, 1940), p. 210.
† Stark, *op. cit.*, p. 19.

pansion. It is this knowledge that is destroying any sense of Asian unity that ever existed. For while an external danger may create unity, external opportunity can create nothing but dissension. Asian pride in Japan's first achievement is giving place to rivalry. Which people is to lead after the Western forces have withdrawn? In attempting to answer that question, we must remember, first of all, that the Chinese have a sense of mission. They have always had a certain urge to civilize the barbarians, to extend the benefit of their own internal peace to such people as could be persuaded to join their universal state. As dwellers in the Middle Kingdom (central to the inhabited world), it was peace, above all, that they have had to offer. The equivalent of the European national wars ended in the China of the second century B.C., since when all conflicts have been internal. Rival groups might strive to control the central government, but few denied for long that government should be centralized. The very names given to the different parts of the Forbidden City at Peking serve to illustrate this aspect of Chinese ideology: Gate of Heavenly Peace, Gate of Supreme Harmony, Hall of Precious Harmony, Palace of Earthly Tranquillity, and Hall of Majestic Peace. These are names, surely, of great significance.

Expansion is thus consistent with Chinese tradition. It is incompatible, nevertheless, with the traditional Chinese way of life. For the family as a social unit cannot survive in an industrialized community. To equip China with the means to assert itself as a world power means the end of the village and the clan. To provide China with effective emigrants, whether soldiers or colonists, must again weaken the ties of kinship as also the loyalties to local and trade associations. To revive in China the old sense of mission, but informed with a new sense of energy, there must be a new Oriental religion. Only a religion can take the place of Islam in modern Asia, spearheading the movement for expansion. It is clear, moreover, that the religion must fulfill certain requirements. It must replace the family by an organization which offers the same sense of membership and security. While Oriental in spirit it must be consistent with the Western ideas which have been found essential for defense against the West. It must satisfy the Chinese tradition of rule by an intellectual elite, as also the Chinese sense of superiority over other peoples. It should satisfy, if possible, the Indian abnegation of self and the Arab sense of conflict between Good and Evil. It must, in fact, be Communism. That is the religion which seems destined to give the renascent East its cutting edge. Watchword of this new Islam is the revised call to prayer, "There is no God but economic Determinism, and Marx is the Prophet of God." *

* L. Cranmer-Byng, *op. cit.*, p. 11.

20

THE DEFENSE OF THE WEST

THE MAIN RELIGIONS of the world fall into two groups. There are the four theistic religions, each claiming a unique revelation: Shintoism, Judaism, Christianity, and Islam. There are, by contrast, the four broadly philosophic or aesthetic religions: Hinduism, Buddhism, Taoism, and Confucianism. To the first group must now be added Marxism — a creed, like the others, of violence, a religion derived ultimately from Judaism. Karl Marx was a Jew, German only in language and education. He was Jewish in his fanaticism, Jewish in his intensity, Jewish in his sense of personal salvation, and Jewish in his hatred. Like Christianity and Islam, Marxism derives thus from the Semitic peoples on the fringe of the desert. Like his rabbi ancestors, Marx saw the world as a place of contrast between Good and Evil, between the believers and the damned. He looked exactly what he was, an Old Testament prophet calling destruction on the cities of the plain. He was one of the chosen, persecuted, but sure of delivery at some future time. A stateless Jew, a professor without a chair, an author without a public, Marx gave all that was in him to a single tremendous task; one to which he brought an immense learning, a complete selfishness, a fanatical devotion, and an impressive intellect. The result was *Das Kapital*.

In form a textbook of economics, *Das Kapital* is actually a sort of bible, long, impressive, and obscure — a source of texts for the preacher, a source of consolation to the poor. It offers a mixture of moral fervor and scientific jargon, with more hatred shown against the heretic than against the avowed enemy. Published in 1867, *Das Kapital* attracted little attention at the time, being addressed to the communists of Europe; people who were then dwindling in numbers and importance. The communist *International* had almost ceased to exist by 1874, and Marx was of no importance whatever when he died in 1882. But *Das Kapital* had been translated into and published in Russian in 1872, one copy coming into the possession of Alexander Ulyanov. When he was executed in 1887 (for conspiracy to assassinate the Tsar), his copy was inherited by his younger brother, Vladimir Ulyanov, who made it the textbook of Russian Communism. Under the name of Lenin, Vladimir made himself leader of the party in 1903. With the Revolution of 1917, he came to power, and made Marxism the orthodox canon of belief. Tsarist rule had been based upon three principles: autocracy, nationalism, and orthodoxy. Lenin ruled in the same fashion but with a new orthodoxy. In this state religion, Marx became the first person of a new trinity, with Lenin as the second, and the current ruler — after Lenin's death — the third.

The Marxist doctrine involves a few economic ideas, all obviously obsolete, an evolutionary theory of history, based on insufficient evidence, and a prophecy relating to an apparently static and utopian future. For the initiate, for the party member, Marxism has a fairly complex theology based on the concept of dialectical materialism. For the populace as a whole, it has its gods, its priesthood, its holy book, its literature, its liturgy, its heretics, its inquisition, its images, hymns, and place of pilgrimage. In this highly developed form it reached China in 1921, when Mao Tse-tung was a delegate at the first Party Congress. Although anxious to develop Marxism on Chinese lines, Mao Tse-tung was always strictly orthodox. He would have no compromise with the nationalist movement headed by Sun Yat-sen until his death in 1925. For him, as for Stalin, party membership is a way of life, a spiritual experience, a creed.

Where the Chinese Marxists differed, however, from the Russians was in offering on the one hand a reduction in taxes, on the other a deliberate defiance of the West. They were never more popular than in clearing foreign warships out of Shanghai harbor, snubbing the British ambassador or humiliating the United States consul-general. By 1949 their triumph over the Kuomintang was complete. With a surprising amount of American connivance and sympathy, the Communists took over the government of China.

With the story of Communism, we are not at present concerned. Its interest, for our present purpose, lies in its special appeal as an Oriental religion. Basically it lends coherence to anti-Western emotions. In addition, however, it offers what various other religions have offered. From the Jews the Marxists have taken the idea of the Chosen People, as also the prophecies of doom to fall on their rivals — the belief that the West is dying of its own internal cancer. From the Christians they have taken the idea of rescuing souls from damnation and so recruiting the ranks of the Chosen. From Buddhism comes the idea of conversion leading to enlightenment, and stability. From Islam the Marxists have taken the idea of a Holy War and a brotherhood superseding all ties of kinship. From the West they have taken, without understanding, the theory of evolution, as also, to some extent, the worship of efficiency. Where they are most totally opposed is in India, for Hindus reject both materialism and humanism, believing, as they have always done, in the mystical experience of union with God. As against that, Communism is especially attractive to the Chinese in that it replaces the family tie by another and wider form of association, one in which the individual counts for little, but has the reassurance of an all-embracing faith. The party, it is said, becomes family, school, church, and barracks, with all else to be destroyed and built anew.

There can be no doubt that Marxism is superseding Islam

as the inspiration of a renascent Asia. As Michael Edwardes observes in *Asia in the European Age*, "Marxism offers the exhilaration that once sent the hordes of Islam upon the campaign of a holy war against the Infidels."

Nor is there any doubt that the danger to the West has been at least instinctively perceived. The early medieval reaction to the threat of Islam took the form of movements toward political and religious unity. Hitherto rival nations are feeling their way toward a United States of Europe, the medieval concept of empire. Hitherto rival churches are feeling their way toward a united Christendom, the medieval concept of papacy. The Jews once more have been massacred, and the heretic's fate may well be what it has always been under conditions of external pressure. McCarthy has at least shown the way, and the Ku Klux Klan has raised the fiery cross. And just as these panic measures reveal a defensive complex in the West, so the growth in Oriental confidence produces measures which are exactly opposite. Fear might push the Eastern communities into some form of temporary alliance. "We have no interest," said Dr. Hu Shih, "in Mr. Gandhi's spiritual reformation. But we will be glad to talk with him about how to eliminate the white man's domination from Asia and humble his conceit." Mere resentment could thus keep them together. It is the sense of opportunity which drives them apart, causing conflict between China and India, between Singhalese and Tamil, between Muslim and Hindu. Such unity as they ever had was based upon fear of the West. Their quarrel now is over how they are to divide the spoils.

In previous offensives, of the kind that are to be expected, the momentum has been maintained by successive waves, each exhausted group being replaced by one not hitherto engaged. Either side drew, in effect, upon uncivilized but vigorous reserves — the Huns adding strength to Hungary and the Slavs to Yugoslavia, the Mongols giving leadership to India, and the

Orthodox Turks to the Muslim Near East. Comparison with the present day may be thought misleading in that no such barbarian tribes remain uncommitted. But in Africa such tribes do exist with primitive energies unspent, as proved in the boxing ring or stadium. It was from Africa that Hannibal drew his Numidian troops. From Africa came the Arabs' infantry and from Africa the French Zouaves. There remains in Africa something more than the source of American popular music. What remains could be an intellectual battlefield or a scene for eventual peacemaking between the representatives of the United States and China — both, as it might happen, as black as ink.

Faced with the menace of Asia, the Western powers have done what they could to avert conflict. In the United Nations they have set up an organization for settling disputes without resort to war. Were the world threatened by mysterious creatures from outer space, something might be made of world unity on these lines. As things are, the effort is obviously futile. For the attempt to ensure international friendship and peace means, essentially, maintaining things as they are. And while this may suit those whose ascendancy has been assured for centuries, it can be of no obvious advantage to those whose recovery has only just begun. To have frozen the existing power relationships in 1900 could have been as advantageous to Britain as a present stabilization would be to the United States. The result would be the seesaw fixed in position with the one end permanently uppermost. Asians and Africans can see no merit in that. Their professed aim is to see the plank in the horizontal position, an aim which will certainly alter as that position is approached. If anything could intensify rivalry it is the prospect of a universe to explore, with rare mineral deposits to be fetched from the moon. When new worlds were discovered in 1493, the achievement was due to a Western application of Oriental knowledge. It would seem likely that some comparable achievement may result, some day, from Western knowledge as applied by Eastern enterprise.

The United Nations idea must fail again in terms of leadership. The Oriental nations are far too backward to aim at world leadership in present circumstances. Insofar as their leaders are sophisticated, it is because they are westernized, and insofar as they are westernized, they are no longer representative. But those unable to offer leadership are not necessarily willing to accept it. Nor is it clear that the West will for long have much leadership to offer. As Michael Edwardes points out:

> The challenge of Marxism was a challenge not only to imperialism but to the civilisation from which it emerged. The colonial struggle has now been extended into a world struggle. The failure of the West in Asia, as in Africa to-day was a failure of inspiration. The West had no clear-cut faith to offer those it ruled because it had none that it really believed in itself.*

This is indeed the crux of the matter, the Western loss of confidence. It has been remarked upon by a score of authors, but it is most clearly manifest in the decadence of Western art. The prices now paid for old paintings are the surest indication of how little our current art is valued. But Lewis Mumford has explained how this has come about:

> . . . by our own preoccupation with the practical, we condemn the artist, if he seeks to gain attention, to sheer exhibitionism, or at worst, to committing a nuisance, just to attract some small modicum of attention. The Salvador Dalis and the Ezra Pounds are obvious examples of artists who use infantile means to recapture the normal status of the artist in a balanced society and just because our world is unwilling to meet the artist half way, it either forces him to make his secret more impenetrable, causing him to invent a private language, even a private mythology, like that of William Blake or James Joyce, to hide his lack of audi-

* Edwardes, *op. cit.*, p. 239.

tors; or its rejection has the effect of turning his love into hate. In that mood . . . even the artist's original narcissism becomes negative: instead of self-love there is self-rejection and, what is worse, self-hatred. What the esthetic symbols then say, more plainly than downright words is: "I hate myself: I hate the world: I hate you. *Drop dead!*" *

This is not the mood in which the West can offer a constructive leadership.

What leadership it *can* offer is best illustrated by the United Nations building itself, on which again Lewis Mumford provides the best commentary. The initial and significant mistake was to place the building in New York. The next mistake was to plan a 42-floor structure, high enough to be inconvenient, but low enough to be dwarfed by adjacent buildings of greater height and better design. Third mistake was to lend that symbolic prominence to the purely secretarial functions — at the expense of the actual assembly. Fourth mistake was to orientate the buildings incorrectly for sun and wind. Fifth mistake was to make the Secretariat Building, "that great oblong prison of steel and aluminium and glass," an empty abstract form, "a frozen geometrical concept, that reflects the emptiness and purposelessness of modern technics." Sixth and last major error was to sacrifice practical convenience to the symmetry of this metal box, leaving some offices without daylight and allocating vast window space to the women's lavatories.

> In short, the Secretariat Building exhibits both a breakdown of functionalism and a symbolic black-out. Though mechanically new, it is architecturally and humanly obsolete.†

Mumford adds the significant comment that a far better design was produced for the capital of the East Punjab. As an organization, the United Nations died almost at birth.

* Lewis Mumford, *Art and Technics* (Oxford, 1952), p. 30.
† *Ibid.*, p. 128.

Behind the efforts made to achieve world unity are the dreams often discussed for reconciling the differences between East and West. There is already a literature on this subject, going back, as we have seen, to Alexander the Great. Radhakrishnan thus hopes that "we will unite the peoples of all races in a community, catholic, comprehensive and co-operative." Conferences have been held, papers have been read and fervent ideals have been explained, doing credit to all concerned. One approach is through a unification of religion:

> The moment is coming . . . to seek amid the multiplicity of religions the one religion of the One God that is revealed by reason, foreshadowed in the universal religions, and perfected in Jesus Christ; to realise the version of Ram Moham Roy, the union of Asia and Europe in which neither shall sacrifice its individuality . . . Beneath the outward multiplicity of religions beats the one religion that is the heart of all.*

Any such idea breaks down at the onset, for all religious thinkers see unity in terms of other people being converted to the religion they themselves profess — monotheism in the above instance. But, apart from that, religious unity would solve nothing. No significant clash of interests has ever been averted as a result of the communities concerned having the same faith.

Other thinkers pin their faith on world unity considered as an aim in itself and as "the key to man's survival." Edmond Taylor sees the need for a religious "conversion" in the hearts and minds of those who pursue this ideal:

> . . . To be completely effective, this moral conversion of individuals must be reflected in workable international political institutions, but the institutions themselves will only be workable in so far as they reflect the changed personalities of the individuals who support them.†

* H. N. Spalding, *Civilization in East and West* (Oxford, 1939), p. 322.
† Edmond Taylor, *op. cit.*, p. 430.

But how can such a "conversion" be urged with success upon people who are "converted" already — to Communism? For they have their own ideal of world unity, one which allows other countries to become so many additional provinces of China. World peace was a Chinese discovery of the remote past (221 B.C.), one which they are willing to share. It is far from clear that the West has anything comparable to offer. And the sense of insecurity which haunts the United States does not produce an urge toward world unity. It tends rather to produce bigotry and violence, or an addiction, at the least, to the fiction written by Mickey Spillane.

Granted, moreover, that it were possible to abolish the conflict between East and West, it is by no means certain that it would be desirable. Maurice Collis tells us that the Europeans who first appeared on the China coast were invited to join the universal state, "the greatest blessing imaginable," which their merely national interests prevented them doing. He calls now for a new universal state comprising the whole world:

> . . . In this we are all agreed, and our agreement makes us Confucians for Confucianism is a universal political philosophy: in the *Li Chi*, one of its original classics, the ideal stage of civilisation is called the 'Great Similarity' and defined as a universal state animated by the common aim of each for all regardless of race or language or creed. That ideal is not peculiar to China, it has always been the stuff of mortal dreams, but China is the only living country which has sought to give it practice and effect, for there alone was it woven into the political structure . . .
>
> If then China and the Western World have found at last that their political aims are the same, the union of East and West is feasible . . .*

But feasible or not, the aim is *not* one upon which we are all agreed. For a universalism on these lines would lead to mental

* Maurice Collis, *The Great Within* (London, 1941), p. 327.

stagnation, would lead in fact to that "Great Similarity" which we have every reason to dread. By the abolition in China of the separate nations which have caused such friction in Europe, peace was, very largely, secured. But China, in its Great Similarity and isolation, lacked the mental stimulus of disagreement. It retained, for example, and still retains, an absurdly antique script which has been all along its self-inflicted handicap. It retained its top-heavy bureaucratic machine, its obsession with classical scholarship. It suffered constantly — as it suffers still — from a lack of external contact. To set up a world state, eliminating all sources of friction, would be to make stagnation the first principle of government. To have widespread intermarriage between the races would be to make dull uniformity the second. For most of the world's most brilliant ideas have been the result of friction between East and West. No reader of this book could doubt that the piston movement, back and forth, has been beneficial, keeping the mind alert and allowing different ideas to mingle and conflict. The brightest waters are in movement, and it is the stagnant pools that are covered with the slimiest slime.

The conflict must go on and the initiative lies now or will soon lie with the East. But if we are glad that the East has managed to survive its period of eclipse, we can wish no less for the West. In the last resort, the frontier must be held. But how? To the historian the answer is clear. It will presumably be held as it was held once before, and probably before that again. In addition to the obvious moves toward European unity there should be — and there already is — a movement to absorb from the East all, or rather nearly all, that the Oriental world has to give. There is, throughout the Western world but more especially in the United States, a feeling that life is becoming impossible, that all sense of security and balance has been lost. People feel that they are at the end of their tether, driven to smoke, to drink, to tranquilizers, and finally to mari-

juana. Problems are multiplying, and range from juvenile crime
to mental disturbance. Sir George Birdwood refers sadly to
"the secular, joyless, inane and self-destructive, modern civilization of the West." Amid the stream of fast-moving traffic,
driven by the urge to go somewhere, anywhere, many think of
the Eastern philosopher, whose advice to each hectic driver
would be to stay where he is and meditate. That is not something of which they are capable, but they feel, nevertheless,
that the East may have something to offer them, some way of
escape from the wheel of life.

For those who have this feeling there is a growing literature.
F. S. C. Northrop points out that the East has its own type of
knowledge based on experience of "the immediately apprehended aesthetic component in the nature of things." Ananda
K. Coomaraswamy observes that Asian people sing at their
work and that work without song is soul-destroying: "In a voca-
tional hierarchy, it is never a question of 'doing what one likes,'
but of liking what one does . . ." "We have much to learn
from the East," says the Earl of Portsmouth, "from high farming, to high philosophies." René Guénon quotes the Hindu
comment on the philosophical books of Europe "that the ideas
in them would only do credit, at the most, to a child of eight."
The everyday men of the West, writes L. Cranmer-Byng,
"walk faster and talk louder and seek refuge in speed and sound
from the self whose narrowing limit they would escape and the
non-self whose eternity appals them." Edmond Taylor thinks
that our first task, in the West, is "to correct the disorders or
deficiencies which our culture has produced in us." Marco
Pallis concludes sadly that "in conquering the world physically,
we seem to have lost much that was great or worth while in
our own heritage," in saying which he points the way to the
Tibetan ideal as revealed in Mila Repa's masterpiece.

To end these comments on the West, here is one, finally,
from Mahatma Gandhi:

You glory in speed, thinking not of the goal. You elevate process, rather than ultimate product. You think your souls are saved because you can invent radio. Of what elevation to man is a method of broadcasting when you have only drivel to send out? What mark of civilisation is it to be able to produce a one hundred and twenty page newspaper in one night, when most of it is either banal or actually vicious and not two columns worth preserving? What contribution to man has aeronautics made which can overbalance its use in his self-destruction? You are children playing with razors.*

Even those who read little or nothing can see for themselves which way the tide is running. Chinese restaurants are to be found in English cathedral cities and in American midwestern towns. Judo clubs have sprung up everywhere so that even schoolchildren have come to speak some words of Japanese. In architecture, the Japanese style is to be seen in California and for that matter in New York. Zen Buddhism is the talk of many a Western circle, and books about Asia are on every shelf. Most significant of all is the change in men's clothing. The classical tradition had given the Victorians a uniform of black and white, austere, manly, and correct. In the East this became a uniform of white alone, the symbol as it were of white authority, contrasting with the gay colors worn by the populace. This black tradition was copied by all Asians who aspired to any social status, and is widely copied still. But a change began in about 1930, when the barriers began to crumble. More gaily colored clothes began to be seen, even in London, for leisure at first, and later even at the desk. White remained the colonial uniform until perhaps 1955, when pastel shades began to diversify the rigid patterns. This illustrated the decay of authority, pointing the way to the final degradation of the Hawaiian shirt, the Bermuda shorts, the symbols of collapse.

The medieval world of the West wore very bright colors in-

* Upton Close, *The Revolt of Asia* (New York, 1927), p. 232.

deed, a tribute to the Orient, but it relied for much of its defense upon the towers of Byzantium. When the Western half of the Roman heritage was largely lost, the Eastern half was stoutly maintained. How was this possible? Simply because the Byzantine forces were too orientalized to fall the victim of an Oriental attack. They were not Oriental in tradition or outlook, but they had so copied their opponents as to become almost Oriental in Frankish eyes. And it was they who for centuries held up the advance of Islam. In this modern age the same story has been repeated. The heritage of the West has again been divided, half to center upon Washington, D.C., and the other (Byzantine) half upon Moscow. And upon Russia will fall, inevitably, the major burden of defense. This was perceived as long ago as 1912.

> Russia, whose frontiers lie athwart Manchuria, Mongolia, Turkestan, Persia, Afghanistan and Turkey, has been singled out by Nature to be the protecting bulwark of Western civilisation. Her peasantry are awakening at a time when the borders of Asia, too are bestirring themselves. The Russian Government have realised that they cannot hold territories that they do not develop and populate — hence the Amur railway to the Far East, and emigration to Siberia. Thus we may say that an outpost of Western civilisation is being converted into a barrier — a barrier composed of sturdy Russian peasants whose industrial activities and, if necessary, whose strong right arm will stem the tide of Asiatic aggression. For in no circumstances can the West assimilate with the East; it can only raise a breakwater against the East. We may yet be thankful that the progress of Russia has been retarded until to-day, and that she still has in reserve those millions of sturdy sons of the soil. Both as a man and as a soldier, the Russian peasant is unsurpassable . . . he will work as hard as in time of war he will fight courageously. He is, indeed, well worthy to represent the liberty-loving manhood of Europe in the coming keen struggle against the economic forces of Asia.*

* Lancelot Lawton, *op. cit.*, p. 810.

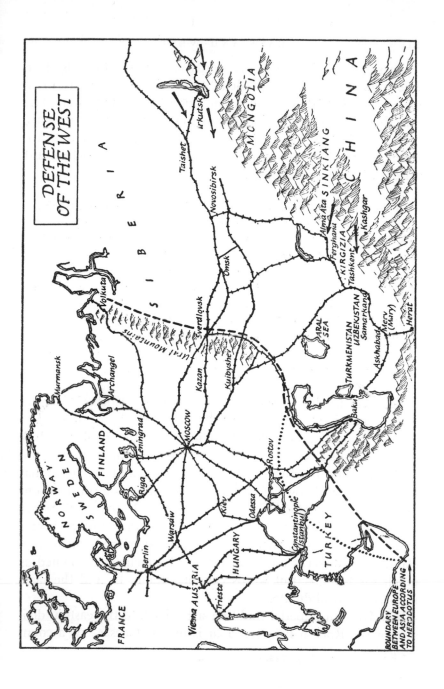

DEFENSE OF THE WEST

S I B E R I A

MONGOLIA

CHINA

SINKIANG

Irkutsk
Taishet
Novosibirsk
Omsk
Vorkuta
Sverdlovsk
Ural Mountains
Kazan
Kuibyshev
ARAL SEA
TURKMENISTAN
UZBEKISTAN
Samarkand
Askhabad
Merv (Mary)
Herat
KIRGIZIA
Tashkent
Ferghana
Alma Ata
Kashgar
Murmansk
Archangel
Leningrad
MOSCOW
FINLAND
Riga
Warsaw
Kiev
Odessa
Rostov
Baku
NORWAY
SWEDEN
Berlin
Vienna AUSTRIA
Trieste
HUNGARY
Constantinople (Istanbul)
TURKEY
FRANCE

BOUNDARY
BETWEEN EUROPE
AND ASIA ACCORDING
TO HERODOTUS

These prophetic and ironic words remain substantially true. There are those who will deny this, pointing out, as many have done, that Russia is an Asian, not a European power. This was the belief of some Victorians and others, more recently, have thought that Soviet Russia has deserted, as it were, to the Asian camp. Typical of these commentators is Michael Edwardes who writes as follows:

> In the withdrawal of Russia from the Western Community, and its severance from its own imperial past, a new independent ASIAN nation, hating the West and proclaiming a new dignity for the colonial struggle, emerged upon the scene. Sun Yat-sen immediately recognised the importance of the momentous event. "At present" he wrote, "Russia is attempting to separate from the white peoples in Europe. Why? Because she insists upon the rule of Right, and denounces the rule of Might. She advocates the principle of benevolence and justice. Recent Russian civilization is similar to our ancient civilization. Therefore she joins with the Orient and separates from the West." *

Believers in this thesis can point to some aspects of Soviet policy since 1922: to Russian support of Mustapha Kemal, to Russian policy in Persia and Afghanistan, to the ideological link between Russia and China. But Russian policy proves, on analysis, to be mostly for Russia's benefit, and the idea that Russia can, by its own decision, change sides, is against all our experience of what can actually be done. It may suit Soviet policy, at one moment, to pretend that Russian history begins in 1917. It may suit Soviet policy, at another moment, to proclaim that Russia is an Asian power. Disraeli once claimed as much for Britain. But words cannot alter facts, and the facts in this case are obdurate.

The Russian imperial tradition dates back to the eastern division of the Roman Empire. Tsar is merely Caesar. As a coun-

* Edwardes, *op. cit.*, p. 235.

try, Russia was in eclipse when the rest of Europe was in eclipse. It revived when the rest of Europe revived. Its history of colonial expansion closely parallels that of Britain. In the invasion of the Far East, Russia was perhaps the most aggressive of the European powers, and foremost in suppressing the Boxer Rising in 1900. In any other anti-foreign riot, then or since, a Russian would be as readily attacked as any other white man. It was the defeat of the Russians by the Japanese which started the great Asian revival in 1905. As for the Revolution, it gave Russia, as an earlier revolution had given France, some openings for subversion. To Russian foreign policy it made no difference at all. Methods might be revised, but the objects remained the same. How could it be otherwise? A country's foreign policy is firmly based, as a rule, on physical facts which are perfectly obvious: position, area, distance, population, production, and trade routes. Its basic interest can be read from the map. And Russia's interests include space for defense and development and an outlet to the Pacific, objects which have been pursued consistently for centuries and are still kept clearly in view.

Misconceptions about Soviet Russia arise from a misinterpretation of the map. Studying the vast land mass between the Baltic and the Sea of Okhotsk, we see that the greater proportion of the Soviet territories are in Asia. We realize, moreover, that the population of the more distant regions must be Asian in character and even perhaps Muslim in religion. We jump to the conclusion that the Russians are Asian, encouraged by their own pronouncements on the subject. But a colonial empire is not the less colonial for being contiguous. The Russian motherland is west of the Urals. Eastward the territories fall into the two familiar categories of colonial expansion: areas of settlement like Siberia, areas of occupation like Turkistan; the one equivalent to Australia and the other to, say, Algeria. The first type they must either populate or lose, and these are extremely difficult to defend. The second type may rebel at any time, with

assistance from the East. And just as British policy has centered, in years past, on the southern trade routes between
Europe and Asia, so Russian policy is centered now upon the
northern trade route between Asia and Europe. It is not as
good a route, but it is the only one the Russians have. But why,
the Chinese will eventually ask, should Russia have the whole
of this route and the whole of the territory through which it has
to pass? It could as reasonably be controlled from the eastern
end. And Siberia, like Australia again, could afford a useful
space for Chinese settlement.

Soviet Russia is not only a colonial power, but one of the
earlier group, chronologically level with Britain. And just as the
British leapfrogged the Portuguese and Dutch, moving eastward
beyond the limits of earlier expansion, the Russians have always
had reason to fear that some other power would leapfrog them.
France first made the attempt, since which time Germany has
tried twice. But just as the thirteenth-century British intervened sufficiently in Europe to draw attention away from their
colonial expansion, so the Russians have always intervened with
exactly the same purpose. It is their rearguard actions and cover
plans that other Europeans have noticed, not their colonial
acquisitions. But if the Europeans pay more attention to events
which happen nearest their own frontiers, the Chinese and
Japanese do exactly the same. It was the Japanese neutralism
over two centuries which allowed the Russians to advance as far
as they did. Neither they nor the Japanese will make that mistake again. About Russia the Oriental leaders have no illusions
at all, and if there has been some semblance of ideological alliance between the Communist powers, that has been due almost
entirely to American foreign policy. But even the State Depart-
ment, at its most inept, could not sustain that alliance forever.

As against China, the Soviet Union is the new Byzantium.
The Russians have no more reason than the Byzantines to sacrifice themselves in their defense of the West. But what else can

they do? The alternative is to see the Chinese at Irkutsk, at Krasnoyarsk, at Omsk or Magnitogorsk. As against such a movement along the trade route, the Urals represent the main line of defense, with Moscow as the inevitable headquarters and the whole of Europe as the base area. For such a conflict the Russians are well placed and equipped. By their previous advance they have gained a vast forward area in which to maneuver. As a population engaged until recently in agriculture, they have so far retained the energies which a people derives from the soil. As a country partly industrialized, they can equip themselves for a conflict with modern weapons. As Marxists, they have the same religious enthusiasm as their opponents, and indeed the same religion. Nor can there be any doubt that the other Western powers, led by the U.S.A., must come to Russia's aid. The crusaders may have had their misgivings about Byzantium, but they went to war on its behalf, creating the diversion where it was needed and prolonging its resistance until the Oriental momentum had been lost.

There are some leaders who will say that this strategic picture is obsolete and that nuclear weapons have created a new situation, one to which the old principles no longer apply. Since August 6th, 1945, they will say, the world has been a different place. It may be so. But we can surely add that there is no proof of it. We can point, instead, to a whole series of conflicts in which conventional means have been used to gain quite predictable ends. The central event has been the destruction of the British Empire, attacked by its enemies and undermined — still more successfully — by its friends. The "axis of Empire," the southern trade route between Europe and Asia, has been severed at different points and notably at Suez. There have been operations in Kenya and Cyprus, in Egypt and Malaya, in Kuwait and Brunei. In no instance would a hydrogen bomb have been of the slightest use. In every instance — as in Korea, Indochina, Algeria, and Nepal — the urgent call has been for battalions and batteries, bayonets and boots. The things needed, whether carriers or cruisers, have always been those our ministers have agreed to abolish. Should they ever turn from science-fiction to fact, the politicians would see that their world can be destroyed piecemeal, and has been very largely destroyed already, without anyone resorting to anything much larger than a three-inch mortar.

If experience can teach us anything, it is that the Asian offensive will be pursued by the current methods: propaganda, infiltration, subversion, negotiation, covert assistance, and eventual revolt. Why should anyone change the methods that have served so well and that are laid down, moreover, in the official textbooks? And behind these preliminaries will be a perfectly orthodox strategy, such as might induce the Chinese to neutralize India (as a possible threat on the left flank) before venturing too far into central Asia. But behind all these familiar operations, and behind the top-hatted and gaslit Marxist jargon, there looms something far greater, the spirit of renascent Asia. From this movement the West has many lessons to learn, lessons which comprise, among other things, the secret of how to resist. In the last resort it is upon this resistance that the world's future must hang — the future of East and West alike. Mahatma Gandhi once predicted "terrific catastrophe and misery" for the West. To an American he said:

> Such of you as survive will come back to Asia for another way of life . . . If I should now allow the West in its boyishly confident rowdyism utterly to crush out an opposing system of life and ideals through political power and material influence, would I not be playing traitor not only to my own people but to you very Westerners as well? *

This was an extremely wise observation. But the time will come when some Western sage may speak to the same effect:

* Upton Close, *op. cit.*, p. 232.

Such of you as survive will come back to Europe for another way of life . . . If I should now allow the East, with its dogmatic Victorian bigotry, utterly to crush out our opposing system of life and ideals, through political subversion and economic aid, would I not be playing traitor not only to my own people but to you very Orientals as well?

Or should we, perhaps, end with the words with which this book began:

Sing the wrath, O Goddess, the baleful wrath of Achilles son of Peleus, that laid on the Achaeans ten thousand sorrows, and sent away goodly souls of heroes to Hades, and themselves it gave to dogs and all the birds; and the counsel of Zeus was fulfilled, from the day when first Atreides, king of men, and the divine Achilles quarrelled and stood apart. Who among the gods set them twain to fight?

BIBLIOGRAPHY
AND INDEX

BIBLIOGRAPHY

Allen, G. C. A *Short Economic History of Modern Japan*. London: George Allen & Unwin, Ltd., 1946.
Apollonius of Rhodes. *The Voyage of* Argo. Translated by E. V. Rieu. London: Penguin Classics, 1959.
Arberry, A. J. (ed.). *The Legacy of Persia*. Oxford: Oxford University Press, 1953.
Atiyah, Edward. *The Arabs*. London: Pelican, 1955.
Atkinson, William C. *A History of Spain and Portugal*. London: Penguin, 1960.

Bagchi, Prabodh Chandra. *India and China: A Thousand Years of Cultural Relations*. 2nd ed. New York: George J. McLeod, Ltd., 1951.
Bearce, George D. *British Attitudes Towards India, 1784–1858*. Oxford: Oxford University Press, 1961.
Bevan-Jones, V. R. and L. *Woman in Islam*. Lucknow: 1941.
Blegen, C. W. *Troy*. Cambridge: Cambridge University Press, 1961.
Blyth, R. H. *Japanese Humour*. Tokyo: 1957.
Brown, Benjamin H. (ed.). *The East and West Must Meet: A Symposium*. East Lansing, Michigan: Michigan State University, 1959.
Bury, J. B., S. A. Cook, and F. E. Adcock (eds.). *Cambridge Ancient History*, Vol. IV. Cambridge: Cambridge University Press, 1926.

Carman, W. Y. *A History of Firearms*. London: Routledge & Kegan Paul, Ltd., 1955.
Cazamian, Louis. *The Development of English Humor*. North Carolina: Duke University Press, 1952.
Childe, V. G. *The Dawn of European Civilization*. 4th ed. London: Routledge & Kegan Paul, Ltd., 1947.
Close, Upton. *The Revolt of Asia*. New York: G. P. Putnam's Sons, 1927.
Coke, Richard. *The Arab's Place in the Sun*. London: Butterworth & Co., 1929.
Collis, Maurice. *The Great Within*. London: Faber and Faber, Ltd., 1941.
———. *Foreign Mud*. London: Faber and Faber, Ltd., 1946.

Cook, J. M. *Greek Settlement in the Eastern Aegean and Asia Minor.* Cambridge: Cambridge University Press, 1961.
Coomaraswamy, Ananda K. *Indian Culture and English Influence.* New York: 1946.
———. *East and West,* n.d.
Cottrell, Leonard. *Enemy of Rome.* London: Evans Bros., Ltd., 1960.
Cranmer-Byng, L. *The Vision of Asia.* London: John Murray, Ltd., 1947.
Curzon, George Nathaniel, Lord. *Russia in Central Asia.* London: 1889.
———. *Problems of the Far East.* London: 1894.

Daniel, Norman. *Islam and the West: The Making of an Image.* Edinburgh: Edinburgh University Press, 1960.
Davis, S. *Race Relations in Ancient Egypt.* London: Methuen & Co., Ltd., 1951.
Dubs, Homer H. *A Roman City in Ancient China.* London: China Society, 1957.

Eastern and Western World. Symposium of lectures delivered in Holland, 1951–52. Forward by S. Hofstra. The Hague: van Hoeve, 1953.
Easton, Stewart C. *The Heritage of the Past.* New York: Holt, Rinehart & Winston, 1955.
Edwardes, Michael. *Asia in the European Age: 1498–1955.* London: 1961.

Fauconnier, Henry. *The Soul of Malaya.* London: Penguin, 1948.
Ffoulkes, Charles. *The Gun-founders of England.* Cambridge: Cambridge University Press, 1937.
Forbes, R. J. *Man the Maker: A History of Technology and Engineering.* London: Constable & Co., Ltd., 1950.
Forster, E. M. *A Passage to India.* London: Penguin, 1960.

Gaury, Gerald de. *Rulers of Mecca.* London: George G. Harrap & Co., Ltd., 1951.
Ghirshman, R. *Iran.* Translated from the French by M. E. L. Mallowan. London: Pelican, 1961.
Gibbon, Edward. *The History of the Decline and Fall of the Roman Empire.* 7 vols. 1776–88.
Goodwin, Astley J. H. *Communication Has Been Established.* London: Methuen & Co., Ltd., 1937.
Gregory, J. W. *The Story of the Road.* London: A. & C. Black, Ltd., 1938.
Grunebaum, G. E. von. *Medieval Islam.* Chicago: University of Chicago Press, 1953.

Guénon, René. *East and West.* Translated by William Massey. London: Luzac & Co., 1941.

Hall, A. R. *See* Singer.
Harden, Donald. *The Phoenicians.* London: Thames & Hudson, Ltd., 1962.
Hatano, Isoko and Ichiro. *Mother and Son.* Boston: Houghton Mifflin Co., 1962.
Herodotus. *The Histories.* Translated by Aubrey de Selincourt. London: Penguin Classics, 1954.
Hogarth, D. G. *The Ancient East.* London: 1914.
Holmyard, E. J. *See* Singer.
Homer. *The Iliad.* Translated by E. V. Rieu. London: Penguin Classics, 1950.
————. *The Odyssey.* Translated by E. V. Rieu. London: Penguin Classics, 1961.
Honour, Hugh. *Chinoiserie: The Vision of Cathay.* London: John Murray, Ltd., 1961.
Hornell, James. *Water Transport: Origins and Early Development.* Cambridge: Cambridge University Press, 1946.
Hsu, Francis L. K. *Americans and Chinese: Two Ways of Life.* New York: Henry Schuman, Inc., 1953.

Jarvis, C. S. *Three Deserts.* London: John Murray, Ltd., 1936.
————. *Oriental Spotlight.* London: John Murray, Ltd., 1937.

Khaldûn, Ibn. *An Arab Philosophy of History.* Translated by Charles Issawi.

Lawrence, T. E. *The Seven Pillars of Wisdom.* London: Jonathan Cape, Ltd., 1935.
Lawrence, T. E. *Oriental Assembly.* London: Williams & Norgate, Ltd., 1939.
Lawton, Lancelot. *Empires of the Far East.* 2 vols. London: Grant Richards, 1912.
Lovat, *Life of Sir Frederick Weld.*

MacKay, Ernest. *Early Indus Civilizations.* London: Luzac & Co., 1948.
Maitra, S. K. *The Meeting of the East and the West in Sri Aurobindo's Philosophy.* Pondicherry: Luzac & Co., 1956.
Mallik, Mannath C. *Orient and Occident: A Comparative Study.* London: T. Fisher Unwin, 1913.
Mumford, Lewis. *The Story of Utopias: Ideal Commonwealths and Social Myths.* London: G. G. Harrap & Co., 1923.

Mumford, Lewis. *Technics and Civilization*. London: Routledge & Kegan Paul, Ltd., 1934.
———. *Art and Technics*. Oxford: Oxford University Press, 1952.

Needham, Joseph. *Science and Civilisation in China*. 4 vols. Cambridge: Cambridge University Press, 1954–62.
Nehru, Jawaharlal. *Glimpses of World History*. London: Lindsay Drummond, Ltd., 1942.
Neill, Desmond. *Elegant Flower: First Steps in China*. London: John Murray, Ltd., 1956.
Northrop, F. S. C. *The Meeting of East and West*. New York: Macmillan, 1946.

Oman, Sir Charles. *The Art of War in the Middle Ages*. Vol. I. London: 1924.
Owen, S. J. (ed.). *A Selection from the Despatches, Memoranda and other papers relating to India, of the Marquess Wellesley, K.G.* Oxford: 1877.

Paleologue, Maurice. *The Turning Point*. Translated by F. A. Holt. London: 1935.
Pallis, Marco. *Peaks and Lamas*. London: Cassell & Co., Ltd., 1940.
Pannikar, K. M. *Asia and Western Dominance*. London: Allen & Unwin, Ltd., 1953.
Parkinson, C. Northcote. *The Evolution of Political Thought*. London: University of London Press, Ltd., 1958.
———. *British Intervention in Malaya*. Singapore: 1960.
Partington, J. R. *A History of Greek Fire and Gunpowder*. Cambridge: W. Heffer & Sons, Ltd., 1960.

Radhakrishnan. *East and West: Some Reflections*. London: George Allen & Unwin, Ltd., 1955.
Ridgeway, William. *The Origin and Influence of the Thoroughbred Horse*. Cambridge: Cambridge University Press, 1905.
Riencourt, Amaury de. *The Coming Caesars*. London: Jonathan Cape, Ltd., 1958.
Rostovtzeff, M. *The Social and Economic History of the Hellenistic World*, Vol II. Oxford: Oxford University Press, 1941.
Rowland, Benjamin. *Art in East and West*. Cambridge, Mass.: Harvard University Press, 1954.

Saggs, H. W. F. *The Greatness That Was Babylon*. London: Sidgwick & Jackson, Ltd., 1962.
Sarton, George. *History of Science*. Oxford: Oxford University Press, 1953.

Seltman, Charles. *Wine in the Ancient World.* London: Routledge & Kegan Paul, Ltd., 1957.
Sethna, K. D. *The Indian Spirit and the World's Future.* Pondicherry: Luzac & Co., 1953.
Singer, C., E. J. Holmyard, and A. R. Hall. *A History of Technology.* 4 vols. Oxford: Oxford University Press, 1954–58.
Sitwell, Osbert. *Escape With Me! An Oriental Sketch-Book.* London: Macmillan & Co., Ltd., 1939.
Spalding, H. N. *Civilization in East and West.* Oxford: Oxford University Press, 1939.
Spear, Percival. *India: A Modern History.* Ann Arbor, Michigan: University of Michigan, 1961.
Stark, Freya. *Alexander's Path.* London: John Murray, Ltd., 1958.

Taylor, Edmond. *Richer by Asia.* Boston: Houghton Mifflin Company, 1947.
Thomson, Ian. *The Rise of Modern Asia.* London: John Murray, Ltd., 1957.
Thucydides. *History of the Peloponnesian War.* Translated by Rex Warner. London: Penguin Classics, 1954.
Torr, Cecil. *Ancient Ships.* Cambridge: Cambridge University Press, 1894.
Toutain, Jules. *The Economic Life of the Ancient World.* Translated by M. R. Dobie. London: Routledge & Kegan Paul, Ltd., 1930.
Toy, Sidney. *A History of Fortification.* London: William Heinemann, Ltd., 1955.
Toynbee, Arnold J. *East to West: a journey round the world.* London: Oxford University Press, 1958.
Trevelyan, G. O. *The Life and Letters of Lord Macaulay.* London: 1931.
Tsuji, Masanobu. *Singapore: The Japanese Version.* Translated by M. E. Lake. London: Constable & Co., Ltd., 1962.
Turner, Ralph. *The Great Cultural Traditions.* Vols. I and II. New York: McGraw-Hill, 1941.

Van Straelen, H., S.V.D. *The Far East Must Be Understood.* London: Luzac & Co., 1945.

Ward, Barbara. *The Interplay of East and West.* London: George Allen & Unwin, Ltd., 1957.
Warmington, B. H. *Carthage.* London: Robert Hale, Ltd., 1960.
Wellesley, Marquess. *See* Owen, S. J.
Wilson, John A. *The Burden of Egypt.* Chicago: University of Chicago Press, 1951.
Wint, Guy. *The British in Asia.* London: Faber & Faber, Ltd., 1947.

Woodrooffe, Thomas. *River of Golden Sand*. London: Faber & Faber, Ltd., 1936.

Wurtzburg, C. E. *Raffles of the Eastern Isles*. London: Hodder & Stoughton, Ltd., 1954.

Wycherley, R. E. *How the Greeks Built Cities*. London: Macmillan, 1949.

Xenophon. *The Persian Expedition*. Translated by Rex Warner. London: Penguin Classics, 1961.

Yahya, Ahmad Ibn. *The Origins of the Islamic State*. New York: 1916.

Zinkin, Maurice. *Asia and the West*. London: Chatto & Windus, 1951.

INDEX